CALLING THE SPIRITS

CALLING
THE SPIRITS

A HISTORY OF SEANCES

LISA MORTON

REAKTION BOOKS

This book is dedicated, with gratitude and undying respect, to all the librarians (with a particular nod to my friend Becky Spratford) who help to ensure that we are not forever condemned to repeat the past

Published by
REAKTION BOOKS LTD
Unit 32, Waterside
44–48 Wharf Road
London N1 7UX, UK

www.reaktionbooks.co.uk

First published 2020
First published in paperback 2022
Copyright © Lisa Morton 2020

Printed and bound in Great Britain
by TJ Books Ltd, Padstow, Cornwall

A catalogue record for this book is available from the British Library

ISBN 978 1 78914 649 3

CONTENTS

A seance in 1910.

INTRODUCTION

A group of London's nineteenth-century elite gather in an ornate drawing room to participate in a seance. The medium, Madame Kali, directs the guests to be seated around a large glass-topped table and to place their hands, all touching, on the tabletop. The gas in the room is turned down as the medium asks them to join her in suspending disbelief and to 'imagine your minds floating in the darkness of time'. She summons the dead, and abruptly convulses, when she speaks again, her voice is altered, deeper and heavily accented. Soon, mayhem erupts as spirits possess a woman in the circle, who re-enacts the excruciating death of another sitter's daughter. Gusts of wind blow out the remaining candles, doors slam, the glass tabletop shatters and the possessed woman is wrenched into impossible positions as the other guests scream in horror.

This scene, from the second episode of the television series *Penny Dreadful*, epitomizes what many of us might think of when asked to imagine a seance. Or we might, perhaps, imagine that moment at a Halloween party when someone pulled out a Ouija board, placed the planchette on the lettered surface and watched it glide beneath the fingers positioned atop it.

The common perception of a seance has been indelibly shaped by decades of popular culture. Horror novels and movies have imprinted the seance with images of terror, while the Ouija board has moved from an innocent game to a piece of occult equipment

Eva Green and Reeve Carney in *Penny Dreadful*'s 'Séance'.

condemned by believers in a variety of religions, apparently because of its effectiveness in producing spirits.

The original form of the seance, however – before it was haunted by the spectre of mass entertainment and consumerism – was a very different creature. Consider this description from an 1873 edition of a Spiritualist newspaper:

> Mrs. Everitt and Rev. F. Monck, both of them good mediums, offered to give us a sitting, so we commenced in the usual way with singing and prayer, after which the spirits chose some appropriate portions of Scripture to be read. Our invisible friends then commenced giving us a series of raps in all parts of the room ... our party numbered fifteen, all intimate friends. At the beginning of the séance, Nippy, one of Mrs. Everitt's spirit friends, raised up the table-cloth from beneath with his materialised hand, and each person present felt his fingers distinctly through the cloth, in the light. We then lowered the gas and sang again, when we had quite a shower of lights, varying in size. We carried on a conversation with the lights, which signaled answers in the usual way, each spirit claiming some friend by the light passing towards

him. Three flashes were given quickly for 'Yes,' and one for 'No'... We next had cool breezes laden with perfumes ...

We commenced singing again, and Mr. Monck was lifted, chair and all, into the air, after which his boots were pulled off and thrown to the other end of the room. He then was entranced by the spirit 'Sam', who asked that an accordion which Dr. Hitchman had brought should be tied tightly with string, so that it could not be pulled open. It was accordingly tied with strong twine passed about eight times round. The spirit then played it quite melodiously on each of our shoulders, the string remaining firmly bound on it the whole time. 'Sam' next asked for his medium to be bound to a chair. Three of our circle bound him tightly and securely, all of us examining the tying. We began to sing, and in four seconds the medium was released, and among us; the rope was found under the sofa, tied and knotted in such an intricate way that it will take twenty minutes for an ordinary mortal to undo it. Thus ended one of the most convincing séances I ever witnessed.[1]

The original form of the seance was created by the Fox sisters, two teenage American girls who, in 1848, discovered that they could entertain groups of curiosity-seekers by seating them around a table and producing rapping sounds that they claimed came from spirits, but it took the Spiritualists on both sides of the Atlantic to refine it. As evidenced from the description above, it was initially one part joyful church meeting (or revival show), one part social gathering and one part thrilling display of what the participants fully believed was proof of life after death. Spiritualism, a movement born as a counter to the rapid progressions in science, industry and urbanization in the nineteenth century, presented itself as the first religion that allowed its followers to routinely witness proof of their belief in survival after death.

However, the seance also presents as one of that century's great frauds, forcing Spiritualists to become adept at defending themselves against debunkers. Take, for instance, the medium who led the enthusiastic Liverpool gathering noted above: Francis W. Monck, a former Baptist minister turned Spiritualist medium, would – four years after that seance – become the first medium to be convicted (under the UK's Vagrancy Act, which covers 'every person pretending or professing to tell fortunes, or using any subtle craft, means, or device, by palmistry or otherwise, to deceive and impose on any of his Majesty's subjects'[2]) and to serve a sentence of three months. Monck's practices would come under the legal spotlight again thirty years later, when one of his most ardent supporters, the Anglican reverend Thomas Colley, battled the magician and sceptic John Nevil Maskelyne in court after Maskelyne reproduced Monck's spirit materialization effect. Maskelyne lost the case after he failed to pull the manifestation back into his body at the conclusion of the act, which Monck had purportedly done.

Spiritualism had, in fact, begun with 'imposture' (the preferred word at the time for fraud) when the Fox sisters began to communicate with spirits in 1848. The Foxes were a middle-class family living in a small house in upstate New York when strange phenomena began to occur. Sounds were heard throughout the house, and two of the girls, Katie and Maggie, soon claimed to be in communication with spirits. When the girls called on their otherworldly contacts, loud rappings could be heard around them. They soon took their act on the road, their performances referred to as 'table-rappings' or 'table-sittings'. When the first British Spiritualist newspaper, the *Yorkshire Spiritual Telegraph*, began publication in 1855, the word 'seance' wasn't present, and gatherings were referred to as either 'spirit rappings' or 'table movings' ('seance' would appear in issues from 1856, however).

Although the word 'seance' wouldn't come into popular use for gatherings of those hopeful of contacting spirits until the late 1850s,

Maggie, Katie and older sister Leah in 1852.

the word had already acquired an interesting history. Originally a French word (the root means 'to sit') that referred to any large gathering, especially those of a political nature, 'seance' first took on a more unusual meaning in the 1830s, when it was used to describe gatherings of those practising 'animal magnetism' or 'mesmerism', a popular belief at the time that was the immediate precursor to Spiritualism. Animal magnetism postulated that all living fauna possess an energy that can be directed by skilled practitioners to heal illness, although it was eventually extended to also encompass telepathy and communication with the dead. It was immensely popular in England and Europe in the 1840s; note a brief newspaper article entitled 'Society in Paris – Somnambulism' from 1843: 'Animal magnetism has become the rage and professional somnambules are invited to give a *séance* for the entertainment of a select circle.'[3] This is one of the earliest examples of 'seance' used in the context of a group seeking an esoteric entertainment in the

This sheet music from 1853 is testament to the popularity of spirit rappings.

form of a circle. Meanwhile, even this nascent version of the word drew sceptics, as in an 1843 article on a demonstration of 'animal magnetism' by one Mr Robinson: 'Will antics be cut any longer in small towns, where *gulls* will be *clawed* at the rate of two shillings per *séance*, and the completest delusion that the human mind ever entertained be persevered in any longer? We certainly hope not.'[4]

That same year saw what was likely the first use of 'seance' to describe a gathering specifically dedicated to contacting spirits of the dead. Eliot Warburton's *Episodes of Eastern Travel*, originally serialized in the *Dublin University Magazine* and then gathered together for publication in a single volume, describes an evening Warburton has in Cairo in which an Egyptian magician summons the dead by casting spells on a young boy, who then gazes into ink poured into his hand and can see the spirits therein. Warburton, whose travelogues were beloved throughout Britain, noted that the 'séance' broke up late in the evening.

Outlining the etymology of 'seance' is one thing, but defining its form is just as important. There are festivals all over the world, such as the *Día de los Muertos* in Mexico or the Hungry Ghost Festival in China, that allow for interaction between the living and the dead, but these celebrations are almost diametrically opposed to the seance. In these festivals, participants accept that the dead will return of their own volition, and choose to honour them with favourite foods and other mortal enjoyments; however, in a seance, the spirits return at the will of the medium and are then used for their knowledge, rather than feted.

A seance is also not, strictly speaking, necromancy. Erika Bourguignon, who prepared the entry on necromancy in the *Encyclopedia of Religion*, says that necromancy, 'the art or practice of magically conjuring up the souls of the dead, is primarily a form of divination. The principal purpose of seeking such communication with the dead is to obtain information from them, generally regarding the revelation of unknown causes or the future course of events'; Bourguignon also notes that, because necromancy involves magical conjuration, it 'does not include communication employing mediums'.[5] *The Catholic Encyclopedia* challenges this latter notion: 'In recent times, necromancy, as a distinct belief and practice, reappears under the name of spiritism, or spiritualism.'[6] However, the seance can be traced as a direct descendent of the earliest forms of necromancy, dating back to Egyptian, Babylonian, Greek and Roman accounts. Both the necromancer and the medium employ metaphysical or magical practices (casting spells for the former, entering a trance state or evoking spirit manifestations for the latter) to force the return of dead spirits in order to do the bidding of the caller (although the necromancer may also be summoning divine entities, including gods or demons).

If the modern version of the seance, with its Ouija boards and phone apps, doesn't look much like the nineteenth-century Spiritualist model, the basic methods and goals nonetheless remain the same: to facilitate communication with spirits of the dead. The Ouija board sprang out of the 'talking boards' sometimes employed by Spiritualist mediums; a twenty-first-century paranormal investigation, with its use of K-II meters (to measure electromagnetic fields) and 'spirit boxes', represents the natural evolution of the seance's obsession with providing scientific proof of ghostly visits. When the ethereal going gets tough, the twenty-first-century ghosthunters will still call in a medium.

Is, then, a medium a necromancer or a magician? The use of the word 'medium' to describe an individual who facilitates contact with the spirits had a similar evolution to 'seance'. For a while, as mesmerism and animal magnetism sat side by side in Britain and America with the new religion of Spiritualism, 'seance' and 'medium' were applied interchangeably within both systems. 'Medium', in fact, wouldn't show up in a dictionary in regards to either of these beliefs until 1860, when Joseph Worcester's *A Dictionary of the English Language* gave, as the eighth definition of 'medium', 'One capable of being put under the influence of animal magnetism; one through whom the phenomena of animal magnetism are manifested.'[7]

Just as with 'seance', some of the earliest references to the Spiritualist use of 'medium' are editorials that decry the gullibility of believers. An 1852 article from the *New York Sun* (and carried by other newspapers around the world) entitled 'Spirit Revelations' first refers to '"knockers" and other impostors in the United States', and then goes on to opine:

> It is a sad thing to see human reason perverted ... We can scarcely keep our temper as we glance over the pages of the blasphemous trash now almost daily issued from the press ... We see these blasphemous, pretended revelations of disembodied spirits ... issued in superior typographical style, and we must infer that their circulation not only pays expenses, but brings profits ... the warning, therefore, which we give to all is – avoid these spirit medium revelations as you would the forger's money.[8]

In December 1852 the *New York Daily Times* went so far as to aver that the world had 'suffered a retrograde movement' and noted that 'mediums [are] as plenty as hystericky ladies.'[9]

'Medium' also represents the Catholic Church's troubled history with Spiritualism and seances. The word does not appear in the King James translation of the Holy Bible, where Deuteronomy 18:11 proscribes against using 'a consulter with familiar spirits, or a wizard, or a necromancer', while Leviticus 20:27 goes even further and states, 'A man also or woman that hath a familiar spirit, or that is a wizard, shall surely be put to death: they shall stone them with stones: their blood shall be upon them.' The word 'medium' wasn't substituted into these passages until the New English Bible and New American Bible translations of 1970.

The intent, however, is clear: death is the punishment for those who seek to converse with spirits. In the past, the Church did indeed follow this instruction, as the history of the Inquisition, when tens of thousands of innocents were stripped of their property, tortured, hanged or burned at the stake, ably demonstrates (although it must be noted that the majority of those victims were tried, convicted and sentenced in secular courts). Fortunately, the modern-day Church has proven to be more tolerant, if not approving.

So where does the Church stand on Spiritualism? How is it possible that a practice that once led to the brutal execution of so many became not just acceptable, but even transmogrified into a parlour entertainment? Surely this represents an extraordinary and significant change in Western thought, doesn't it?

It does. The seance – how it came into existence, how it was defined by a generation seeking comfort against materialistic philosophies, how it became both a religion and an entertainment, and how it came to coexist (nervously, at least on the Church side) alongside Christianity – is the story of a massive cultural shift.

But in order to understand how that transformation came about, it's necessary to begin by examining where it all came from.

1

SUMMONING THE
OLD SPIRITS

Before the birth of modern science – when technology was likelier to be about how many oxen were required to pull a heavy plough – magic was a significant part of daily life. The divine forces that controlled the universe – the pantheons of gods and goddesses – were plentiful and approachable. The gods could be propitiated or invoked; they fought and loved among themselves, but also with mortals. The ancients relied on magic, which they believed connected them directly with the gods, whom they worshipped and considered the cause of everything from increasing wealth to healing insect bites. Death came more often and earlier, but if a god could be called upon, surely summoning the mere spirit of a deceased mortal was possible.

Dead souls have always occupied a literal place; in nearly all of the ancient religions, ghosts were believed to reside in an underworld, a realm that could be accessed by caves (if one knew where to find these caves, that is). Having been released from their physical shells, the spirits existed outside of normal time; they knew the past, the present and the future. In his dialogue *On Heroes*, Flavius Philostratus offers this explanation for the all-knowing state of the dead:

> To be cleansed of the body is the beginning of life for divine
> and thus blessed souls. For the gods, whose attendants

they are, they then know, not by worshipping statues and conjectures, but by gaining visible association with them. And free from the body and its diseases, souls observe the affairs of mortals.[1]

In his *Thebaid*, the poet Statius offers an additional rationale: when the seer Tiresias is called upon by the Thebans readying for war and anxious for insight, he tells them:

> . . . lavish slaughter
> of heifers, flickering wing-texts, entrails pulsing
>   with truth,
> the subtle tripods, calculations tracking the stars,
> spicy smoke drifting over the altars – not one of
>   these
> methods makes the Gods' will nearly so clear as
>   do ghosts
> ordered to rise from Death's enduring doorway.[2]

Historians have suggested that only certain spirits, known as the 'unquiet dead', could be summoned for consultation; they had died in acts of murder or battle, or were deprived of a proper burial.[3]

The First Necromancies

Necromancy, or the art of summoning dead or divine spirits (usually to deliver prophecies), comes from the Greek words *nekros*, or 'dead', and *manteia*, or divination, and does indeed figure prominently in the mythology and histories of early Egypt, Babylonia, Assyria, Greece, Rome, the Norse and the Irish Celts. Unlike the modern seance, necromantic rituals took days to prepare for; they often involved travel (going to a tomb, a battlefield or an entry to the underworld) and sacrifice. They varied in other key ways from the seance as well: they were not group activities, even though both the seance and the necromantic practice require a single practitioner who is adept at obtaining answers from the dead. The recalled dead of the ancient world were rarely insubstantial shades, but often seemed to reinhabit their bodies (in fact, there was another word, sciomancy, for divination by shade or ghost). Those summoned up from Hades, for example, frequently complained of being called upon, and typically provided little beyond the required prophecy. However, one area where the ancient necromancers often aligned with the later seance mediums was in how often the production of the spirits was accomplished via trickery and fraud.

Throughout history, humanity has been divided in its approach to magical resurrection, finding it both fascinating and repellent, and this certainly applied to the ancient world, where it was condemned alongside being celebrated: in *Laws*, Plato calls for the imprisonment of those who 'charm the souls of the dead',[4] and the later Roman emperors called for strict punishment of guilty necromancers.

The oldest mentions of necromancy date from Mesopotamia, where a second millennium BC list of professions (a group of tablets known as Lu) includes two terms for necromancer (*ša eṭemmi* and *mušēlûeṭemmi*), while Lu Excerpt II mentions a female necromancer (*mušēlitum*).[5] An Old Assyrian letter makes note of 'female diviners and the spirits'.[6] A partial tablet from the collection of the British Museum dates from the first millennium BC and includes (in Babylonian script) an incantation for summoning a ghost. The ritual includes placing a skull on the ground and ordering the spirit to enter the skull: 'I call [upon you], O skull of skulls: may he who is within the skull answer me.' A potion made from animal parts is left to stand overnight and then used to anoint the skull (although this latter action is unclear). Another tablet contains a spell for creating an ointment that is applied to the eyes, which then enables the one thus anointed to see and speak with ghosts.[7] Other tablets feature incantations for protection against raised spirits, since encounters with ghosts usually resulted in death.

The Babylonian Talmud (in Tractate Sanhedrin 65b) also mentions those who consult with skulls, and a medieval commentary (from 1450) by Bar-tenura notes: 'He takes the skull of a dead person after the flesh has decomposed, and he offers incense to it, and asks of it the future, and it answers.'[8]

The earliest literary reference to any form of necromancy occurs in the ancient epic of *Gilgamesh, Enkidu and the Nether World*. This text, probably dating from around 2000 BC and found in both Sumerian and Akkadian versions, tells of how Gilgamesh once lost his beloved *ellag* and *ekidma* (gaming equipment) in the netherworld. His servant Enkidu offers to retrieve them, but Gilgamesh warns him that a journey into the netherworld is perilous and outlines the rules that must be strictly observed:

> You should not put on your clean garments: they would recognise immediately that you are alien. You should not anoint yourself with fine oil from a bowl: they would surround you at its scent. You should not hurl throw-sticks in the nether world: those struck down by the throw-sticks would surround you. You should not hold a cornel-wood stick in your hand: the spirits would feel insulted by you. You should not put sandals on your feet. You should not shout in the nether world. You should not kiss your beloved wife. You should not hit your wife even if you are annoyed with her. You should not kiss your beloved child. You should not hit your son even if you are annoyed with him. The outcry aroused would detain you in the nether world.[9]

Enkidu, however, fails to follow any of the rules and is unable to return. Desperate, Gilgamesh consults first with Enlil (the chief god of the Sumerians), who won't help, then with Enki (a Sumerian god of water, knowledge and creation – known as Ea in Akkadian and Babylonian mythology), who does assist. Enki calls on the young warrior Utu (who is also the god of the sun, and would later be worshipped as Shamash) and tells him, 'Open a hole in the nether world immediately, and then bring up his servant from the nether world!' Enkidu is brought up from the netherworld and provides a picture of the realm that is sometimes joyful (men who had seven sons are now companions to the gods) and frequently tragic (the leper 'twitches like an ox as the worms eat at him'[10]). The different versions of the epic vary as to whether Enkidu returns from the netherworld as a ghost (the Akkadian version) or a living mortal (the Sumerian version).

Egypt

Necromancy is often credited as having originally come from the ancient Egyptians. Most of the historical and literary references to Egyptian necromancy are found in either Greek or biblical records. Isaiah 19:3 refers to the Egyptians consulting the spirits of the dead, and this passage is often taken to suggest that necromancy was commonplace in Egypt. The second-century AD Greek Christian philosopher Clement of Alexandria (Titus Flavius Clemens) wrote in his *Exhortation to the Heathen*:

> Let the secret shrines of the Egyptians and the necromancies of the Etruscans be consigned to darkness. Insane devices truly are they all of unbelieving men. Goats, too, have been confederates in this art of soothsaying, trained to divination; and crows taught by men to give oracular responses to men.[11]

The Greek Magical Papyri (also known as PGM, from the Latin *Papyri Graecae Magicae*) is a collection of hundreds of Egyptian spells and invocations, dating from the second century BC to the fifth century AD. PGM IV: 222 sets forth a ritual in which the seeker must fill a bronze vessel with spring water, place it on the knees, pour green olive oil around and, bending over the vessel, speak this incantation (throughout the PGM, 'NN' is used to indicate a name to be inserted by the magician):

AMOUN AUANTAU / LAIMOUTAU RIPTOU MANTAUI
IMANTOU LANTOU LAPTOUMI ANCHŌMACH ARAPTOUMI,
hither to me, O NN god; appear to me this very hour and
do not frighten my eyes. Hither to me, O NN god, be
attentive to me because he wishes and commands this.
ACHCHŌR ACHCHŌR / ACHACHACH PTOUMI CHACHCHŌ
CHACHCHŌCH CHAPTOUMĒ CHŌRACHARACHŌCH APTOUMI
MĒCHŌCHAPTOU CHARACHPTOU CHACHCHŌ CHACHCHŌ
PTENACHŌCHEU [a hundred letters].

The spell also includes instructions on how to dismiss the summoned soul and how to create a protective charm.[12]

Many of the rituals in the PGM suggest the use of elaborate and mysterious-sounding words, a practice that would inform occult rituals for the next 2,000 years. However, not all of the incantations in the PGM are so arcane; some, like this general incantation for evoking spirits, read more like poetry:

I invoke you, ye holy ones, mighty, majestic, glorious
Splendours, holy, and earth-born, mighty arch-daimons;
compeers of the great god; denizens of Chaos, or Erebus
and of the unfathomable abyss; earth-dwellers, haunters
of sky-depths, nook-infesting, murk-enwrapped; scanning
the mysteries, guardians of secrets, captains of the hosts
of hell; kings of infinite space, terrestrial overlords, globe-
shaking, firm-founding, ministering to earth-quakes;
terror-strangling, panic-striking, spindle-turning; snow-

scatterers, rain-wafters, spirits of air; fire-tongues
of summer-sun, tempest-tossing lords of fate; dark shapes
of Erebus, senders of necessity; flame-fanning fire-darters;
snow-compelling, dew-compelling; gale-raising, abyss-
plumbing, calm-bestriding air-spirits; dauntless in courage,
heart-crushing despots; chasm-leaping, overburdening,
iron-nerved daimons; wild-raging, unenslaved; watchers
of Tartaros; delusive fate-phantoms; all-seeing, all-hearing,
all-conquering, sky-wandering vagrants; life-inspiring,
life-destroying, primeval pole-movers; heart-jocund
death-dealers; revealers of angels, justicers of mortals,
sunless revealers, masters of daimons, air-roving, omnipotent,
holy, invincible AO'TH ABAO'TH BASYM ISAK SABAO'TH IAO'
IAKO'P MANARA SKORTOURI MORTROUM EPHRAULA
THREERSA; perform my behests.[13]

The above incantation, while artful if read by itself, is nonetheless accompanied by specific actions involving an assembly
of materials – a complete ritual, in other words. It's worth nothing that most necromancy involves a ritualistic mix of language
and action. As anthropologist S. J. Tambiah notes, 'Words excel
in expressing enlargement, physical actions in realistic presentation.'[14] Ritualistic necromancy usually combines the two; even
the later seance would employ an invocation from the medium,
although the language of this summons was not strictly prescribed,
but left to the medium more as a form of improvisation, mark-
ing one way in which the seance differs from the earlier forms of
necromancy.

One more extraordinary necromantic rite in the PGM is unusual
in asking the gods to release the spirit of the deceased from the
underworld. After placing a pair of wax dolls (pierced with needles)
on the grave (at sundown) of someone who has died a violent or
untimely death, this is the spoken invocation:

I place this charm down beside you, subterranean gods,
Kore Persephone, Ereschigal and Adonis ... Hermes, the
subterranean, Thoth and the strong Anubis, who hold
the keys of those in Hades, the gods of the underworld
and the daimons, those untimely reft away, men, women,
youths and maidens, year by year, month by month, day
by day, hour by hour. I conjure you, all daimons assembled
here, to assist this daimon. And awaken at my behest,
whoever you may be, whether male or female. Betake
yourself to that place and that street and that house
and bring her hither, and bind her. Bring NN hither,
daughter of NN, whose magic stuff you have.[15]

Pliny describes the Egyptian scholar Apion using the plant
cynocephalia, known in Egypt as osirites, in divination practices,
and mentions that Apion claimed to have raised the spirit of Homer
and questioned it, although Apion said that 'he does not dare ...
disclose the answer he received.'[16]

Thessalos, a Greek scholar of healing and magic from the first
century AD, studied in Alexandria, but failed to reproduce a healing
described by King Nechepso. He consequently travelled to Thebes,
where he befriended a high priest who offered to help. The priest
instructed Thessalos to maintain purity for three days. At the end
of the third day, Thessalos was led to a special chamber and asked
whom he would like to speak to – a god, or a spirit of the dead.
Thessalos asked for Asclepius, the Greek name for the Egyptian
god Imhotep, and gained knowledge about why Nechepso's spell
had failed.[17]

In *Aethiopica*, or *Ethiopian Tales*, Heliodorus includes a scene
in which the novel's heroine, Charicleia, and an elderly Egyptian
priest stumble across a woman practising necromancy on the body
of her own son, recently slain in battle. They are resting under a
bright moon in the desert when they overhear the ritual, in which

the woman pours one jug each of water, wine and honey into a ditch beneath a burning pyre around her son's body, throws a dough figure into the ditch and then uses a sword to cut her arm while reciting spells. She flings the blood into the ditch, and a short time later the dead body rises. When the corpse refuses to speak, the necromancer redoubles her efforts, and her son finally answers her request for prophecy (regarding a second son, missing in battle) by telling her that she has sinned and violated the laws of the Fates, her missing son is dead, and she herself will die shortly because of her terrible deeds. Lastly, the corpse warns her of the observers, and she turns, raising the sword and determined to find them, only to accidentally impale herself on a spear.[18]

In the classic work by Apuleius *The Golden Ass*, Zatchlas, an Egyptian priest and 'a prophet of the first rank', is asked to restore the murdered Thelyphron to testify against his killer. In front of a large crowd, Zatchlas 'laid some sort of herb on the corpse's mouth and another on his breast. Then turning eastwards he silently invoked the majesty of the rising sun, arousing among the witnesses of this impressive performance excited expectations of a great miracle.' The corpse sits up and does indeed reveal the circumstances surrounding his murder by poison.[19]

Herodotus, in *The Histories*, also recorded an African tribe called the Nasamones who communicated with the spirits of their ancestors by going to the tombs, offering prayers and then falling asleep there, in order to be gifted with oracular dreams.[20]

An 1819 reference work, *Encyclopædia Londinensis*, uses references from the Book of Exodus to suggest methods by which Egyptian necromancers may have committed deception. Because the Book of Exodus mentions both the power of the Egyptian pharaoh's magicians (who are ultimately bested by God) and that the Israelite women possess mirrors (which they donate to the construction of a washbasin for the priests), it is suggested that the Egyptian magicians would certainly have known the use of mirrors to create trickery: 'Now a mirror of a particular form, and properly illuminated at the instant required, might easily be made to reflect, in a cavern from which all other light was carefully excluded, the image of the deceased, who was called upon by the necromancer; and . . . a person might be concealed prepared to give such ambiguous answers as would satisfy the inquirer.'[21] It's worth noting that at about the time of the writing and publication of the *Encyclopædia Londinensis*, phantasmagoria performances, which used magic lanterns to create illusions of spirits, were much in vogue.

Greece

When we look from the Egyptians to the Greeks, we find possibly the single most famous example of necromancy in literary history: the *Odyssey*, finalized around 700–650 BC, is also the earliest example of necromancy in Greek literature or history. The *Odyssey*, of course, is Homer's account of the hero Odysseus' journey home after the Trojan War. The voyage is long and episodic, and at one point Odysseus and his crew land on the island of the witch Circe, who changes Odysseus' men into pigs. The god Hermes intervenes, giving Odysseus a herb that will protect him from Circe's spells and instructing him in how to defeat her. Odysseus prevails, and after his men have been restored to human form they spend a year with Circe. When Odysseus tells her they need to set sail again, she tells him he must first go to Hades and speak with the shade of the Theban seer Teiresias. In Book x, Circe directs Odysseus regarding how to find the cave mouth that leads down to Hades: 'You will find it near the place where the rivers Pyriphlegethon and Cocytus [which is a branch of the river Styx] flow into Acheron, and you will see a rock near it, just where the two roaring rivers run into one another.'[22] Odysseus and his men follow the witch's directions, find the cave that goes to Hades and enact the ritual to draw forth the spirits:

Here Perimedes and Eurylochus held the victims, while
I drew my sword and dug the trench a cubit each way.
I made a drink-offering to all the dead, first with honey
and milk, then with wine, and thirdly with water, and
I sprinkled white barley meal over the whole, praying
earnestly to the poor feckless ghosts, and promising them
that when I got back to Ithaca I would sacrifice a barren
heifer for them, the best I had, and would load the pyre
with good things. I also particularly promised that Teiresias
should have a black sheep to himself, the best in all my
flocks. When I had prayed sufficiently to the dead, I cut
the throats of the two sheep and let the blood run into the
trench, whereon the ghosts came trooping up from Erebus
– brides, young bachelors, old men worn out with toil, maids
who had been crossed in love, and brave men who had been
killed in battle, with their armour still smirched with blood;
they came from every quarter and flitted round the trench
with a strange kind of screaming sound that made me turn
pale with fear. When I saw them coming I told the men
to be quick and flay the carcasses of the two dead sheep
and make burnt offerings of them, and at the same time
to repeat prayers to Hades and to Proserpine; but I sat
where I was with my sword drawn and would not let the
poor feckless ghosts come near the blood till Teiresias
should have answered my questions.[23]

Odysseus first converses with his recently departed crewman
Elpenor, whose remains have yet to be buried, and Elpenor instructs
Odysseus in how to complete his funeral; next, the hero encounters the spirit of his mother, Anticlea, whom he had last seen
alive. Finally, the spirit of the oracle Teiresias appears, and – after
being allowed to drink the blood of the slaughtered sheep – offers
Odysseus advice on how to reach his home on Ithaca. Odysseus then

lets his mother drink from the blood, asks her about her death and begs for news of his wife and son back home. When he attempts to embrace his mother's shade she leaps back in alarm. Odysseus is then met by a string of heroes, including his old friend King Agamemnon, who doesn't recognize Odysseus until he's drunk from the blood. Finally comes Hercules, who is nothing but a phantom because he feasts now on Mount Olympus with the gods.

Aeschylus offered another view of Odysseus' necromancy, one that emphasizes its location on a lakeshore:

> be stood on the grassy sacred enclosure of the fearful
> lake. Slash the gullet of the neck, and let the blood of
> this sacrificial victim flow into the murky depths of the
> reeds, as a drink for the lifeless. Call upon primeval earth
> and chthonic Hermes, escort of the dead, and ask chthonic
> Zeus to send up the swarm of night-wanderers from the
> mouths of the river.[24]

Aristophanes also mentions Odysseus in his play *The Birds*, as the chorus periodically breaks into the action with historical anecdotes like this one:

> Near by the land of the Sciapodes there is a marsh, from
> the borders whereof the unwashed Socrates evokes the
> souls of men. Pisander came one day to see his soul, which
> he had left there when still alive. He offered a little victim,
> a camel, slit his throat and, following the example of
> Odysseus, stepped one pace backwards. Then that bat
> of a Chaerephon came up from hell to drink the
> camel's blood.[25]

(The Sciapodes are one-footed men found in a number of Greek histories and tales; Pisander was a corrupt politician who also appears in Aristophanes' *Lysistrata* and *Peace*; Chaerephon was an associate of Socrates whom Aristophanes featured in multiple plays.)

In other Greek accounts of offering a ram to a spirit in order to gain information, the seeker is instructed to sleep on the fleece after the sacrifice. This process – performing a specific ritual before going to sleep to communicate with spirits in dreams – is known as 'incubation'. Strabo, for example, mentions this procedure in his *Geography*, noting that it was practised at a shrine to Calchas on a hill in Daunia called Drium.[26]

Necromancy was frequently performed either in caves or on lakeshores. The cave on the shore of Lake Acheron that supposedly led down to Hades was called Cheimerion. It is a famous nekromanteion (prophecy-place of the dead), thanks largely to the *Odyssey*. The exact site has been sought by historians and archaeologists for decades. An archaeological site located in Epirus in 1958 and excavated off and on over the next twenty years was

Excavation at Acheron once believed to be the nekromanteion.

believed by archaeologist S. I. Dakaris to be the long-sought-after nekromanteion. The site, which included a large underground vault and the remains of machinery, was later established as a defensive structure, but in speculating, Dakaris suggested that priests might have used the machinery to produce fraudulent apparitions.[27]

The Acheron nekromanteion figures prominently in one other story – that of Periander, a Greek tyrant who ruled over Corinth and died in 585 BC. Periander was said to have murdered his wife Melissa in a violent rage. Herodotus, in *The Histories*, offers a ghost story of what happened when Periander dispatched a legate to Acheron:

> Periander had sent messengers to the Oracle of the Dead on the river Acheron in Thesprotia to enquire concerning a deposit that a friend had left, but Melissa, in an apparition, said that she would tell him nothing, nor reveal where the deposit lay, for she was cold and naked. The garments, she said, with which Periander had buried her had never been burnt, and were of no use to her. Then, as evidence for her husband that she spoke the truth, she added that Periander had put his loaves into a cold oven.[28]

When this message is relayed to Periander, he recognizes the reference to 'loaves into a cold oven' as a recollection of a necrophiliac act he committed with his wife's corpse. After that, Periander orders all the women of Corinth to the temple of Hera, where they are stripped naked. Their clothes are thrown into a pit and burned as Periander prays to Melissa. Upon sending his messengers back to Acheron, Melissa's ghost is satisfied with the offering of clothes and reveals the location of the deposit.

There were four significant nekromanteia in ancient Greece: the one that Odysseus visited on the shore of Lake Acheron and three others, found at Avernus in Campania, Heracleia Pontica and Tainaron on the Mani Peninsula.[29] The ritual for a visitor at a nekromanteion was to sleep there, hoping for prophetic dreams from the spirits (the process known as incubation). The nekromanteia were not officially recognized by the state, although they were sometimes associated with a nearby temple.

The Heracleian nekromanteion (which supposedly included a tunnel to the underworld that Heracles had used when he pulled the three-headed dog Cerberus up from Hades) doesn't appear in literature as much as those in Acheron and Avernus, but it does provide the setting for one of the most famous tales of necromancy in classical literature. In the sixth chapter of Plutarch's *Life of Cimon*, the debased leader Pausanias accidentally kills a girl, Cleonice, whom he has demanded be brought to his bed. Haunted in his dreams by the ghost of Cleonice, he seeks the ghost oracle of Heracleia, who summons the girl's spirit, which is then beseeched by Pausanias to leave him.[30]

The nekromanteion at Tainaron is the only one that is not associated with a body of water. It's famous for being near a cave that Orpheus and Theseus used to journey to the underworld; this same cave was also sometimes said to be the one through which Heracles pulled Cerberus. The famous traveller Pausanias (not to be confused with the fifth-century-BC leader who was haunted by the spirit of Cleonice) was disappointed, though, to find no easy way down: 'Some of the Greek poets state that Heracles brought up the hound of Hades here, though there is no road that leads underground through the cave, and it is not easy to believe that the gods possess any underground dwelling where the souls collect.'[31] Tainaron also figures in the story of Corax, who has killed a man in war who was a favourite of the god Apollo. After he tries to explain to Apollo that it was a 'kill or be killed' situation, Apollo offers to forgive him if he will go to Tainaron, call up the soul of the man he slew and 'conciliate him with libations'. Corax does, and is spared the wrath of the god.[32]

If Pausanias was disappointed to find no route down to Hades, the same was not true of Orpheus, the hero at the centre of the most famous story in the ancient world of a mortal travelling to the underworld to seek a spirit. Orpheus, the greatest poet and musician in Greek mythology, first appears in literature (in a two-word fragment by the poet Ibycus) around the sixth century BC; he travels with Jason and the Argonauts in search of the Golden Fleece, using his music to drown out the lethal song of the Sirens. However, his most well-known adventure occurs after his wife, Eurydice, dies from a snakebite. Both Virgil and Ovid rendered versions of Orpheus' journey into the underworld, using his musical gifts to pass Cerberus. He makes his way through 'the grove gloomy with black horror' until he comes upon Pluto, king of the dead, who allows him to take Eurydice away on one condition: Orpheus must take the lead in returning to earth and must not look back until they are both completely above ground. In his anxiety, Orpheus misjudges the final steps and turns to look back before Eurydice is completely out of the underworld; she is lost to him forever.[33] There is one final haunting legend associated with Orpheus: he died when he was torn apart by a mob of women (possibly Maenads sent by Dionysus, who was upset because Orpheus worshipped Apollo over him). The parts of his body were thrown into a nearby river, where the head was heard to still be mourning Eurydice. The head floated to the island of Lesbos, where it continued to speak, serving as an oracle.

Other heroes who journeyed to the underworld included Hercules and Theseus. Theseus accompanied his friend Pirithous, who intended to kidnap Persephone from Hades; however, Theseus made the mistake of resting by sitting on a rock from which he could not rise, even when Pirithous was overcome by the Furies. It took Hercules, completing the last of the labours assigned to him by King Eurystheus (who sent him to capture and bring back Cerberus), to free him, although Pirithous remained in the underworld forever.

It wasn't always necessary, however, to journey to a nekromanteion to commune with the dead in ancient Greece; speaking with great heroes of the past could also be accomplished by going to the place where they had died, such as a battlefield, or to a place where they had been encountered, such as around their shrine or birthplace. These heroes appeared in physical form, often engaging in warlike exercises, hunting or assisting with agriculture. In *On Heroes*, Philostratus provides a list of dead heroes who are regularly seen; a vinedresser, one of the two characters in the dialogue, regularly communes with Protesilaos, the first soldier to perish in the Trojan War. He does, however, win over the hero (who is described as being ten cubits – or 4.6 metres (15 ft) – tall) by offering him wine every evening, sweetmeats every day at noon and milk when the moon is full in early spring.[34] The vinedresser goes on to describe how local shepherds and herdsmen on the Trojan plain encounter the spirits of the great war heroes, whose appearance foretells the future (for example, if the heroes are sweaty, floods are imminent).

Statius' *Thebaid* offers a particularly detailed instruction for communing with the shades of soldiers: when asked by the Thebans for prophecies regarding an upcoming battle, Tiresias directs them to graze their black-fleeced flocks on the blood-drenched soil that was the site of the Spartans' last battle; next, he hangs garlands on the rams' horns. A trench is dug and filled with wine, honey, milk and blood. Pyres are lit, the sheep are slaughtered and Tiresias calls first on the denizens of the underworld to release the shades. Then – when that fails – he threatens the goddesses. Finally, the dead appear, but they immediately fight among themselves, more interested in each other's blood than that of sheep.[35]

Leonidas of Tarentum, a third-century-BC Greek poet who wrote mostly about death, penned a stanza that seems to propose that the best way to prepare the dead for raising is to propitiate them far in advance (or to create the 'grateful dead'):

O shepherds, who roam over this mountain ridge feeding
your goats and fleecy sheep, do, in the name of Earth,
a little kindness, but a pleasant one, to Cleitagoras, for
the sake of Persephone underground. May the sheep
bleat to me, and the shepherd seated on the unhewn
rock pipe soft notes to them as they feed, and may the
villager in early spring gather meadow flowers and lay
a garland on my grave. May one of you bedew it with
the milk of a ewe, mother of pretty lambs, holding her
udder up and wetting the edge of the tomb. There are
ways, I assure you, even among the dead of returning
a favour done to the departed.[36]

The first time that an act of necromancy takes place at a tomb
in Greek literature appears in Aeschylus' play *The Persians*. Atossa,
the widow of the great Persian king Darius, leaves the royal palace,
dressed in black robes, and journeys to his tomb, where she calls
forth his shade with the following offerings:

> ... delicious milk, that foams
> White from the sacred heifer; liquid honey,
> Extract of flowers; and from its virgin fount
> The running crystal; this pure draught, that flow'd
> From the ancient vine, of power to bathe the spirits
> In joy; the yellow olive's fragrant fruit,
> That glories in its leaves' unfading verdure;
> With flowers of various hues, earth's fairest offspring
> Is wreathed. But you, my friends, amid these rites
> Raise high your solemn warblings, and invoke
> Your lord, divine Darius; I meanwhile
> Will pour these off'rings to the infernal gods.[37]

The chorus joins her in calling forth Darius, who finally rises.

The Greeks and Romans often cited areas of the Near East (Persia, Mesopotamia, India) as home to great magicians. In Philostratus' *Life of Apollonius of Tyana*, Apollonius calls up the spirit of Achilles not by sacrificing an animal, but by reciting an Indian prayer to heroes: 'a slight earthquake shook the neighborhood of the barrow, and a youth issued forth five cubits high, wearing a cloak of Thessalian fashion ... but he grew bigger, till he was twice as large and even more than that; at any rate he appeared to me to be twelve cubits high just at that moment when he reached his complete stature, and his beauty grew apace with his length.' Achilles answers five questions about the veracity of Homer's record of the Trojan War, then vanishes 'with a flash of summer lightning'.[38]

In *Menippus: A Necromantic Experiment*, Lucian, a second-century-BC author who was born in Roman Syria but wrote entirely in ancient Greek, relates the story of Menippus, who, desiring to learn about life from the great philosophers of the past, journeys to Babylon and finds a mage named Mithrobarzanes who agrees to take him into Hades. The preparation of Menippus is thus:

Taking me under his charge, he commenced with a new moon, and brought me down for twenty-nine successive mornings to the Euphrates, where he bathed me, apostrophizing the rising sun in a long formula, of which I never caught much; he gabbled indistinctly, like bad heralds at the Games; but he appeared to be invoking spirits. This charm completed, he spat thrice upon my face, and I went home, not letting my eyes meet those of any one we passed. Our food was nuts and acorns, our drink milk and hydromel and water from the Choaspes, and we slept out of doors on the grass. When he thought me sufficiently prepared, he took me at midnight to the Tigris, purified and rubbed me over, sanctified me with torches and squills and other things, muttering the charm aforesaid, then made a magic circle round me to protect me from ghosts, and finally led me home backwards just as I was; it was now time to arrange our voyage.

The mage finally leads them down the Euphrates to a marshy area, where they leave their boat, dig a pit and sacrifice a sheep. The mage shouts an invocation and the earth cracks open, revealing the underworld. Mithrobarzanes leads Menippus past Cerberus and across the River Styx, and they encounter the shades of numerous ghosts before Menippus reascends, none the wiser from the great philosophers.[39]

Lucian also mentions a necromantic incident in his *The Lover of Lies*: a Hyperborean mage, who has been hired to bring young Glaucias the love of Chrysis, first produces the spirit of Glaucias' father to approve the match. In the courtyard of the father's house, on a night when the moon is waxing, the necromancer digs a pit and then at around midnight raises the spirit.[40]

Rome

As might be expected from the civilization that gave history gladiatorial games, the Roman descriptions of necromancy tend to be bloodier and more spectacular than those provided by the Greeks. They often involve fearsome and vain witches, such as Canidia, who appears in Horace's Ode XVII boasting of being able to 'raise the dead after they are burned'.[41] In Seneca's *Medea*, the eponymous sorceress who helped Jason in his quest for the Golden Fleece seeks terrible revenge, not just calling on 'the silent crowd . . . the gods of doom, the dark Chaos', but recalling terrible monsters like the Hydra – slain by Hercules – to life.[42]

No witch in the history of necromancy, though, can equal the bloodthirsty, horrific Erichtho. This disturbing episode is found in Lucan's *Pharsalia*, about the war between Julius Caesar and Pompey the Great. On the eve of a battle, Sextus, son of the great Pompey, wanting to know his fate, decides to seek out 'the occult knowledge of the cruel sorcerers that are an abomination to the gods'. Sextus manages to locate the Thessalian witch Erichtho, whose mere appearance is terrifying: 'The face of the loathsome witch is haggard, hideous, and decomposed; her features inspire fear because of their hellish pallor; they are covered with disheveled hair and are never seen on a bright sky: only if rain and black clouds conceal the stars does the witch emerge from the tombs she has stripped.'[43] Sextus tells the witch he must know the outcome of the battle, and she answers that she requires the corpse of a soldier. Erichtho chooses one from the battlefield, inserts a hook into its throat and, using a rope from a gallows, drags the corpse to a rock in the mountains that looks down over deep caverns. Once there, she fills the body with boiling blood and a spell made from various occult ingredients, finally offering this invocation:

I invoke the Eumenides, Hell's horror, and the Avengers;
I invoke Chaos, eager to disorder countless worlds,
I invoke the ruler of the earth, tormented for long future ages
by the drawn-out death of the gods; I invoke
    the Styx, and the Elysian fields
no witch of Thessaly may reach; I invoke
    Persephone, loathing sky
and mother; and the lowest form of
    our Hecate, through whom
the shades and I in silent utterance may commune;
I invoke the porter of the wide abode,
    who tosses human entrails
to the savage hound; I invoke the Sisters
    soon to spin a second thread
of life, and you, a ferryman of the blazing water,
old man already tired out by shades returning to me:

heed my prayers. Do I summon you with mouth sufficiently
abominable and polluted? Do I ever chant these spells
without consuming human entrails? How
     many times have I cut out
breasts filled by deity and washed them with warm brains?
Are there no babes, about to enter life, who laid
their head and heart upon your dishes? Then obey my prayer.
A soul I ask for, not one lying hid in the cave of Tartarus
and long accustomed to the darkness, but a soul on its way
     down,
life's light just fled, a soul still hesitating at the door
to pallid Orcus' chasm, a soul which,
     though he drain these drugs,
will join the dead once only. Let the
     ghost of a soldier with us
recently foretell all Pompey's future to the leader's son,
if civil wars have earned your gratitude.[44]

The ghost of the dead soldier appears beside its corpse, afraid
to re-enter it. Enraged, Erichtho whips the corpse with snakes
and shrieks threats at the Fates unless they allow the shade to
reunite with its corpse. The clotted blood begins to boil, and the
corpse opens its eyes. Erichtho promises the corpse eternal protection from future witchcraft if he will deliver the prophecy, which
he does (assuring Sextus a place of honour in the afterlife). After
delivering the message, the dead man walks to a pyre Erichtho has
made for him and is at last released.

A number of the Roman emperors supposedly employed necromancers. Cicero, in his letter 'Against Vatinius', accused this
servant of Caesar of seeking 'to evoke the spirits of the shades
below, and to appease the Dî Manes with the entrails of murdered
boys'.[45] Tacitus records the history of Libo Drusus, great-grandson
of Pompey and a 'short-sighted youth, who had a foible for

absurdities'. Libo, already under suspicion of the Roman senate, seals his doom when he seeks the services of Junius, whom he solicits 'to raise departed spirits by incantations'. His situation goes to trial, but Drusus kills himself rather than face the Senate. From AD 180 to 217, Commodus, Didius Julianus, Caracalla and Elagabalus all practised necromancy, while Valerian and Maxentius (AD 253 to 312) conducted magical rites that were very similar; both were said to sacrifice newborn babies in an attempt to read the future in the entrails.[46]

The most famous case of an emperor employing necromancy, though, is surely that of Nero, who was hounded by the ghost of his mother after he had her killed. He finally called on the magi to summon the ghost and beg its forgiveness.[47]

Where the Greeks had largely ignored necromancy on a legal level, the Romans legislated against it, with increasing severity in the later part of the Empire. In 33 BC Agrippa addressed magic as a form of nationalism:

Those who attempt to distort our religion with strange rites you should abhor and punish, not merely for the sake of the gods (since if a man despises these he will not pay honour to any other being), but because such men, by bringing in new divinities in place of the old, persuade many to adopt foreign practices, from which spring up conspiracies, factions, and cabals, which are far from profitable to a monarchy. Do not, therefore, permit anybody to be an atheist or a sorcerer. Soothsaying, to be sure, is a necessary art, and you should by all means appoint some men to be diviners and augurs, to whom those will resort who wish to consult them on any matter; that there ought to be no workers in magic at all. For such men, by speaking the truth sometimes, but generally falsehood, often encourage a great many to attempt revolutions.[48]

Agrippa also warns against philosophers.

In AD 357 Constantius II prohibited all forms of divination, specifically night-time sacrifices, incantations to demons and certain forms of necromancy (such as summoning ghosts to destroy your enemies).

Despite the bloodier witchcraft of the Romans, necromancy sometimes still involved gentler, familiar forms. The seeker of knowledge, such Aeneas or Orpheus, might undertake a fanciful journey into the underworld. Spirits appeared in the form of dreams, as with Elysius, whose son Euthynoüs died of unknown causes. Anxious to discover his son's cause of death, Elysius 'visited a place where the spirits of the dead are conjured up, and having offered the preliminary sacrifice prescribed by custom, he lay down to sleep in the place, and had this vision'. Both his son and his own father appear to him, and his son hands him a piece of paper that suggests he died of natural causes.[49]

As with the Egyptians, herbs sometimes played a part in necromantic rituals. In Virgil's *Eclogue* VIII, the shepherd-singer Alphesiboeus describes powerful herbs from Pontus that can change a man into a wolf or 'summon spirits from the tomb's recess'.[50]

While not technically a form of necromancy, one description of an oracular rite from Ammianus Marcellinus is nevertheless interesting as being possibly the first recorded use of a 'talking-board'. Two men, Hilarius and Patricius, on trial for the criminal act of consulting an oracle about the fate of an emperor, explain the process to their judges:

we constructed from laurel twigs under dire auspices this unlucky little table which you see, in the likeness of the Delphic tripod, and having duly consecrated it by secret incantations ... we at length made it work ... It was placed in the middle of a house purified thoroughly with Arabic perfumes; on it was placed a perfectly round plate made of various metallic substances. Around its outer rim the written forms of the twenty-four letters of the alphabet were skillfully engraved, separated from one another by carefully measured spaces. Then a man clad in linen garments, shod also in linen sandals and having a fillet wound about his head, carrying twigs from a tree of good omen, after propitiating in a set formula the divine power from whom predictions come ... stood over the tripod as priest and set swinging a hanging ring fitted to a very fine linen thread and consecrated with mystic arts.[51]

The ring goes on to spell out the name of Theodorus. Unfortunately for Hilarius and Patricius, they also reveal that the ring had foreseen the death of Emperor Valens, and so they are put to death.

Northern Europe

In Norse mythology, Odin, the father of the gods, was said to be skilled with runic magic. In one oft-quoted passage, Odin says, 'If I see a man dead, and hanging aloft on a tree, I engrave runic characters so wonderful, that the man immediately descends and converses with me.'[52] In the ode 'The Descent of Odin', the great king rides his eight-legged horse Sleipnir down into the realm of Hela (Death), makes his way past the terrifying dog – its jaws full of gore – that guards the entrance, and arrives at the eastern gate. Once there, Odin casts a spell:

> Facing to the northern clime,
> Thrice he trac'd the Runic rhyme;
> Thrice pronounc'd, in accents dread,
> The thrilling verse that wakes the dead;
> Till from out the hollow ground
> Slowly breath'd a sullen sound.[53]

Odin has called up a legendary prophetess who tells him of the coming death of his son Balder, murdered by his brother Hoder.

In the *Ynglinga* saga, the two tribes of Norse gods, the Æsir and the Vanir, have been at war; to effect a truce, two of the Æsir – Mímir and Hœnir – are offered as hostages. When the Vanir become suspicious of Mímir, he is decapitated and his head sent back to Odin, who 'embalmed it with herbs so that it would not rot, and spoke charms over it, giving it magic power so that it would answer him and tell him many occult things'. This, and the ability to restore life to dead men, earned Odin the title 'Lord of Ghouls'.[54]

In *The Danish History* (*Gesta Danorum*), Saxo Grammaticus relates the tale of Hadding, a heroic mortal who is the beloved of Hardgrep, a magical giantess. While journeying through Hadding's homeland, they find a household where the master has just died. Desiring to obtain knowledge from the dead man, Hardgrep engraves spells on a piece of wood which Hadding places beneath the dead man's tongue. The corpse comes to life, enraged:

> Perish accursed he who hath dragged me back from those below, let him be punished for calling a spirit out of bale! Whoso hath called me, who am lifeless and dead, back from the abode below, and hath brought me again into upper air, let him pay full penalty with his own death in the dreary shades beneath livid Styx.

The corpse forecasts death at the claws of demons for Hardgrep, although Hadding survives. Later on, Hadding – like heroes before him – takes a journey to the underworld, where he finds a rushing river, herbs growing in perpetual sunshine and armies made up of the spirits of those who died at war and are now perpetually fighting. Further on in the tale, Hadding receives advice from his late wife in a dream.[55]

Illustration from W. G. Collingwood, *Groa's Incantation* (1908).

Another Norse tale involving a dream is strikingly similar to the ancient Greek practice of sleeping on a tomb to commune with the interred: an unskilled poet named Hallbjǫrn sits on the burial mound of the great skald (poet) Þorleifr, trying to improve his art. When he falls asleep atop the barrow, he sees the *haugbui*, or ghost, of Þorleifr step out of an opening in the mound and approach him. Þorleifr takes hold of Hallbjǫrn's tongue, recites a spell that Hallbjǫrn must remember and tells him to compose a great ode to Þorleifr upon awakening. Hallbjǫrn does so, and finally acquires the talent he's sought for so long.[56]

Grógaldr, or *The Spell of Gróa*, is an Eddic poem in which a young man raises his mother, who was a *völva* (a seeress), from the dead in order to learn protective spells from her. Svipdag, the son, calls her: 'Awake, Groa, good woman, awake! From the door of the dead I wake you: see now how badly your son to your grave-hill has wanted to visit?' Groa responds: 'What ailment have you my only son, what makes heavy your heart, that your mother you call, who under the grave mould does lie, and has left the world of the living?'[57] Svipdag goes on to explain that his stepmother has cursed him with a difficult journey, and Groa offers nine spells to shield him.

In the Icelandic sagas, there are several events in which dead warriors have been magically resurrected to do battle. In the tale of Sorli, soldiers are brought back to life by the goddess Freyja; in the saga of King Hrolf, Queen Skuld sits on a special scaffold for witches and brings back the dead.[58]

The Celts

Celtic legend provides one of the eeriest tales of necromancy, from 'The Adventures of Nera' (a 'fore-tale' associated with the *Táin Bó Cúailnge*, or *The Cattle Raid of Cooley* or the *Táin*). The story begins on Samhain (the Celtic precursor to the modern-day Halloween), as Queen Medb and her husband Ailill are preparing a feast. Ailill offers a reward to any warrior who can loop a long twig around the foot of one of two men who were hanged the day before. After a number of others go out into the dark, demon-haunted night, only to return in failure, Nera takes up the challenge. His first three attempts at fastening the twig around one of the corpses' feet fail, but when he finally prevails the corpse begins to speak, telling Nera that he died thirsty and would like a drink. Nera agrees to carry the corpse to a nearby house, and after finding two houses that are unapproachable, they enter the third house they come across. Once inside, the corpse takes a drink, and immediately spits it back out at the residents of the house, killing all of them. Nera returns the corpse to the gallows after that.[59]

An account of how the *Táin Bó Cúailnge* was rescued from oblivion sounds intriguingly like the Norse tale of Hallbjǫrn, the incompetent poet who gains great talent after communing with the spirit of a legendary skald in a dream. *The Book of Leinster* recounts the story of Muirgen, a poet who is journeying with a band of his fellows in search of the *Táin*. When they come to the burial mound of the great hero Fergus mac Roich, Muirgen sits alone on the mound as the others continue on to find a lodging house. Muirgen recites a poem to the memorial stone on the mound, in which he mentions some of the hero's great deeds and ends by crying out, 'O Fergus!'[60] The spirit of Fergus then appears in a mist, and recites the entirety of the *Táin* to Muirgen.

In Scotland various forms of Celtic-inspired necromancy were still practised in the western islands well into the seventeenth century. One custom involved pouring cow's milk on a small hill to summon a spirit called Browny, described as 'a tall man, having very long brown hair';[61] calling up Browny brought good fortune. Other rituals, however, were more typically necromantic, seeking prophecies. In one, four men accompanied a fifth to a river that bordered two villages, and then, taking the fifth man by the arms and legs, they flung him against the riverbank as they called out an incantation; soon, 'a number of little Creatures came from the Sea' to answer their questions.[62]

The Scottish Gaelic word *taghairm* was usually translated as 'spirit-call' and applied to necromantic practices, which often involved donning a cow or ox hide:

> [Another] way of consulting the Oracle was by a Party of Men, who first retir'd to solitary Places, remote from any House, and there they singled out one of their number, and wrapt him in a big Cow's hide, which they folded about him: his whole Body was cover'd with it except his Head, and so left in this posture all night, until his invisible Friends reliev'd him, by giving a proper Answer to the Question in hand; which he receiv'd, as he fancy'd, from several Persons that he found about him all that time. His Consorts return'd

to him at Break of Day, and then he communicated his News to them; which often prov'd fatal to those concern'd in such unwarrantable Enquiries.[63]

A gentleman named John Erach, from the Isle of Lewis, testified to having endured this ritual, 'during which time he felt and heard such terrible things, that he could not express them; the Impression it made on him was such as could never go off, and [he] said that for a thousand Worlds he would never again be concern'd in the like performance, for this had disorder'd him to a high degree'.[64]

If those who sought an oracle via the above method desired confirmation, they 'took a live Cat and put him on a Spit', until other cats appeared and were asked the same question that the man in the hide had put forth. If the cats provided the same answer, it was considered an infallible confirmation.[65]

Some versions of the cow-hide *taghairm* specify that it must take place near a cascade or waterfall. The cow-hide ritual is also similar to part of the *tarbfeis* ('bull-feast') described in *The Book of the Dun Cow*, a manuscript that pre-dates 1106, and includes a scene in which the death of a king is followed by a bull-feast, wherein one man eats of the bull, falls asleep and has a dream that reveals who the next king will be. Scholars have noted the similarity of this rite to the scene in the *Odyssey* in which Odysseus sleeps on the hide of two sacrificed rams to be visited by spirits of the dead in his dreams.[66]

2

EARLY NECROMANCY

With the decline of the Roman Empire and the expansion of the Catholic Church, the Western world entered the Middle Ages. The Church struggled with the pagan beliefs of the past, sometimes ignoring them, sometimes co-opting them and sometimes attempting to stamp them out altogether. Early theologians also wrestled with the question of pagan magic versus Christian miracles. Were spirits and the ability to invoke them even possible when souls were supposed to leave their bodies and depart the earth immediately upon death (and who, after all, would want to return from the paradise of Heaven or could come back from the prison of Hell)? Could enchantments enacted with old magic be used to demonstrate the truth of Christian beliefs?

Rather than claim that all earlier acts of magic had been fraudulent, Christian scholars argued that these earlier enchantments were controlled by demons who ensnared humans with these gifts, so necromancy moved from being the calling up of the dead to the summoning of demons. St Augustine, possibly the greatest Christian philosopher of all time, rejected the existence of ghosts by offering a poignant and personal rationale in a text from AD 422: 'If the souls of the dead could indeed involve themselves in the affairs of the living, and if it were really they themselves who are speaking to us when we see them in our sleep, I cannot speak for others, but my pious mother, who followed me over land and sea in order to live with me, would never miss a single night in visiting me.'[1] Augustine suggested that good revelations from 'ghosts' were actually from angels, while malignant messages came via demons.

The early and prolific writer Tertullian (AD 155–240) was one of the first to argue that pagan magic was essentially demonic in origin. In *A Treatise on the Soul*, he lays out his long (and frequently confusing) argument, asking, 'what after this shall we say about magic? Say, to be sure, what almost everybody says of it – that it is an imposture.' However, the imposture Tertullian mentions is not that of human fraud, but of a different variety: 'Under cover, however, of these souls, demons operate . . . This imposture of the evil spirit lying concealed in the persons of the dead, we are able, if I mistake not, to prove by actual facts.' Tertullian goes on to state that exorcism forces these evil spirits to speak the truth; he also notes that 'the fact that Hades is not in any case opened for (the escape of) any soul, has been firmly established by the Lord in the person of Abraham.'[2] Scholars also debated how demons could possess such powers. Thomas Aquinas (1225–1274) later discussed the question of demonic power at length in his *Summa theologiae*, wherein he expresses the opinion that their knowledge is limited because they can never know God.[3]

Another writer who preceded Augustine, Justin Martyr, treated ancient magic as proof of one of Christianity's central tenets, saying,

> For let even necromancy, and the divinations you practise
> by immaculate children, and the evoking of departed human
> souls, and those who are called among the magi, Dream-
> senders and Assistant-spirits (Familiars), and all that is done
> by those who are skilled in such matters – let these persuade
> you that even after death souls are in a state of sensation.[4]

If the pagans needed more persuading, the Bible gave numerous examples of miraculous resurrections. In 1 Kings 17, God commands Elijah the Tishbite, of Gilead, to go to Zarephath and to stay with a widow and her son. While Elijah is there, the son becomes ill and dies. The widow curses him until Elijah takes the corpse from the grieving mother, carries it to his own room, lays it on the bed there and cries out, 'O Lord my God, have You also brought tragedy on the widow with whom I lodge, by killing her son?' Elijah prostrates himself three times and begs God to let the child's soul return, and the Lord restores the child to life. When the mother sees her living son, she accepts God.

The saints frequently raised the dead, always (of course) in the service of God. St Macarius the Great of Egypt was reported to have raised a corpse to convince a heretical sect that denied the resurrection of the dead of their error (one account of the resurrection noted that Macarius brought the dead man back just long enough to speak, then released him).[5] Macarius was also the subject of a curious account involving a skull:

> Walking in the desert one day, I found the skull of a dead man, lying on the ground. As I was moving it with my stick, the skull spoke to me. I said to it, 'Who are you?' The skull replied, 'I was high priest of the idols and of the pagans who dwelt in this place; but you are Macarius, the Spirit-bearer. Whenever you take pity on those who are in torments, and pray for them, they feel a little respite.'

Macarius converses briefly with the skull before burying it.[6] Note the similarity between this, a talking skull, and the ancient Babylonian method of necromancy in which a spirit is ordered into a skull to converse with the magician.

The story of St Martin of Tours restoring a dead catechumen (a recent convert yet to receive baptism) is fascinating since the resurrected man offers a description of the afterlife. St Martin restored the dead man to life three days after his passing by stretching 'himself at full length on the dead limbs of the departed brother'. After two hours of maintaining this position while engaged in prayer, the dead man began to move, causing Martin to shout joyously. The man immediately obtained baptism and lived for many years, offering testimony to Martin's miracles. The man told of this experience while in the deceased state:

> when he left the body, he was brought before the tribunal
> of the Judge, and being assigned to gloomy regions
> and vulgar crowds, he received a severe sentence. Then,
> however, he added, it was suggested by two angels of
> the Judge that he was the man for whom Martin was
> praying; and that, on this account, he was ordered to
> be led back by the same angels, and given up to Martin,
> and restored to his former life.[7]

The ancient Irish manuscript *Lebor na hUidre* (*The Book of the Dun Cow*) recounts the tale of St Patrick attempting to convert the monarch Loegaire (or Laery mac Neill) by producing the spirit of the great Celtic hero Cuchulain. Patrick successfully resurrects not just Cuchulain but his chariot, his famous horses the Liath Macha and the Dub-Sainglend, and his charioteer Loeg,[8] all of whom emerge from a mist that follows a blast of icy wind (which Patrick's companion St Benen calls the wind of Hell). The spirit of Cuchulain proves his identity by reciting certain facts, and wins Loegaire's sympathy by describing his fate in the afterlife:

> What I suffered of trouble,
> O Laery, by sea and land –
> Yet more severe was a single night
> When the demon was wrathful!
> Great as was my heroism,
> Hard as was my sword,

The devil crushed me with one finger
Into the red charcoal!⁹

Patrick's ability to produce the spirits convinces Loegaire to convert.

Of course the second most famous biblical scene of resurrection (after Christ's) is the raising of Lazarus of Bethany – after four days in the tomb – by Jesus. Biblical scholars have long debated both this and the passages surrounding John the Baptist and Jesus, who in the Gospel of Mark is imagined by Herod Antipas to be John risen from the dead. Some theologians have noted that the resurrection of Lazarus is not strictly necromancy, since Lazarus is not raised in order to deliver prophecy; nor, obviously, is this sciomancy, as Lazarus is made once again fully human and lives out his life for many years thereafter.

Even heathen necromancers were converted after witnessing miraculous resurrections. Onkelos, son of Koloniko, was one such who was considering converting to Judaism. He first raised Titus, who advised against it, then Balaam, who told him that it wouldn't happen. The next resurrection is sometimes inferred as referring to Jesus, although other translations give it as 'the sinners of Israel'. This time, Onkelos is told, 'Seek their welfare, seek not their harm.'¹⁰ Onkelos converted and went on to produce the *Targum Onkelos*, a translation of the Five Books of Moses. Similarly, the fifteenth-century reformer and writer Johannes Nider writes of a notorious necromancer who was huge and frightening-looking; after his sister converted him, he sought admittance to numerous monasteries, all but the last turning him away because of his monstrous appearance. He ended up becoming a devout holy man, but was tormented by demons throughout his life.¹¹

The Bible and the Books of the Apocrypha also recount the famous story of one unsuccessful attempt to convert a pagan necromancer: Simon Magus. In Acts 8 Philip journeys to the city of Samaria, where he performs miracles that include casting out unclean spirits. A Samarian named Simon, a sorcerer who has long bewitched the people of his city, sees Philip's miracles and agrees to be baptized with the rest of the city. The apostles Peter and John are then sent to the city to bring down the Holy Ghost upon the new converts; Simon is so impressed with this that he offers the apostles money to learn their skills. They instead tell him to repent, and he begs that they pray for him.

In the apocryphal book Acts of Peter, Simon is given many more magical abilities, including levitation and the power to cause a dog to speak. Peter travels to Rome to confront Simon, where he is staying with the senator Marcellus. Peter and Simon engage in a long battle of wills and miracles that includes a sequence in which Peter challenges Simon to resurrect a dead man. Simon accepts the challenge, and succeeds: 'Simon went to the head of the dead man and stooped down and thrice raised himself up . . . and showed the people that he [the dead man] lifted his head and moved it, and opened his eyes and bowed himself a little unto Simon.' At first the onlookers are convinced, but then Peter points out that the corpse hasn't risen or spoken. When it returns to its deathly state, the people turn against Simon, but Peter asks them to allow the necromancer to repent; then Peter raises the dead man, who rises and speaks. Simon, however, does not repent, but continues to work against Peter, accusing him of not truly believing in God; Simon moves among the wealthy, where 'in dining chambers he made certain spirits enter in, which were only an appearance, and not existing in truth.' The battle between Peter and Simon comes to a head when Simon tells the people of Rome that he is going to fly to Heaven, but as he begins to move upward Peter asks God to cause him to fall but not die. Simon plummets, breaking his leg, and that night he flees Rome, eventually arriving in Terracina, where he dies a short time later, unrepentant.[12] Simon would go on to become the archetypal heretical necromancer, appearing in such later texts as the *Golden Legend* and

Studio of Pompeo Batoni, *The Fall of Simon Magus*, c. 1745–50, oil on canvas.

the romantic *Clementine Recognitions*, Book II (in Chapter XIII of that work, Simon Magus relates how he accomplishes his magical works: 'I have made the soul of a boy, unsullied and violently slain and invoked by unutterable adjurations, to assist me, and by it is done all that I command'[13]).

While resurrecting the dead for purposes of convincing heathens fell into the realm of miracles, by the fourth century AD the Church had positioned itself firmly against the practice of necromancy; where the pagan Roman emperors had once tolerated and even practised necromancy, the Christian emperors established severe punishment for this unholy practice. As Tertullian noted, 'We must after all this turn our attention to those scriptures also which forbid our belief in such a resurrection as is held by your Animalists (for I will not call them Spiritualists), that it is either to be assumed as taking place now, as soon as men come to the knowledge of the truth, or else that it is accomplished immediately after their departure from this life.'[14] Not only was the first of God's Ten Commandments 'Thou shalt have no other gods before me' (which would include the pagan gods and demons that enabled necromancy), but the Bible also contains numerous instances in which the practice of necromancy is condemned. Leviticus 19:31 instructed, 'Regard not them that have familiar spirits, neither seek after wizards, to be defiled by them.' God promised that as punishment for those who sought out necromancers, He 'will even set my face against that soul, and will cut him off from among his people' (Leviticus 20:6), while the necromancer himself would be stoned to death (Leviticus 20:27). Deuteronomy 18:11 forbids the use of a necromancer, while 12 adds, 'For all that do these things are an abomination unto the Lord: and because of these abominations the Lord thy God doth drive them out from before thee.' In 2 Kings 21, the story of Manasseh is related, who reigned in Jerusalem for 55 years, during which time he committed terrible abominations, including (in verse 6) dealing 'with familiar spirits'; for this action, the Lord responded with terrible vengeance ('I will wipe Jerusalem as a man wipeth a dish, wiping it, and turning it upside down').

However, the greatest biblical warning against the promise of necromancy is undoubtedly the story of Saul and the Witch of Endor, found in 1 Samuel 28:3–25. The prophet Samuel has just died and been buried, and King Saul has banished all necromancers

Gustave Doré, *Saul and the Witch of Endor*, 1866, engraving.

and wizards. The Philistines are preparing to go to war with the Israelites, and when Saul sees their forces massed, he's terrified. He calls out to the Lord, but receives no response, neither by dreams nor prophets nor the special divinatory equipment (Urim and Thummim, two enigmatic objects worn on a breastplate) of the high priest. Saul then tells his servants to find 'a woman that hath a familiar spirit' (even though he's just banned all the necromancers), and they locate a witch at Endor. Saul disguises himself and, taking two men with him, travels by night to visit the woman. When he orders the woman to call forth her familiar spirit, she reminds him of Saul's recent prohibitions, upon which he promises that she will be safe from punishment. The witch agrees to work for him then, asking whom he wants to see, and he asks for Samuel. When the spirit of Samuel appears, Saul's identity is revealed to the witch, who cries out, but Saul assures her again of her safety; however, he's seen nothing and asks her to describe the apparition. She describes seeing Samuel 'ascending out of the earth', and Saul falls to the ground. Samuel – in the tradition of so many spirits before him – complains that he's been 'disquieted', and Saul tells him of the Philistine army and God's refusal to answer his pleas. Samuel tells Saul that the Israelites will be conquered by the Philistines, and Saul and his sons will die tomorrow. Samuel departs then, and Saul is too frightened and hungry to get up, so the witch offers him food. He and his men eat and then leave. The next day the Philistines triumph, Saul falls on his sword rather than be captured and three of his sons also die.

Because this important story is the Bible's clearest confirmation of the powers of necromancy, scholars have debated it for centuries. Some focus on the way the witch cries out when she sees the spirit of Samuel, suggesting that she has never actually accomplished producing a spirit before. In the Septuagint (the earliest Greek translation of the Torah, dating from the second century BC) a word that translates to 'ventriloquist' is used to describe the woman. In

Greek 'ventriloquist' (ἐγγαστρίμυθοι or *eggastrimthouoi*) translates more literally to 'the one who has words in his belly'; it's how the Greek translators chose to represent the Hebrew word *'ôb*, or spirit, although this can also mean a leather water bag (in *The Discoverie of Witchcraft* from 1584, Reginald Scot suggested that the translators actually used it because it meant 'water bag', because the Old World oracles spoke hollowly from 'the bottome of their bellies'[15]). The word first appears in a medical text from the fourth century BC, when a woman with a throat inflammation is described as producing sounds like 'those produced by the females we call ventriloquists'.[16] Its use could also be due to the sounds of the voices the necromancers produced, which might have been heard emanating from the chest or the belly; or it may have been employed because, in ancient necromancy, spirits were described as emanating or speaking from the ground. 'Ventriloquist' probably didn't have necromantic associations until the translators chose it for the Septuagint.

The Christian Mages

By the fourth century AD the Roman emperors were calling for severe punishment for pagan magical practices. Valentinian I (reigned 364–75), often named as the last great Western emperor, authorized death for those who engaged in 'necromantic sacrifices'. Even wearing a talisman or practising a medical charm could cause a citizen to be subjected to capital punishment. People burned magical texts rather than risk being caught with them; such texts thus became scarce, which later added to their desirability by occult practitioners. Some religious officials – such as the Archbishop of Paris, in 1277 – specifically condemned all written necromantic works. The fourteenth-century Dominican inquisitor Nicholas Eymericus wrote of confiscating and burning such texts as the *Table of Solomon* and the *Treasury of Necromancy*. There are numerous legends involving infamous necromancers disposing of their books: Solomon,

Simon Magus, Roger Bacon and St Germain were all said to have destroyed theirs rather than be discovered with them. Magical manuscripts that survived from this period were sometimes kept in monasteries or royal courts.

Despite the Church's official stance on necromancy throughout the Middle Ages, there are a significant number of accounts of priests, friars and even popes who practised the black arts. This is not entirely surprising, given that those in religious orders had education (they could read Latin) and access to the manuscripts; they were also trained in exorcism, and so already had an understanding of – and possible interest in – demonic forces. One of the more infamous cases was Gerbert of Aurillac, who became Pope Sylvester II at the end of the tenth century, and who was also alleged to be a 'practitioner of necromancy and magic' whose rise had been fuelled by occult practices. Pope Gregory VII and Benedict XIII were also accused of necromancy; the latter was even said to have kept a book on necromancy in his bed.

Gilles de Rais (1405–1440) is the notorious Bluebeard of fairy tales, but he was once a knight who fought alongside Joan of Arc. Gilles, after squandering a significant fortune, turned to sorcerers in the hopes of replenishing his wealth. He sought the services of a Florentine priest named François Prelati who was said to be skilled at summoning up demons. Prelati's usual demon was named Barron, but neither Barron nor any other spirit put in an appearance at any of the three invocations conducted by Prelati that Gilles attended (during which the priest drew a circle and read from a book).[17] In 1440 Gilles and two servants were arrested on charges of child murder and sodomy, and Gilles was executed later that year. The fate of Prelati is unknown.

In his autobiography, Florentine artist Benvenuto Cellini describes a necromantic ritual that he witnessed in 1534. He had recently engaged a priest in conversation about necromancy, and the priest invited him to witness an invocation:

We went together to the Coliseum; and there the priest, having arrayed himself in necromancer's robes, began to describe circles on the earth with the finest ceremonies that can be imagined. I must say that he had made us bring precious perfumes and fire, and also drugs of fetid odour. When the preliminaries were completed, he made the entrance into the circle; and taking us by the hand, introduced us one by one inside it. Then he assigned our several functions; to the necromancer, his comrade, he gave the pentacle to hold; the other two of us had to look after the fire and the perfumes; and then he began his incantations. This lasted more than an hour and a half, when several legions appeared, and the Coliseum was all full of devils. I was occupied with the precious perfumes, and when the priest perceived in what numbers they were present, he turned to me and said: 'Benvenuto, ask them something.' I called on them to reunite me with my Sicilian Angelica. That night we obtained no answer; but I enjoyed the greatest satisfaction of my curiosity in such matters.

Cellini returned for a second night, bringing with him (per the priest's instruction) a 'little boy of pure virginity'. On this occasion, even more spirits appeared; after assuring Cellini that he would see Angelica again in one month, the mass of spirits began to threaten those inside the circle. A terrifying time ensued as the necromancer entreated the spirits to leave peaceably, and at last they did.[18] Cellini did indeed see Angelica one month later.

Religious clerics who pursued necromancy were occasionally found out and punished. A fourteenth-century Florentine monk called John of Vallombrosa became very learned during his first few years at the monastery, reading his way through the library. Unfortunately, he developed a keen interest in necromancy, spent time with books on that subject and began to practise. After he was discovered, he spent several years in a dungeon, emerging broken but repentant.[19] In 1340 a priest named Lucas de Lafond of Grenade was tried by the Inquisition for practising necromancy.

The Grimoires

What were the texts that led to the fall of these clerics? Scholars of magic often point to a document known as *The Testament of Solomon* as the magical dividing line between the classical world and the Middle Ages. Based on the biblical character of Solomon and drenched in Jewish folklore, it's impossible to establish a date for the *Testament*, although it stems from about the same time that the Greek Magical Papyri were created, and is also written in Greek. *The Testament of Solomon* revolves around demonology, a common theme for magical practices of the next thousand years; it recounts Solomon's capture of Beelzebub and a number of lesser demons, and how he puts them to use in building the Temple of Jerusalem. The text lists dozens of lesser demons, detailing the characteristics and associations of each, along with spells on how to summon and control them. Although there is direct necromancy in the book, it consists of calling demonic and angelic spirits (not the dead), and offers an interesting perspective into how those who are summoned know the future:

> We demons ascend into the firmament of heaven, and fly about among the stars. And we hear the sentences which go forth upon the souls of men, and forthwith we come, and whether by force of influence, or by fire, or by sword, or by some accident, we veil our act of destruction; and if a man does not die by some untimely disaster or by violence, then we demons transform ourselves in such a way as to appear to men and be worshipped in our human nature.[20]

There is also a corresponding belief in Islam that suggests that, before the arrival of the Prophet Muhammad, *jinn* – invisible supernatural entities that were created before man – would fly to the heavens, listen in on the conversations of angels and return to report what they heard to men as divination. However, after the Prophet, angels guarded the heavens more closely.

The Testament of Solomon is also notable for the way it combines elements from so many previous belief systems; the demons' names derive from Assyrian, Babylonian, Egyptian, Greek, Jewish/Kabbalistic and early Christian sources.

The name of Solomon – a figure who appears in many of the great religions and is often associated with magic – has been given to many occult texts over the centuries, most notably *The Key of Solomon*. This influential volume has appeared in many editions, although it has also been argued that all printed editions are useless since the spells it contains would work only if the magician himself copied them with a consecrated pen onto consecrated paper.[21] The spells often call for purification (a period of chastity and fasting before attempting the ritual) and use the Kabbalistic names of God and angels. Although the spells may be conducted in the magician's own abode (provided it has been properly prepared), the *Key* suggests the use of a secret place:

> The places best fitted for exercising and accomplishing
> Magical Arts and Operations are those which are
> concealed, removed and separated from the habitations
> of men. Wherefore desolate and uninhabited regions are
> most appropriate, such as the borders of lakes, forests,
> dark and obscure places, old and deserted houses, whither
> rarely and scarce ever men do come; mountains, caves,
> caverns, grottos, garden, orchards; but best of all are
> cross-roads, and where four roads meet, during the
> depth and silence of the night.[22]

Note the similarities here to rituals from the ancient world: 'borders of lakes' sounds like a direct reference to the Acheron nekromanteion, 'caves' recalls the underworld entrances, and 'orchards' sounds like the story of Protesilaos, the Trojan War soldier who appears to a vinedresser. Warnings about the importance of cross-roads play a major part in later folklore, especially from Ireland, Scotland and rural America.

In her 1949 study *Ritual Magic* E. M. Butler comments on how often these early grimoires centre on ancient heroes: 'Magic, always conscious of a remote and glorious golden age, seeks in the distant past and its memorials for the secrets of knowledge, wisdom and power.'[23] Another volume rooted in history and Jewish mysticism, and employing yet another great biblical hero, was *The Sword of Moses*. Like *The Testament*, this document lists names of divine entities (angels here), and offers a process of purification that must be followed before any of the spells can be attempted. The purification process – three days of light fasting and prayer – is reminiscent of certain episodes from the classical world involving similar practices; note, for example, the story of Thessalos, the Greek scholar who travelled to Egypt in search of necromancy, and who was instructed to purify himself for three days prior to the ritual. Similarly, visitors to a nekromanteion prepared themselves before 'incubation', or sleeping in order to communicate with the spirit in dreams. Once the three days of purification are complete, *The Sword of Moses* offers detailed instructions for enacting dozens of different rituals. They all begin by praising God and his angels and by calling for their assistance, then move on to specifics. To speak with the dead, it's necessary to write several angelic names on a saucer and place it in the roots of a genip tree.[24]

As indicated by the use of Old Testament heroes in their titles, these books make considerable use of Jewish religious writings, especially the richly detailed tradition of the Kabbala, which claims to offer secret knowledge that is buried within the Old Testament (and was gifted either by fallen angels or by God himself). The Kabbala, as outlined in the massive multi-volume study the Zohar, offers means of magical encryption that appeal to the magician's use of language and names, while its description of the Tree of Life provides an elegant visual illustration.

Jewish mysticism includes numerous names for necromancers: the person who invokes the dead is called *ba'alat-'ôb*, the 'mistress of the 'ôb' or 'mistress of the spirits'; a *yidde-oni* literally means 'gainer of information from ghosts'; and a *doresh el ha-metim* is one who questions corpses.[25] According to the Talmud, the *yidde-oni* used a bone of the animal called 'yaddua' in his mouth, which is made to speak by magic.

Although later occult scholars would frequently cite both Jewish and Arabic influence on medieval magic, Islam doesn't offer the possibility of ghosts. Black magic or sorcery, known as *Sihr*, are recognized in the Quran, but ghosts are not. Sorcerers may call on *jinn* and *jinn* may impersonate ghosts, but the spirits of the dead don't return.

There are a number of other necromantic texts that survived from the Middle Ages, most associated with authors who have attained fame as legendary necromancers. One of the most famous of the later Solomon-inspired texts is *The Grand Grimoire*, the full subtitle of which runs: *with the Powerful Clavicle of Solomon and of Black Magic; or the Infernal Devices of the Great Agrippa for the Discovery of All Hidden Treasures and the Subjugation of Every Denomination of Spirits, together with an Abridgment of All the Magical Arts*. Dates for the origin of this text have been placed at everything from 1421 to the early 1800s; not all versions of the book, which is also known as *The Red Dragon*, include that subtitle. Worth noting here is the mention of Agrippa: Heinrich Cornelius Agrippa (1486–1535) was a German mercenary, writer and occultist who is the author of the influential *Three Books of Occult Philosophy*, first published from 1531 to 1533 (a fourth book was added much later, although the authorship of that volume is suspect). The books are a substantial collection of occult lore, covering everything from astrology to herbal remedies to summoning spirits. Agrippa tells us there are two kinds of necromancy: traditional necromancy, which offers a blood sacrifice to resurrect the carcass; and sciomancy, which calls up only the spirit.[26] He also divides ceremonial magic into two parts: *Goetia* and *Theurgia*. Goetia involves 'the commerces of unclean spirits' and is essentially black magic, which is 'abandoned and execrated by all laws'; by contrast, theurgia calls upon divine entities and is often thought of as white magic.[27] Agrippa even suggests that every man has a 'good Demon' that has come from 'God himself, the President of Demons, being universall, above nature'.[28]

In Book iv of his *Occult Philosophy*, Agrippa offers a spell for reuniting a soul with its body: an offering of milk, honey, oil and other materials is made and 'compounded according to a true rule,

A medieval necromancer at work.

Circle for invoking tribal spirits from Johann Faust's *Magia naturalis et innaturalis* (1849).

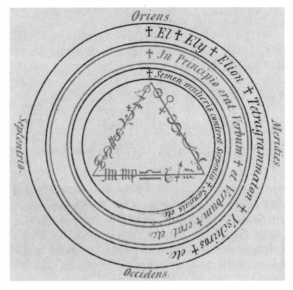

with congruent inscriptions of Names and Seals, [it] very much avail[s] to the raising up of departed souls'.[29]

Although Agrippa's works are still sought after and even practised, he isn't as universally known as Johann Georg Faust (1480–1540), who inspired both Marlowe's *The Tragical History of the Life and Death of Doctor Faustus* (1604) and Goethe's *Faust* (1808). The real Faust was a German magician, probably born in 1480, a date that technically places Faust at the beginning of the German Renaissance, but it can be argued that his life and legend – the wandering necromancer who makes deals with spirits (or, in literature, the Devil) – plant him firmly in the Middle Ages. Faust's legend has survived not only on stage, but as the author of one of the classic grimoires: *The Threefold Coercion of Hell*, so titled because it begins with Faust boasting of his ability to control spirits:

> With this book I, Dr Johannes Faust, have coerced all the spirits so that they had to bring to me whatever I desired: be it gold, silver, treasures large and small, also the spring-root,

and whatever else is available on Earth. All that did I get with this book. I was also capable to dispel the spirits after they had done what I asked them for.[30]

Faust begins his instructions with a strong warning to practise necromancy only within a protective circle, otherwise the spirits may end up controlling the magician. The necromancer should begin only after receiving Holy Communion and should be skilled in prayer. The circle is scratched into the ground with a specially inscribed sword, sigils (magical symbols) are drawn and placed, and incantations are spoken. Although Faust's spells are really meant to summon demons, some of the rituals attributed to him are also designed to call human spirits. The instructions are typical for occult texts of this period in calling for items that are difficult, if not impossible, to obtain. Look, for example, at the first three steps listed in his 'Deals with the citation of the tribal spirits of deceased men' ('tribal spirits' were those that guarded treasure):

1   Go silently on the night to the place where a beggar talked to you. Give to the same person 1 good peny [sic], and give him 3 pieces again and let yourself be surrendered 3 pieces back thereon.
2   You must make holy water for yourself.
3   A diaper-cord, which must have been used thrice on the baptism.

The citation goes on to involve creating a circle inscribed with sacred names and symbols. When ready, the necromancer steps into the circle, incites a few preliminary prayers and then conjures the spirits with the main invocation spoken three times. An incense made of white mastic, frankincense, myrrh, aloe, dragon-blood and rosemary is burned.[31]

The Inquisition and Witchcraft

Around the beginning of the thirteenth century, the Catholic Church began to suppress sects such as Catharism, which it considered heretical; it soon established inquisitions to investigate and deal with heretics, even offering absolution to inquisitors who used torture. In addition secular courts also began to deal out harsh punishments for sorcery and witchcraft. Four centuries earlier, Charlemagne had declared that all those found guilty of sorcery or divination should be turned over to the Church as slaves, while those who sacrificed to the Devil should be executed.[32] The trial of the Templars (1307–14) established many of the patterns of later trials: there were charges surrounding magical practices, both the Church and secular courts were involved and confiscation of property was likely a reason for pursuing the case.

Throughout the fourteenth century, the inquisitions focused mainly on religious heretics. When inquisitors occasionally brought charges against cunning folk – those minor magical workers who created simple love charms or healing potions – they were counselled to pursue charges of magic only if heresy was the overriding factor. However, things changed during the fifteenth century, as inquisitors and others sought to charge large groups in what they conceived of as a widespread diabolical conspiracy. The friar Bernardino of Siena took the concept of mass charges further by suggesting that anyone who failed to report on a known practitioner of magic shared in the guilt. Inquisitorial texts like *The Errors of the Gazarii* created and furthered the popular image of witches' sabbaths, meetings during which new converts might be required to kiss the Devil's posterior or anoint themselves with an ointment made from unbaptized infants (thus giving them the ability to fly). In 1484 a Dominican priest named Heinrich Kramer sought and received a papal bull to prosecute witches. Three years later, Kramer's notorious *Malleus Maleficarum* (The Hammer of Witches,

An early engraving depicting an Inquisition torture chamber.

supposedly co-authored with a friar called Jacob Sprenger, although his contribution is subject to debate) was published, and further fuelled the witch-hunts that spread across Europe for the next two hundred years. Perhaps the most hysterical of the witchcraft texts at this time was Jean Bodin's *On the Demon-mania of Witches*, which argued in favour of believing virtually all accusations of witchcraft, and for the strongest punishments possible. Bodin's book calls necromancy 'perhaps among the first and most ancient kinds of witchcraft',[33] and includes some of the most lurid descriptions ever recorded, such as this one, which Bodin claimed to have heard from someone with intimate knowledge of those involved:

> one of the great kings of Christendom wishing to know the fate of his state, sent for a Jacobin necromancer, who said Mass, and after having consecrated the host had the head cut off a young first-born child of ten years old, and had his head placed on the host; then uttering certain words

and using symbols, which it is not necessary to know, asked what he wanted. The head only answered these two words, 'Vim patior.' Immediately the king went into a frenzy, crying endlessly, 'Take away this head,' and died mad in this way. This story is considered certain and beyond doubt.[34]

Bodin goes on to note that he believes the spirits of the dead are always devils, and even that the oracles of the ancient world were possessed by the Devil.

Reginald Scot's *The Discoverie of Witchcraft* (1584) also collects spells and rituals. As with the earlier texts, the spells are a strange mix of Christianity and paganism. A spell for imprisoning a summoned spirit in a crystal begins in a familiar fashion, involving two days of prayer and fasting, begun at a new moon. Next, the magician utters this prayer:

> I desire thee O Lord God, my mercifull and most loving God, the giver of all graces, the giver of all sciences, grant that I thy welbeloved *N.* (although unworthy) may knowe thy grace and power, against all the deceipts and craftiness of divels. And grant to me thy power, good Lord, to constraine them by this art: for thou art the true, and livelie, and eternall GOD, which livest and reignest ever one GOD through all worlds, Amen.

This spell next outlines the use of five swords, one of which is used to create a magical circle, and the invoking of the names of the 'five kings of the North': Sitrael, Malanthon, Thamaor, Falaur and Sitrami. Once the spirit kings appear, the magician orders them: 'I conjure, charge, and command you, and everie of you, Sirrael, Malanthaon, Thamaor, Falaur, and Sitrami, you infernall kings, to put into this christall stone one spirit learned and expert in all arts and sciences, by the virtue of this name of God

Tetragrammaton.' At the conclusion of the spell, the kings will call a spirit and place it into the crystal, at which point the crystal will turn black.[35]

However, much of *The Discoverie of Witchcraft* offers a far more rational look at witchcraft; it dares to suggest that most cases can be easily ascribed to other, more natural causes (for example, it notes that elderly witches are likelier to simply be suffering from 'melancholie' or dementia). Scot takes on Bodin's text by name, arguing that witches don't summon spirits ('this is a stale ridiculous lie'), and offering a wryly sarcastic answer to the notion that witches can bring storms and fly: 'Then I will worship them as gods; for those be not the works of man, nor yet of witch.'[36] Scot even includes instructions for performing basic magic tricks and tips on juggling.

By the time the witch persecutions faded, an estimated 40,000 to 50,000 victims had been executed,[37] often by being burned at the stake. Most of the victims were female, a fact which many historians attribute at least in part to the extraordinary misogyny of the *Malleus* (see chapter headings such as 'Whether Witches May Work Some Prestidigatory Illusion so That the Male Organ Appears to Be Entirely Removed and Separate from the Body'). The self-proclaimed 'Witchfinder General' Matthew Hopkins roamed parts of England in search of witches from 1644 to 1646, justifying his actions (in a pamphlet entitled *The Discovery of Witches: In Answer to Severall Queries, Lately Delivered to the Judges of Assize for the County of Norfolk*) by explaining that witches possessed extra breasts (which he referred to as 'teats' or 'papps') in order to suckle 'imps' and evil spirits.[38] Hopkins oversaw around three hundred executions before his death in 1647.

The witch-hunt craze is often thought to have come to a finale with the trial and execution of nineteen witches in Salem, Massachusetts, in 1692 and 1693. That famous case, which has inspired dozens of books, films and plays (most notably Arthur Miller's *The Crucible*), is one of the best documented, and looking at the transcripts provides insight into the belief that the so-called witches operated with familiar spirits:

> Martha Carrier was Indicted for the Bewitching of certain Persons, according to the Form usual in such Cases. Pleading Not Guilty, to her Indictment, there were First brought in a considerable number of the Bewitched Persons; who not only made the Court sensible of an horrid Witchcraft committed upon them, but also deposed, That it was Martha Carrier, or her Shape, that Grievously Tormented them, by Biting, Pricking, Pinching, and Choaking of them. It was further deposed, that while this Carrier was on her Examination, before the Magistrates, the Poor People were so Tortured that every one expected their Death upon the very Spott; but that upon the binding of Carrier they were eased.[39]

Edward Kelley and John Dee

A man who was possibly the last great necromancer of the Renaissance demonstrates the conflicting ways in which the summoning of spirits was viewed towards the end of this era. Doctor John Dee (1527–1608/9), a man learned in mathematics, science and astrology who had served as a royal adviser, is famous for his occult writings, which include messages supposedly dictated by angels and mediated by his associate, Edward Kelley.

The preface (by Arthur Edward Waite) from the 1893 edition of Kelley's works describes him as 'a sordid impostor, who duped the immeasurable credulity of the learned Doctor Dee, and subsequently involved his victim in transactions which have permanently degraded an otherwise great name'.[40] Kelley was born in England in 1555, and may have been educated at Oxford (he could read and write in Latin and some Greek). Although early parts of his life are vague, he may have committed fraud involving forged deeds; his ears were removed, possibly as punishment for crimes as a young man. He travelled the English countryside, finally arriving in Glastonbury, where he encountered an old alchemical manuscript (according to legend, this was *The Book of St Dunstan*) which he purchased from an innkeeper, along with some unnamed powders that were supposed to be useful in alchemical transmutations. By 1582 he was in London, in the company of Dr John Dee, who was in his fifties and more interested in magic than mathematics or science. Dee was most enamoured with the idea of communing with spirits, and Kelley proved to be a willing medium specializing in scrying (peering into a reflective surface to receive visions or messages). Over the course of many sessions, Dee claimed to channel messages from angels, creating along the way an 'Enochian language'. However, Kelley may have also been practising less angelic forms of spirit-calling, as detailed in this report published after his death:

This diabolicall questioning of the dead, for the knowledge of future accidents, was put in practice by the foresaid *Kelley*; who, upon a certaine night, in the Parke of Walton in le dale, in the county of Lancaster, with one *Paul Waring* (his fellow companion in such deeds of darknesse) invocated some one of the infernall regiment, to know certaine passages in the life, as also what might beeknowne by the devils of foresight, of the manner and time of the death of a noble young Gentleman, as then in his wardship. The blacke ceremonies of that night being ended, *Kelley* demanded of one of the Gentlemans servants, what corpse was the last buried in Law-church-yard, a Church there unto adjoining, who told him of a poore man that was buried there but the same day. He and the said *Waring* intreated this foresaid servant, to go with them to the grave of the man so lately interred, which hee did; and withal did helpe them to digge up the carcase of

'Edward Kelly, a Magician, in the Act of Invoking the Spirit of a Deceased Person', 1806, engraving.

the poore caitiffe, whom by their incantations, they made him (or rather some evill spirit through his Organs) to speake, who delivered strange predictions concerning the said Gentleman.[41]

In 1583 Kelley convinced Dee that they should travel to Europe, meeting with kings and demonstrating alchemy. Kelley and Dee had brought their families with them, and while in Europe, Kelley claimed to receive a spirit directive that he and Dee should use 'their two wives in common'. When Kelley was unable to produce the desired alchemical effects at the court of Emperor Rudolph II, King of Hungary and Bohemia, the emperor ordered him to be imprisoned, although Dee was left free. Kelley was allowed to return to Prague – under guard – to consult with Dee, but while there he murdered one of the guards and was returned to prison, where he died in an escape attempt in 1597. After Kelley's death, Dee returned to England, where he found that occult practices were falling out of favour. He spent his final years in poverty, dying in 1608 or 1609. To this day, scholars of the occult study his Enochian writings, as Dee called them, while historians suggest that he fell victim to one of history's great fraudulent mediums.

3

DARKNESS ACROSS THE ENLIGHTENMENT AND THE ROMANTIC GOTHIC

During the fifteenth and sixteenth centuries, the Renaissance held sway in the Western world. Alongside the Inquisition, the Renaissance (which some scholars believe is really just the conclusion of the Middle Ages) brought advances in science, particularly astronomy; art, with the works of such masters as Leonardo da Vinci, Michelangelo and Raphael; literature, as illustrated by the plays of Shakespeare; religion, when in 1517 Martin Luther began the Reformation with his 95 Theses; exploration, with improved ships and navigation allowing Europeans to map the globe; and (perhaps most importantly) the spread of information, after Johannes Gutenberg invented the first movable-type printing press around 1439.

The Renaissance led on to the Age of Reason, or the Enlightenment. As thinkers like Francis Bacon and René Descartes established empiricism and rationalism in modern philosophy, the Church sought to rein in the persecution of witches. In 1611 the Spanish Inquisitor Alonso de Salazar Frías wrote, 'I have not found even indications from which to infer that even a single act of witchcraft has really occurred.'[1] In 1614 the Spanish Inquisition removed the death penalty in witchcraft trials and called for restraint in torture. The influential Prussian lawyer and writer Christian Thomasius argued against both torture and the existence of demons; the year that Thomasius died – 1728 – also saw the last witch-burning in

Prussia. In 1735 the British Witchcraft Act was passed, designating witchcraft as a criminal offence by those who pretended to possess magic abilities or call up spirits, and, despite a few more isolated cases over the next century, the era of the witch trials was dead.

By the eighteenth century great philosophers and writers such as John Locke, Thomas Hobbes and Voltaire were expounding materialism and humanism. Paris was the intellectual and cultural capital of Europe, and its salons became the gathering places for the new thinkers. The atmosphere surely favoured an end to old superstitions about calling forth spirits and demons . . . or did it?

Cagliostro

Instead of consigning magicians to history's dustbin, the eighteenth century made them as big and resplendent as the court of Versailles. None were bigger than Count Alessandro di Cagliostro, whose life and riotous escapades made him the most infamous necromancer since Faust. He was born Giuseppe Balsamo in Palermo in 1743, and at thirteen he was sent to a convent where he apprenticed to the apothecary but was soon expelled. He had to flee Palermo after duping a man out of sixty pieces of gold by promising to help him find treasure in a cave, but when the unfortunate victim arrived he encountered instead a cadre of angry 'spirits', who were Balsamo's confederates. For a time Balsamo found himself in Malta, where he studied alchemy with a man named Pinto. After that, he travelled to Europe, amassing wealth and always keeping one step ahead of the law or a vengeful victim. When he arrived in London in 1776, he had acquired a new name – the Conte di Cagliostro – and a lovely wife who was presented as the Countess Serafina Feliciani, a jar of red powder (à la Edward Kelley before him) that he claimed could transmute baser metals into gold, and a life-prolonging 'Egyptian Wine'. While in England he became acquainted with freemasonry, and was soon declaring himself Grand Master of the Egyptian

Rite. After leaving England, he found himself at the centre of Enlightenment society, holding seances that reputedly involved communication with celestial spirits. At these events, Cagliostro promised his followers they would partake of his secrets of alchemy, immortality and communion with the beyond.

He eventually made his way to Russia, hoping to find favour with Catherine II, but she ordered him out of the country. He next turned up in Warsaw, where witnesses described his seances as using an eight-year-old girl into whose hands he poured oil (an ancient Egyptian form of scrying); she was then placed behind a curtain and mysterious notes that Cagliostro had burned reappeared at her feet. Unfortunately for Cagliostro, the youthful medium confessed the next day to being tutored in the performance of these

Cagliostro faisant de l'alchimie avec le prince de Rohan.

Cagliostro (on the left) learns the craft of alchemy in this
19th-century engraving.

tricks. During another seance in which the spirit of the Grand Kophta (the Egyptian High Priest) was produced, the apparition was revealed to be a disguised Cagliostro.

In 1780 he arrived in Strasburg, where he built a large country villa dubbed 'the Cagliostræum' and presented himself as a miraculous healer. After he befriended Cardinal de Rohan (whom he supposedly cured of asthma), Baroness Oberkirch described Cagliostro's effect:

> No one can ever form the faintest idea of the fervour with
> which everybody pursued Cagliostro. He was surrounded,
> besieged; every one trying to win a glance or a word . . .
> A dozen ladies of rank and two actresses had followed him,
> in order to continue their treatment . . . If I had not seen it,
> I should never have imagined that a Prince of the Roman
> Church, a man in other respects intelligent and honourable,
> could so far let himself be imposed upon as to renounce
> his dignity, his free will, at the bidding of a sharper.[2]

In 1785 he and the cardinal arrived in Paris. One of the most famous stories surrounding Cagliostro is that of a seance he held there, in which he produced some of the late heroes of the Enlightenment:

> Six guests and the host took their places at a round
> table upon which there were thirteen covers. Each guest
> pronounced the name of the dead man whose spirit
> he wished to appear at the banquet table. Cagliostro,
> concentrating his mysterious forces, gave the invitation
> in a solemn and commanding tone. One after another
> the six guests appeared. They were the Duc de Choiseul,
> Voltaire, d'Alembert, Diderot, the Abbe de Voisenon, and
> Montesquieu.[3]

While in Paris, Cagliostro continued to engage in one benevolent practice: he offered free treatment and medicine to the poor. It was said that the indigent of the cities he lived in would routinely remove their hats when passing his residence.

In 1785 Cagliostro was arrested in connection with the notorious Affair of the Diamond Necklace, in which an extraordinary piece of jewellery originally created for Louis xv's chief mistress was swindled away, and the fraudster pointed a finger at Cagliostro. He was acquitted a year later, although historians suspect he may have been involved in the crime.

Cagliostro was then banished from France and returned to London, but his glamour seemed to be waning at last and he soon found himself in tremendous debt; even a pamphlet in which he predicted the fall of the Bastille couldn't restore his failing reputation.

Cagliostro journeyed back to the Continent, but his fraud had finally caught up with him and he was banned from returning to any of his former residences. He wound up in Rome, where in 1789 he was arrested by the Holy Inquisition. Apprehended with damning texts and paraphernalia, Cagliostro was tried, convicted and sentenced to death, but Pope Pius vi commuted the sentence to life imprisonment. Cagliostro died in prison in 1795.

He may have died in ignominy, but Cagliostro's legend lived on after him. Goethe and Alexander Dumas based characters upon him, and a street in his home town of Palermo was named after him. One of the most famous illusionists of all time, Robert-Houdin, invoked Cagliostro's name in one of his tricks. Thomas Carlyle described Cagliostro as:

Pupil of the Sage Althotas, Foster-child of the Scherif of Mecca, probable Son of the last King of Trebisond; named also Acharat, and Unfortunate Child of Nature; by profession healer of diseases, abolisher of wrinkles, friend of the poor and impotent, grand-master of the Egyptian Mason-lodge of

High Science, Spirit-summoner, Gold-cook, Grand Cophta, Prophet, Priest, and thaumaturgic moralist and swindler; really a Liar of the first magnitude, thorough-paced in all provinces of lying, what one may call the King of Liars.[4]

In occult circles there is even a theory that Cagliostro and Balsamo were two separate people, with Cagliostro indeed having been a great magician. This theory is fuelled by two metaphysical books often ascribed to Cagliostro, although the actual author of both remains unknown: *Mémoires authentique pour servir à l'histoire du Comte de Cagliostro* was published in 1785, purportedly written by Cagliostro but attributed to the Marquis de Luchet, and principally concerns the initiation of Cagliostro and his wife into the Rosicrucians by another famous eighteenth-century swindler, Le Comte St Germain;[5] and *La Très Sainte Trinosophie* (The Most Holy Trinosophia) is a 96-page, heavily illustrated occult text attributed to either St Germain or Cagliostro (it's rumoured that a copy was confiscated from Cagliostro when he was imprisoned).

More recently, renowned sceptic James Randi described the death of Cagliostro as an important historical turning point:

> When Cagliostro died, so effectively died a belief in genuine sorcery, though it peeps from out of its grave occasionally even today. The era of the admitted trickster dawned, in which audiences were no longer asked to believe that those who performed mysterious demonstrations did so with divine or demonic assistance.[6]

The Great Light Shows

There has been speculation that Cagliostro may have employed a magic lantern, a device invented by the Dutch scientist Christiaan Huygens in the mid-seventeenth century. The magic lantern swiftly gained in popularity as a unique new form of entertainment, mainly shared among Europe's elite, but it also proved a boon to humbugs.

Although the concept of using a light source to project images wasn't new, Huygens's invention allowed for far more complicated and realistic effects. In his notes from 1659 Huygens describes '*la laterne magique*' as a candle placed in a box with convex lenses extending in front of it; when glass slides are inserted between the candle and the lenses, the images they contain are projected in large format. Huygens's first slides were of hand-painted skeletons in a variety of poses.[7] Movement could be created by moving one slide against another.

It's entirely possible that the first users of the magic lantern were fraudulent necromancers. While the illusions conducted by Cagliostro in his seances – for example, the sudden appearance or disappearance of a costly gem – mostly seemed to fall within the realm of standard magician's sleight of hand (performed with what must have been an inexhaustible source of confidence), other con-men working the Continent at about the same time were holding seances that sound likelier to have made use of the magic lantern. The most famous of these was Johann Georg Schröpfer, a German charlatan who is sometimes credited (albeit erroneously) as being the first to use the magic lantern to create a 'phantasmagoria', or light show of spooky images like skeletons, ghosts and demons. Schröpfer resided in Leipzig just a few years before Cagliostro, and they had much in common: they both travelled Europe presenting themselves as skilled necromancers and highly placed Freemasons; they both moved within elite circles, even hobnobbing with royalty; and they were both frequently discredited, at which point they moved on to the next easy mark. Schröpfer started out as the owner of a Leipzig coffee house, but he accrued a great deal of debt and began to hold seances as a means to pay it off. The seances were popular, Schröpfer's fame spread and he was soon presenting his act in other cities.

Schröpfer created his own personal mythology. He claimed that his summons could produce three types of spirit: the good, the bad or the neutral (he was said to carry two pistols with him at all times to use against the evil sort). He began his performances by invoking the good spirits and asking for their aid in protecting him from the bad.

A Russian traveller named Nicolai Karamsin, who ventured to Leipzig, described attending a show hosted by 'Baron Schröpfer'. He recounts how Schröpfer began the evening by plying his guests with drink (becoming very insistent if they refused); at some point, the guests were led into a large hall hung with black cloth. Schröpfer then drew a circle around the assembly, warning them not to step outside of it. The only light in the room came from some lamps on a small altar, before which Schröpfer knelt. Karamsin then describes Schröpfer's impassioned acting, which included baring his breast and waving a sword as he begged the spirits to appear. This was followed by the sound of thunder, and then something stirred in the air above the altar, 'a light vapour, which grew thicker by degrees, till it assumed the figure of a man'. When Karamsin's companion, determined to unmask Schröpfer, started to step out of the circle, the necromancer pointed the sword at him and shouted, 'You are a dead man, if you stir another step!' Karamsin says that many of the spectators treated the entire performance as theatre.[8]

Another one of Schröpfer's seances offers an even more dramatic scene and became one of the most celebrated occult occurrences of the eighteenth century. In 1773 Schröpfer visited Dresden, where he was called upon by Prince Charles of Saxony. The prince was hoping to locate a treasure said to be hidden somewhere in his palace, and so he asked Schröpfer to summon up the spirits to reveal the secret. On the appointed evening, the prince, Schröpfer and seventeen guests assembled in secret in the Great Gallery of Charles's palace. Schröpfer once again demanded they all drink (all but two did), and – matching Karamsin's description – the necromancer then knelt before an altar, calling for the spirits until thunderous noises sounded. A sound like fingers being rubbed around the tops of fine glasses announced the arrival of the good spirits, while shouting voices foretold the coming of the evil ones. One of the doors to the gallery then burst open, and 'something that resembled a black ball or globe rolled into the room'. This orb, which was surrounded by smoke, held a human face in its centre, and called on the prince, who fell to his knees and begged the spirit's forgiveness. Schröpfer seemed to have difficulty in banishing this spirit; when he finally succeeded, the seance was over and the spectators were 'overcome with amazement, and fully satisfied, as they might well be, of Schrepfer's [*sic*] supernatural powers'. Unfortunately, the location of the treasure was not revealed.[9]

Schröpfer's death is surely one of the most bizarre in occult history: on an October evening in 1774, Schröpfer asked a few friends to take a pre-dawn stroll with him. Although accounts vary regarding exactly what transpired next, it seems that at some point around 5 a.m. Schröpfer excused himself and walked into a nearby grove. His friends heard a single shot. They rushed into the woods to find Schröpfer dead. The death was ruled a suicide, but rumours circulated: was Schröpfer murdered? Or had he shot himself, believing that his necromantic skills assured resurrection? It seems likelier that he shot himself as a result of once again finding himself deeply in debt.

Schröpfer's illusions are often cited as an influence on a man who could be thought of as history's first honest creator of fake seances: Étienne Gaspard Robertson. In 1799 the 36-year-old Robertson presented his first magic lantern shows, eventually moving from Paris salons to an abandoned chapel where the 'Fantasmagorie' (from the Greek for 'phantom assembly') would run for six years. While some Parisians were vigorously debating Enlightenment politics in salons, others were entering Robertson's darkened chapel for a display of ghosts. Robertson began each performance by talking about impostors, then launched into the spook show: after the last light was extinguished, strange sounds were heard (taking, perhaps, a cue from Schröpfer), then the spirits appeared. The sound effects gave Robertson the cover he needed to set up his magic lantern; he employed rear projection onto a screen or smoke. He created the illusion of movement by either moving the projector or using multiple slides; although most of his hand-painted transparencies were surrounded by black to make the central image seem to float, he sometimes used a second projector to create a landscape. Occasionally, his scenarios – which might depict ghosts leaving a tomb, a witches' sabbath or Samuel's spirit appearing before Saul – even employed voices, which Robertson and his assistants provided; other sounds were created by a Chinese gong and the glass harmonica, an instrument created by Benjamin Franklin that span glass cylinders along a rod and produced ethereal sounds when touched. Robertson even employed a technique that would be used

A fanciful depiction of Robertson's phantasmagoria, by Alphonse de Neuville or A. Jahandier, from F. Marion's *L'Optique* (1867).

in the 'ghost shows' that toured America in the 1940s, '50s and '60s: he used planks to fly spectres over the audiences' heads.[10] In fact Marina Warner has suggested that Robertson had an even greater connection to later cinema: 'He – and his contemporary rivals and imitators – set the scene for the coming of the horror video, its ghouls, ghosts, and vampire-infested suburbs.'[11] It's worth noting that several of the earliest horror films – *Nosferatu* (1922) and especially *The Cabinet of Dr Caligari* (1920) – featured villains who put their victims in hypnotic (or mesmerist) trances.

Robertson's performances were quickly imitated, moving to Great Britain and America. In London Paul de Philipsthal called his show a 'Phantasmagoria' and included an even stronger disclaimer, informing audiences that his show 'professes to expose the Practices of artful Impostors and pretended Exorcists, and to open the Eyes of those who still foster an absurd Belief in Ghosts or Disembodied Spirits'.[12] Phantasmagoria shows arrived in America in 1803 and within a few years were showing at museums and theatres around the country. They remained popular in the U.S. until 1839. Although audiences eventually grew bored with these macabre magic lantern displays, interest in a similar effect would appear in the 1860s, when the 'Pepper's Ghost' illusion (employing live actors and specially coated mirrors) took off. John Henry Pepper, the professor who improved upon an idea conceived by Henry Dircks and who began presenting his ghost illusion at the London Polytechnic in 1862, said he had collected a trunkful of letters from guests who had witnessed his plays and insisted that they had seen real spirits.[13]

Ghost Stories

It wasn't only theatres or palace galleries where ghosts were popular from the mid-eighteenth to the early nineteenth century; ghosts seemed to be making a return appearance across other areas of

Western culture. New printing technologies created a public hungry for a good horror story; small, inexpensive pamphlets were popular, and printers rushed to produce accounts of hauntings. 'The Drummer of Tedworth', a famous poltergeist-style haunting from the 1660s, was still being written about, discussed and mocked (see William Hogarth's 1762 satirical print 'Credulity, Superstition and Fanaticism: A Medley'); from 1716 to 1717, the family of John Wesley, the founder of Methodism, was tormented by a spirit they came to call 'Old Jeffrey'; the 'Cock Lane Ghost' had obsessed London in 1762 before being disproven as a hoax; and in America, the 'Bell Witch' was actually a spirit that haunted a rural Tennessee farm from 1817. Publications like Ireland's *Supernatural Magazine* (which appeared in 1809) collected stories, both old and new, of hauntings and necromancy; a 1785 account from the first issue suggests that spirit-calling was practised among Ireland's middle class, and consisted of reciting invocations over a chafing dish holding burning powders and herbs (although the housewife who described her husband engaging in this practice admitted that she 'did not know all the composition of this fumigation, nor did she recollect the words'[14]).

Meanwhile the Gothic novel was taking literature by storm. Beginning in 1764 with Horace Walpole's *The Castle of Otranto* and coming to fruition with the novels of Ann Radcliffe, in whose works the ghosts were invariably proven to be hoaxes perpetuated to frighten the credulous, the Gothic novel was perfected in such classics as Mary Shelley's *Frankenstein* and Bram Stoker's *Dracula*. And this is aside from the flood of 'penny dreadfuls' popular throughout the 1800s.

Was this new interest in frightful spectres the first salvo fired against the materialism of the Enlightenment philosophers? Hobbes, Spinoza, Descartes and Locke had all reduced the glory of the immortal spirit to philosophical arguments that ranged from there being no difference between the mind and soul (Descartes) to there being no immaterial, immortal soul (Hobbes). How to span the gap between philosophy, science and the yearning for individual survival after death?

The Christian mystic Emanuel Swedenborg provided one alternative to cool empiricism and materialism. Born in Sweden in 1688, Swedenborg spent the first 51 years of his life as an inventor, but in 1744 he experienced a 'spiritual awakening' that included, in part, conversations with Jesus, angels and demons. In books like his eight-volume *Arcana caelestia*, Swedenborg argued that Heaven and Hell existed not as physical locations but in what he called 'interspace', or 'the World of Spirits'; upon death, each person's spirit first journeyed to this interspace, where it was prepared for either Heaven or Hell. Swedenborg also wrote of the connection between mind and spirit, and how spirits surrounded us at all times:

> Man's mind is his spirit, which lives after death; and his spirit is constantly in company with its life in the spiritual world, and at the same time by means of the material body with which it is enveloped, it is with men in the natural world. Man does not know that in respect to his mind he is in the midst of spirits, for the reason that the spirits with whom he is in company in the spiritual world, think and speak spiritually, while his own spirit thinks and speaks naturally so long as he is in the material body; and the natural man cannot understand or perceive spiritual thought and speech, nor the reverse. This is why spirits cannot be seen. But when the spirit of man is in company with spirits in their world, he is also in spiritual thought and speech with them, because his mind is interiorly spiritual but exteriorly natural; therefore by means of his interiors he communicates with spirits, while by means of his exteriors he communicates with men.[15]

Swedenborg's work – which almost reads like a set of instructions for trance mediums – would prove tremendously influential on the Spiritualism movement a century later.

Mesmer and Animal Magnetism

It took another radical thinker to provide the main preface to Spiritualism: Franz Anton Mesmer. Mesmer was born in Germany in 1734; in 1766 he completed his doctoral dissertation, *De planetarum influxu in corpus humanum* (On the Influence of the Planets on the Human Body), which suggested that the human body held certain 'tides' which could be affected by the sun and moon. In 1768 Mesmer moved to Vienna, where he befriended Mozart and began experimenting with the effects of magnets on health. After Mesmer failed to permanently cure the blindness of the young musician Maria Theresia von Paradis, he relocated to Paris in 1778.

By 1783, when the Montgolfier brothers proved that invisible, heated air could lift a balloon, Mesmer had become a star in the Parisian cultural milieu. Mesmer theorized that an invisible, superfine fluid surrounded all bodies in the universe; this fluid explained phenomena as large as the movement of planets, and as small as a nerve tic. Illness resulted when the flow of this fluid was blocked in some way, so cures could be wrought by massaging a patient's 'poles', or points on opposite sides of the body; this process might result in hysteria or convulsions (a 'crisis') as the individual's body was brought back into harmony. The poles to be avoided were the north, which, being located on the top of the head, received the magnetism of the spheres; and the south, located at the feet and thus the receiver of terrestrial magnetism. Mesmer had undoubtedly taken some of his ideas from earlier works, especially William Maxwell's 1679 treatise *De medicina magnetica*, which included instructions for the use of magnets in healing.

Mesmer began by employing magnets on his patients, but soon came to believe that he achieved more success by relying on his own 'animal magnetism'. He did, however, utilize some equipment, mainly wooden tubs full of 'magnetized' water with iron rods, which acted as transmitters, extending up from the water; patients rubbed the body parts in need of healing against the rods. Mesmer also taught that a chain of people would amplify the magnetism, so he sometimes had multiple patients tied loosely together around the tubs, all holding hands (an early precursor to the Spiritualist seance). The mattress-lined 'crisis room' awaited those patients who experienced a cathartic event, while some fell into a deep sleep, in which state they manifested extrasensory perception and communicated with spirits of the dead.

In 1784 an English physician visited Mesmer's clinic and recorded his observation:

In the middle of the room is placed a vessel of about a foot and a half high which is called here a 'baquet'. It is so large that twenty people can easily sit round it; near the edge of the lid which covers it, there are holes pierced corresponding to the number of persons who are to surround it; into these holes are introduced iron rods, bent at right angles outwards, and of different heights, so as to answer to the part of the body to which they are to be applied. Besides these rods, there is a rope which communicates between the baquet and one of the patients, and from him is carried to another, and so on the whole round. The most sensible effects are produced on the approach of Mesmer, who is said to convey the fluid by certain motions of his hands or eyes, without touching the person. I have talked with several who have witnessed these effects, who have convulsions occasioned and removed by a movement of the hand.[16]

Nineteenth-century engraving showing mesmeric healing, using a tub of water and iron rods.

For the better part of a decade before the start of the French Revolution in 1788, Paris was obsessed with mesmerism above all else. It inspired dozens of pamphlets, was the frequent target of satire and even appears in Mozart's *Così fan tutte*. Mesmerism's true believers wrote passionately about their practices and their beliefs: 'What are we,' noted the legal philosopher A.-J.-M. Servan, 'if not a more or less admirable organ composed of more or fewer stops, but whose bellows never were and never will be in the pineal gland of Descartes ... nor in the diaphragm, where certain dreamers have placed it, but in the very principle that moves all the universe?'[17]

Mesmer soon discovered a profitable new venture by selling training in his techniques, so that France was shortly filled with students of Mesmer, practising what they had learned. One such protégé, the Marquis de Puységur, focused less on the healing aspects of animal magnetism and more on the trance state that some subjects slipped into. Using what he called 'mesmeric somnambulism' – or, as we now know it, hypnotism – by 1784 the marquis was hypnotizing large groups, sometimes tied together around a magnetized tree. The German philosopher Arthur Schopenhauer attributed both animal magnetism and magic from earlier times to demonstrations of will:

> It is in the will itself that the magic power lies, and that the strange signs and acts together with the senseless words that accompanied them, which passed for the means of exorcising and the connecting link with demons, are in fact merely vehicles and means for fixing the will.[18]

Agrippa, however, had talked about a practice called 'fascination' that was surely hypnotism, and he ascribed an occult meaning to it: 'Fascination is a binding, which comes from the spirit of the Witch, through the eyes of him that is bewitched, entering to his heart.'[19] Some of the marquis's claimed results sound occult: he said he had discovered that a somnambulist could view his own insides and diagnose sicknesses accurately, and that subjects communicated with the dead.[20]

That same year, 1784, the government finally decided to make a serious examination of mesmerism, and appointed a commission of celebrated doctors and scientists, including Benjamin Franklin. They spent weeks serving as mesmerist subjects themselves and applying various tests, only to conclude that Mesmer's superfine fluid did not exist and mesmerism resided only in the imagination. Thomas Jefferson, also in France at the time, called mesmerism 'an imputation of so grave a nature as would bear an action at law in America'.[21]

As mesmerism spread throughout Europe, in some areas it allied itself with other doctrines, including Rosicrucianism and the followers of Swedenborg. In a letter dated 19 June 1787 the Exegetical and Philanthropic Society of Stockholm argued that magnetism (hypnotism) led to the 'sleep-talker' being inhabited by 'angels and good spirits' who would cure the magnetized patient's illnesses. The magnetizer was said to be invoking a 'Divine blessing', with all ailments believed to be the result of 'moral evil'.

> The human soul is a spiritual organ, endowed with free will, reason and power of action, which in proportion as it makes a good or perverse use of these capacities, renders itself apt and fitted to receive the influences of good and wisdom from the Lord, through the medium of angels and good spirits; or the influences of evil and folly from hell, through the medium of devils and malignant spirits.[22]

Mesmerist associations – like Spiritualist associations in the latter half of the nineteenth century – also embraced social and political reform, and in Paris these groups were involved in activities that led to the French Revolution.

An 1842 article in a British periodical examined the history of animal magnetism, offering up a list of three separate schools that had existed in Paris:

1　The original School of *Mesmer*, whose disciples believed in the existence of the universal fluid, and conducted their operations physically, or by passing the hands immediately over, or at a short distance from, the body of the patient.

2 The School of the *Spiritualists*, wherein it was maintained that the magnetic operation depended entirely upon a pure effort of the soul, and was to be conducted only on psychical principles.

3 The School of the *Experimentalists*, who professed to be guided solely by observation; and combined the physical treatment of Mesmer with the psychical theory of the Spiritualists.[23]

Of particular note here is the use of the word 'Spiritualists', roughly ten years before it would come to refer to those who employed mediums in an attempt to communicate with spirits of the dead.

After the French Revolution, it seemed that mesmerism might fade away; it wasn't, for example, immediately embraced in Britain. In a letter printed in the June 1809 issue of the *Supernatural Magazine*, the correspondent describes attending a fashionable party at which a magnetizer was present, but when asked for a demonstration her young subject experienced convulsions and had to be carried to her bed, where she became hysterical. The letter writer goes on to call animal magnetism a 'diabolical practice, which appears to have originated in that antichristian Empire of Atheism, France', and concludes by condemning 'the fictitious miracles of Somnambulism, Magnetism, Mechanism, Chemistry, Galvinism, Phantasmagoria, Ventriloquism, and Acoustics'.[24] However, after some initial resistance, animal magnetism continued to expand and evolve; by the second decade of the nineteenth century, it had spread to America and the British Isles, even if its new form seemed fundamentally different from Mesmer's original notions of animal magnetism and healing. The tubs and iron rods largely vanished, with the new central thrust being the hypnotic element. 'Somnambulists' were now accorded a variety of psychic powers; a British newspaper account from 1817 – which begins with 'This strange delusion is reviving (if, indeed, it ever died) in Germany, with two-fold vigour' – recounts stories of prophecy (a somnambulist seeing the death of a man four years in the future) and a woman dying of consumption who was kept alive by her husband's magnetism (she finally died when he left the room).[25]

Animal magnetism continued its revival into the 1830s and '40s, when it had become a considerable source of curiosity and entertainment in Britain. Audiences flocked to demonstrations, like the one described below from 1838, which did seem to return to some of Mesmer's original practices:

> The magnetiser commences by drawing his hand
> from the head down the whole length of the trunk
> of the body, without touching the patient. He keeps
> his fingers pointed longest and most steadily at the
> forehead and the pit of the stomach, so as to infuse
> the greatest quantity of the magnetic influence into the
> two great centres of the nervous system. These tractions
> or passes are repeated, with slight variations of undulating
> or sprinkling action, until an effect is produced. This effect
> is gradual, and increases in proportion to the number
> of 'séances'.[26]

Note also the appearance of the word 'séance' in that account – the 1830s marked the first use of the word in regards to metaphysical gatherings.

One of the most unusual displays of mesmerism is recorded in an 1847 newspaper review entitled 'Oneiromancie Artistique', of a 'séance' presented at the Hanover Square Rooms: a young lady named Isa Prudence, while under the 'mesmeric will' of a woman called Mademoiselle Laurent, was 'made to represent certain *poses* in illustration of historical, classical and Scriptural subjects'. The reviewer notes that Ms Prudence's 'great beauty and precision . . . surpass anything we have ever seen'.[27]

Mesmerism had inspired artistic and literary endeavours almost from the start. Prior to the French Revolution, mesmerism had been parodied in both plays and cartoons, but it soon crept into more serious works. In 1822 Percy Bysshe Shelley wrote 'The Magnetic Lady to Her Patient' about his experience of being mesmerized two years earlier:

> Sleep, sleep on! forget thy pain;
> My hand is on thy brow,
> My spirit on thy brain;
> My pity on thy heart, poor friend;
> And from my fingers flow
> The powers of life, and like a sign,
> Seal thee from thine hour of woe;
> And brood on thee, but may not blend
> With thine.[28]

Honoré de Balzac, Victor Hugo, Alexandre Dumas and Théophile Gautier all included references to magnetism and mesmerism in their novels; even Charles Dickens – who had experimented with mesmerism after attending a lecture on the subject in 1838[29] – references mesmerism in two of his novels (*Oliver Twist* and *The Mystery of Edwin Drood*). However, probably the two most famous uses of mesmerism are found in Edgar Allan Poe's short story 'The Facts in the Case of M. Valdemar' (1845) and George du Maurier's 1894 novel *Trilby*. In Poe's tale a mesmerist, curious to experiment with a subject who is at the point of death, mesmerizes his friend M. Valdemar; Valdemar dies, but is held in a suspended state for seven months until released from his mesmeric trance – at which point the body immediately dissolves into putrefaction. One of the more interesting lines in the story suggests a sort of blasé attitude to mesmerism's more occult properties: 'His will was at no period positively, or thoroughly, under my control, and in regard to clairvoyance, I could accomplish with him nothing to be relied upon.'[30]

Du Maurier's *Trilby* introduced the character of Svengali, a mesmerist who gains control of young Trilby O'Ferrall, giving her the ability to sing while under his spell; when he dies, she loses the talent and soon follows him in death. The novel became immensely popular and led to numerous film and television adaptations, most recently in 1983, as the television movie *Svengali* (starring Peter O'Toole and Jodie Foster).

The Seeress and the Seer

Any popular field of occult interest can boast its stars, and this later period of mesmerism was no exception, with possibly the biggest being a woman named Friederike Hauffe, or, as she was more commonly known, 'the Seeress of Prevorst'. In the first half of the nineteenth century, just before Spiritualism made the word 'medium' popular (and of course long before the contemporary word 'psychic' was applied to individuals), 'seer' or 'seeress' was the job description for those who were said to possess psychic gifts.

Hauffe's extraordinary story was chronicled in *Die Seherin von Prevorst* (The Seeress of Prevorst) by the poet and physician Justinus Kerner in 1829; the book achieved great success, especially after its translation into English in 1845 during the height of the British animal magnetism craze. In the book Kerner records a variety of phenomena he had either heard of or witnessed from Hauffe, including instances of her own version of animal magnetism: 'She would make me magnetise the water she drank by sounds from the Jew's-harp; and when I had done this unknown to her, on drinking water so prepared, she involuntarily began to sing.'[31] Traditional dowsing and prophecy were apparently simple for Hauffe, given that she could also view phantom limbs when she met those who had suffered amputations, and she could use 'a magnetic wand, with an iron point, held to her right eye' as a telescope, to magnify distant objects.[32]

Hauffe, who suffered from convulsions (she died at just 27 years of age), frequently saw ghosts; her grandmother Schmidgall's spirit was always with her as a protector. It was said that Hauffe could pass on her ability to see ghosts (or, as it was then known, her 'second sight') if she touched someone else in the instant that she saw a spirit. Unlike later mediums, Hauffe rarely called directly on spirits, but one informed her that she served as a conduit; apparently the spirits used Hauffe to facilitate their contact with the human world instead of the more usual other way around. Kerner questioned Hauffe on her communication with this spirit: 'She once asked him, if he could hear other people speak as well as her. He answered, "I hear them through you. When you hear others, you think what they speak; and I read your thoughts."'[33]

Kerner's book and Hauffe would continue to influence mediums for decades after. When Carl Jung studied a German teenage medium, S.W., he noted that she had studied Kerner's book and went on to claim that she had been Hauffe in a previous incarnation.[34]

On the other side of the Atlantic, another seer was born 25 years after Hauffe: Andrew Jackson Davis, the self-described 'Poughkeepsie Seer'. In 1843, when he was seventeen, Davis had attended a lecture on animal magnetism and began to practise magnetic healing (although he was also influenced by the works of Swedenborg). He believed his abilities grew during this time, and in 1847 he released the first of his thirty books, *The Principles of Nature, Her Divine Revelations, and a Voice to Mankind*, which he dictated while in a trance state (the book's title page notes that the book is 'by and through' Davis). In that first book (which spans more than eight hundred pages), Davis's way of explaining magnetism illustrates the convoluted and fantastic thinking that sceptical critics often charged him with:

One system coming in contact with another of less positive power, will be attractive (the attraction depending upon the medium universally established), and will attract the positive power from the patient or subject, with whom the former is in contact; and the positive or magnetic force which is attracted from the subject's system, is that which exists upon the nerves of sensation, which terminate in the serous surfaces. This fluid being withdrawn, the patient is not susceptible of external impressions, simply because the medium by which these are transmitted is absent. He is then demagnetized – leaving sensation only existing upon the internal or mucous surfaces which produce vital action. The negative power remains; the positive does not remain. Vital action becomes torpid and feeble according to the loss of power which previously controlled it. This is the magnetic state; and in this peculiar condition, the patient is in sympathy with, or is submissive to the will or positive magnetic power of, the operator.[35]

As can be seen here, Davis put forth the 'law of attraction', a metaphysical belief that remains popular to this time.

As to the question of who or what Davis is channelling to dictate these words, he speaks not of spirits he is communicating with, but of his own spirit contacting the 'spheres'; he describes himself as 'a mediator, or medium connecting the spirit with the body'[36] (which marks Davis as one of the first to use the word 'medium' in this sense).

Although Davis is now regarded as a central figure in Spiritualism, he was deeply critical of the idea of seances and mediums. He believed in an afterlife he called the Summer-Land, a place of great beauty to which all human spirits went after bodily death (Davis didn't believe in Heaven or Hell), and he saw little reason for spirits to leave the Summer-Land, especially in response to a medium's command. 'If I ever returned after death to this seventh-rate planet,' he tells a man questioning him about the use of mediums, 'it would be to accomplish some object in accordance with my own affections, reason, conscience and will, and not in response to "the call" of some selfish money-hunter or any other special investigator.'[37]

Preparing the Way

Another pseudoscience that had become popular alongside animal magnetism was phrenology. Created by the Viennese Franz Josef Gall but popularized in Paris about the same time that Mesmer was promoting wooden tubs and magnetized iron rods, phrenology proposed that the brain was made up of separate 'organs', that these organs pushed out against the skull and that the brain could therefore be 'read' by the shape of the skull. As with mesmerism, phrenology crossed the Channel in the nineteenth century and became popular first in Britain (where Queen Victoria had her young son's head examined), then America. Although phrenology didn't lead quite so directly to Spiritualism as animal magnetism did, it nevertheless helped to establish a British audience hungry for metaphysical wonders.

In 1843 the Irish novelist Bartholomew Eliot George Warburton gave readers a taste of what was to come in just a few more years when he wrote of an occult adventure in Egypt and became one of the first to use the word 'seance' to describe a gathering around calling forth spirits: Warburton has arrived in Cairo and is eager to experience the local brand of magic he's heard so much about, so his local friends bring the magician Sheikh Abd-el-kader Maugrabee to his rooms. The scene that Warburton describes is something between a necromantic ritual, a true seance and a magic show:

> After some time a boy of about twelve years old was brought in and the performance began. He took the

child's right hand in his, and described a square figure
on its palm, on which he wrote some Arabic characters;
while this was drying, he wrote upon a piece of paper an
invocation to his familiar spirits, which he burned with
some frankincense in a brazier at his feet. For a moment
a white cloud of fragrant smoke enveloped him and the
cowering child who sat before him, but it had entirely
dissipated before the phantasms made their appearance.
Then taking the boy's hand in his, he poured some ink
into the hollow of it, and began to mutter rapidly; his
countenance assumed an appearance of intense anxiety,
and the perspiration stood upon his brow, occasionally he
ceased his incantations to inquire if the boy saw anything,
and being answered in the negative, he went on more
vehemently than before. Meanwhile the little Arab
gazed on the inky globule in his hand with an eager
and fascinated look, and at length exclaimed, 'I see
them now!'[38]

Ink is poured onto paper and read for spirits in this scene of
Egyptian magic from 1880.

The boy describes a camp, and the magician tells Warburton he may ask to speak to anyone. Warburton calls for several acquaintances, whom the boy describes accurately. At length the first boy is dismissed and another boy is brought in, but this boy is unable to see anything. Warburton concludes with, 'The hour was so late that no other boys were to be found, and so the séance broke up.'[39]

Warburton also notes that this practice soon spread: 'A friend of mine at Alexandria said, that he knew an Englishman who had learnt the art, and practised it with success; and a lady mentioned to me that a young female friend of hers had tried the experiment, and had been so much terrified by the first apparition that she fainted, and could not be induced to try it again.'[40] Warburton's travelogues, first published in the *Dublin University Magazine* in 1843, were collected a year later into the book *The Crescent and the Cross*, which was to prove incredibly successful.

Between Swedenborg, advances in science and politics, animal magnetism, phrenology, occult travelogues and the seers, the mid-nineteenth century did seem ripe for the birth of an entirely new belief system, but it needed one last push, which it received from a British female author named Catherine Crowe.

Crowe (1790–1872), born Catherine Ann Stevens, was a writer of both fiction and non-fiction whose works pre-dated the rise of Spiritualism by just a few years and provided much of the impetus for the movement. She started her writing career in 1838 with a series of plays and well-received novels, and then in 1845 translated Kerner's *The Seeress of Prevorst* into English, including a few of her own comments, like this one: 'Magnetic sleep . . . is a condition which resembles the primitive state of mankind, when man lived in intimate connexion with nature.'[41] Crowe goes on to talk about how magnetic sleep was practised by the oracles of the ancient world, and how it separates the spirit from the body and leaves it free to interact with the spirit world.

Her greatest success, though, came in 1848 with *The Night-side of Nature; or, Ghosts and Ghost Seers*. First published in two volumes, *The Night-side of Nature* is a hefty collection of anecdotes regarding hauntings, poltergeists, wraiths, dreams and so on. The material included is a combination of historical recountings and stories collected directly by Crowe (letters and interviews), and she is open about her intent with the book: near the end, she says, 'I shall be better pleased to learn that I have induced any one, if it be *but* one, to look upon life and death, and the mysteries that attach to both, with a more curious and inquiring eye than they have hitherto done.'[42]

It's difficult to underestimate the importance of *The Night-side of Nature* in bridging the gap between mesmerism and Spiritualism. Spiritualists recognized the significance of *The Night-side of Nature*, and even Spiritualism's great enemy, the magician John Nevil Maskelyne, acknowledged the book's influence (although his acknowledgement includes, of course, a mention of how the book adds 'confirmation to those superstitious people'[43]).

Crowe herself was less comfortable with being considered a significant figure within Spiritualist circles. Although she was certainly interested in Spiritualism, she publicly denied being obsessed with it. In response to such accusations that circulated in 1854, she wrote to the major newspapers to correct the suggestion that she had 'gone mad on the subject of the spirit rapping'. She said she suffered from 'chronic gastric inflammation', had been taken very ill in February of that year, and spent five or six days 'in a state of unconsciousness. During this aberration, I talked of the spirit rapping, and fancied the spirits were directing me ... but I was not – and am not – mad about spirits or anything.'[44]

Crowe may not have been mad about Spiritualism, but she seems to have seen its approach with near-prophetic abilities when she wrote, near the beginning of *The Night-side of Nature*, 'The contemptuous scepticism of the last age is yielding to a more humble spirit of inquiry; and there is a large class of persons among the most enlightened of the present, who are beginning to believe that much which they had been taught to reject as fable, has been, in reality, ill-understood truth.'[45] She wrote that in 1848; that same year, America would give birth to both Spiritualism and the modern seance.

4

THE VICTORIANS AND SPIRITUALISM;OR, THE SEANCE IS BORN

By the middle of the nineteenth century, the world was in a period of transition greater than any seen previously. The Industrial Revolution had resulted in steam engines, huge factories (producing mostly textiles, iron and steel, and chemicals[1]) and Britain's dominance of global trade. Gas lighting illuminated the nights, railways started to spread in the 1840s, new forms of paper production and printing technology assured that even those at the bottom of the economic ladder could read, women's suffrage and labour reform were on the horizon, and, in 1859 – when Darwin's *On the Origin of Species* was published – the dynamite of evolution would explode science, religion and culture. As Janet Oppenheim noted in her fine study *The Other World: Spiritualism and Psychical Research in England, 1850–1914*, Darwinism was a significant threat to nineteenth-century religious and spiritual beliefs, 'too convincing a revelation of man's animal origins threatened the very foundations of faith in his immortal spirit, for if he had not been specially created, it was scarcely plausible that he was specially endowed.'[2]

Mesmerism had a revival, especially as it transitioned from the earlier healing practices of animal magnetism into what would later be known as hypnotism, but the old-world necromancy was dead, now regarded (along with witchcraft) as an obsolete superstition. The magic lantern and phantasmagoria shows still touring Great Britain and North America demonstrated that the public maintained a healthy appetite for demons and ghosts, as long as they understood that these were merely characters in a public entertainment. Similarly, the Gothic novel, which gave way to the penny dreadful and the Victorian ghost story, showed (and whetted) the vast appetite for polite terrors. These same tales pushed the past into the realm of haunted ruins; old abbeys and castles – architectural symbols of religious and political systems that had faded – were now the abode of ragged spectres.

When writing about Spiritualism in 1902, Carl Jung commented on its almost inevitable appearance:

> The rise of spiritualism is understandable enough.
> With us, its favourable reception can be explained only
> by the fact that the ground had been historically prepared.
> The beginning of the nineteenth century had brought us the
> Romantic movement in literature, symptom of a widespread,
> deep-seated longing for anything extraordinary and abnormal.
> People adored wallowing in Ossianic emotions, they went
> crazy over novels set in old castles and ruined cloisters.
> Everywhere prominence was given to the mystical; the
> hysterical; lectures about life after death, about sleepwalkers
> and visionaries, about animal magnetism and mesmerism,
> were the order of the day.[3]

The Fox Sisters, Part 1

While Spiritualism seemed almost inevitable, it nonetheless took a spark to set the movement ablaze, a spark found in two teenage girls who lived around five hundred kilometres from Andrew Jackson Davis, the 'Poughkeepsie Seer'. Writing twenty years after the events that transpired around the Fox Sisters in Hydesville, Emma Hardinge conveyed (in a rush of ecstatic, fevered prose) the importance of these historic incidents:

The humble frame dwelling at Hydesville looms up into the proportions of a gigantic temple whose foundations are laid in the four corners of the earth, and the rough and rugged path which the bleeding feet of the Hydesville mediums seemed doomed to tread, amidst tears, shudderings, and nameless horror, has now loomed out into the splendid proportions of the bridge which arches over the awful chasm of the grave, affording a transit for millions of aspiring souls into the glorious realities of eternity, and erecting a telegraph whereby legions of enfranchised spirits can transmit their messages of undying affection, or their glad tidings of immortal life and eternal progress.[4]

On 11 December 1847 a blacksmith named John D. Fox moved his family into a rented house in Hydesville, New York, not far from Rochester; the house would be their temporary residence until construction was completed on their permanent home. John and his wife Margaret had six children: Leah, Elizabeth, Maria and David were all adults who lived elsewhere, while Maggie, fourteen, and Katie, ten, were still at home with their parents. The Foxes were, by all accounts, a respected and ordinary family (although second sight was said to run in Margaret's family), but they were about to become the eye at the centre of an extraordinary cultural storm.

In March 1848, just a few weeks before Katie turned eleven, a series of strange noises began to disturb the family. At night, rapping sounds emanated from the ceiling, walls, doors and furnishings. The Foxes searched the small frame house, but were unable to locate the source of the eerie knocks. The two girls soon discovered that the noises responded to verbal commands or questions: asking, for example, to 'count ten' would lead to ten thumps. By posing a series of questions to their unseen visitor, the Foxes ascertained that the sounds were produced by the spirit of a man who had been murdered in the house and was now buried beneath it.

Word spread to neighbours of the disturbances, and visitors heard the sounds for themselves. Some questioned the spirit further, and a former resident of the house, John Bell, was named as the killer, while the victim had been a pedlar. One neighbour, William Duesler, even determined the motive for the crime and the amount of money involved:

> I then inquired if it was murdered for money, and the
> knocking was heard. I then requested it to rap when
> I mentioned the sum of money for which it was murdered.
> I then asked if it was one hundred? two, three or four? and
> when I came to five hundred, the rapping was heard.[5]

On the evening of 1 April more than two hundred people assembled at the Hydesville house, all curious about the reports of supernatural happenings. A journalist named E. E. Lewis caught wind of what was going on, interviewed John, Margaret and several of the neighbours, and documented the situation in a pamphlet entitled *A Report of the Mysterious Noises, Heard in the House of Mr. John D. Fox, in Hydesville, Arcadia, Wayne County, Authenticated by the Certificates, and Confirmed by the Statements of the Citizens of That Place and Vicinity*, published in April 1848. Witnesses were completely convinced of the phenomena's authenticity. As David Fox's wife Elizabeth notes in her testimony, 'I cannot account for these noises in any way, nor imagine how they could be made by any human means.'[6] Lewis ends his pamphlet by offering a $50 reward to anyone who can prove that the mysteries surrounding the Foxes are 'the work of any *human being*' (the italics are his).[7]

As the year continued, both the disturbances and the notoriety grew until the Foxes were driven from the rented house, only to find that the spirits seemed to follow Katie and Maggie. Their older sister Leah wrote of the return of the spirits on the second night when she and the girls were situated in a newly rented house in Rochester:

We could hear them shuffling, giggling, and whispering, as if they were enjoying themselves at some surprise they were about to give us. Occasionally they would come and give our bed a tremendous shaking, lifting it (and us) entirely from the floor, almost to the ceiling, and then let us down with a bang; then pat us with hands.'[8]

The girls nicknamed the spirit 'Flat-foot' or 'Mr Split-foot', and found that it would dance if they sang for it. Other phenomena, including prophecies, hurled objects and the manifestation of visible human forms, were also reported about this time. Some

'Rapping Spirits' by Honoré Daumier, 1851. This lithograph represents the Fox Sisters.

questioners read the alphabet aloud and asked the spirit to knock when certain letters were announced. Using this method, the name of the spirit (the murdered pedlar) was revealed to be Charles B. Rosna. Several attempts to find Rosna's remains by excavating the cellar beneath the Hydesville house were made, but only a few strands of hair and some bones were recovered, although Maggie later refuted Leah's claim that doctors identified the bones as human, saying that they had likelier belonged to a horse.[9]

The two girls were soon entertaining large groups of the curious; these groups typically convened around a dining table, which would then proceed to sound with raps and move on its own. 'The gatherings or sessions . . . were already assuming a recognizable shape',[10] as Barbara Weisberg notes in her history of the Fox Sisters.

That shape was the seance.

By the summer of 1848 the word 'magnetism' began to appear in reports of Katie and Maggie's sittings,[11] drawing a line from earlier models to the new form of spirit communication. By 1849 older sister Leah was also reporting spirit visitations, although hers arrived while she was under a magnetic sleep, courtesy of a friend who was an amateur mesmerist. That mesmerist was Isaac Post, a well-known abolitionist and supporter of women's rights; Rochester was at the centre of these social movements, and the Fox Sisters' supporters would also include Frederick Douglass, the former slave whose autobiography would become a classic of American literature.

That same year, Katie travelled to Auburn, where she was the guest of journalist Eliab Capron. Capron put her through a series of examinations, pronouncing all the resulting effects genuine. In one case, he and five others attempted to hold down a table only to have it tilt up on one side. The witnesses also reported being touched by phantom hands that 'leave a feeling of electricity where they touch. The hand feels much like one who is in a magnetic sleep, being colder (generally) than the hand of persons in a normal state, and having a moisture like a cold perspiration on it.'[12] Capron also claimed that the hand could change temperature according to requests to do so; additional spirit demonstrations included playing a guitar, taking ladies' combs and opening Bibles to passages regarding spirits.

Early in 1850, Capron published a booklet called *Singular Revelations: Explanation and History of the Mysterious Communion with Spirits, Comprehending the Rise and Progress of the Mysterious Noises in Western New-York, Generally Received as Spirit Communication.* This detailed his experiences with the Foxes and laid out his theories regarding what he'd witnessed. In an introductory chapter, Capron refers to spirit communication as natural rather than supernatural, and aligns it with 'all the great discoveries of science'.[13] Capron draws comparisons between the Foxes' pedlar spirit and John Wesley's 'Old Jeffrey' of a century earlier, and also mentions magnetism, Catherine Crowe's translation of *The Seeress of Prevorst* and the works of Swedenborg and Davis. The pamphlet sold well and was reviewed in the *New York Tribune* with a mix of interest and scepticism by influential critic Horace Greeley.[14] Capron may have taken his title from an earlier opinion piece in the *Tribune*: in December 1849 they responded to a letter about the 'Rochester knockings' by noting, 'For ourselves, we really cannot see that these singular revelations have, so far, amounted to much.'[15]

A number of writers also noted similarities between what the Fox girls were doing and certain traditions within Shakerism. The Shakers were a sect founded in 1747 who subscribed to the notion that they received spiritual messages from God and other divine beings. In 1837 the Shakers' Era of Manifestations began at Watervliet, New York, bringing with it a wave of spirit communications that included table-rappings and automatic writing. The Shakers celebrated this time for providing 'proof of a telegraphic communication established between the two worlds; and no more to be disputed or doubted than is the existence of that marvelous submarine telegraphic cable that connects the Eastern and Western continents'.[16] In fact, in July 1850 two Shakers, Elder Richard and Brother Frederic, went to see the Fox Sisters and were much impressed by their abilities. During the seance, Elder Richard asked several questions, including: 'Are disembodied spirits capable of corresponding with spirits that are embodied?' He received an affirmative rap.[17]

The Foxes' spirits began to regularly demand increased exposure, anxious to convey their message of immortality to the wider world. Capron and George Willets rented the Corinthian Hall, Rochester's largest theatre, for three nights, beginning on 14 November 1849. Four hundred tickets were sold at 25 cents each (or 50 cents for a gentleman and two ladies); Katie was not present, for Maggie and Leah took the stage. Capron delivered an introductory lecture, during which raps were heard throughout the space. Newspaper reviews mocked Capron's speech but expressed admiration of Maggie and Leah's skills in producing spirits. Committees formed to investigate the Fox Sisters (investigations that included stripping the sisters, a procedure which was halted due to Maggie and Leah's sobbing) found no evidence of deception. However, the sisters didn't impress everyone: the third night was interrupted by a firecracker-wielding mob of outraged men who considered the women blasphemers.

One early supporter of the Fox girls' gifts was Horace Greeley, the influential newspaperman and reformer. Greeley had lost his beloved five-year-old son Pickie to cholera in 1849, and afterwards he became an ardent devotee of Spiritualism, hoping for a sign from his boy. He sat in on early sessions with the Foxes, writing about them in the pages of his paper, the *New York Tribune*. In May 1852 he penned a column celebrating the arrival of the first issue of the *Spiritual Telegraph*; in that piece he referred to 'the modern "Spiritualism"'.[18] After that appearance, 'Spiritualism' soon replaced 'spirit-rappings' as the accepted name for this new phenomenon. Greeley also playfully complained about his paper devoting space to the subject (mentioning 'the annoyance given to many readers who detest the "Rappings"'), but praised the new publication for 'affording to the "Spiritualists" a central organ'.[19]

That first issue of the *Spiritual Telegraph* sets the model for the Spiritualist newspapers, combining editorials, articles about spirit communication, news in regards to mediums, poetry and letters from correspondents; in the editorial for the first edition, publisher S. B. Brittan comments on the changing world and the need for his publication:

> The old world – we mean the world of human thoughts, customs and institutions – is fearfully shaken now. To-day we sit musing among the ruins . . . Even now, while earnestly watching the signs of the times, the dim shadows of a new creation pass before us. The new life of the great world, as well as the immortality of the individual man, is disclosed at the door of the sepulcher, and from the very urns in which are garnered the ashes of the Past the spirit of the Present goes forth, at the Divine behest, to quicken the nations of the earth. The old Materialism is startled and driven from its dusty abodes; Facts, illustrative of the intimate relations of mortals to the Spirit-world, are multiplying on every hand; Science is overwhelmed with images – vague and shadowy they may be – of a new world and another life, now opening as the great theater of its future and its final triumphs. The ancient wonders are being confirmed and reenacted . . . this paper will encourage the most unlimited freedom of thought on all the subjects within its appropriate sphere . . . The investigation in which we are engaged calls for the exercise of great calmness and forbearance, and yet we are not unconscious of the fact that possibly the high claims of truth and humanity may require us to deal earnestly with the opposition, to rebuke folly

SPIRITUAL TELEGRAPH

DEVOTED TO THE ILLUSTRATION OF SPIRITUAL INTERCOURSE.

"THE AGITATION OF THOUGHT IS THE BEGINNING OF WISDOM."

PUBLISHED BY CHARLES PARTRIDGE, NO. 3 COURTLAND STREET—TERMS, ONE DOLLAR AND FIFTY CENTS PER ANNUM; SINGLE COPIES, THREE CENTS:

Volume I.   NEW-YORK, SATURDAY, MAY 8, 1852.   Number I.

Front page of the first issue of the *Spiritual Telegraph*.

and fanaticism among our friends, and to expose imposture wherever it may be discovered.[20]

The first few years of the Fox Sisters' adventures as mediums reads as a virtual template for the Spiritualist movement that would spring from it. Katie, Maggie and Leah were seen by half their observers as authentic mediums who could facilitate spirit communication at will, while the other half viewed them as laughable frauds. Intensely religious men and women viewed what they did as blasphemous or heretical, and scientists simply dismissed them. Their appeal to many, however, rested on their timing, arriving as they did when the u.s. was at a crossroads in science and social reform. Rapid advances in biological studies, engineering and technology left many feeling that their spiritual life was receding, while progress in ending slavery and establishing basic rights for women opened minds to the possibilities of a harmonious future. The United States was being covered with telegraph wires which carried messages via Morse code, a series of dot-and-dash tapping that sounded almost like the spirit-rappings surrounding the Fox girls. The works of Franz Mesmer, Emanuel Swedenborg and Andrew Jackson Davis had all paved the way for a new system of belief that would allow its adherents to combine spirituality, science, social reform and philosophy.

The Fox Sisters' rise was indeed rapid and widely followed. Capron's pamphlet went into multiple editions and was followed by hundreds of similar publications. The recently widowed Leah, who was now unable to find time to give the music lessons that had formerly been her source of income, began accepting money from those anxious to experience the mysterious rappings, holding daily seances in her Rochester house with Maggie and Katie. A young visitor named Augustus Strong provided a vivid account of what occurred during these sittings:

That was a memorable evening for me. It began very
solemnly, with the wheeling out of a heavy mahogany
center table into the middle of the parlor. Then the
company gathered tremblingly around it and formed
a closed circle by clasping hands about its edge. Then
we waited in silence. Katy Fox was opposite me. I thought
I observed a slight smile on her face. I was less observant
of the proprieties at that time than I have been since, and
I ventured, alas, to wink at Katy Fox. And I thought that
Katy did something like winking in return. She was a pretty
girl, and why shouldn't she? But she soon composed her
countenance. The séance proceeded solemnly to the end.
But for me there was no more solemnity or mystery. All
the rest of the performance seemed a farce.[21]

By 1852 Leah's popularity as a medium was also advancing, and
she held regular sittings while also managing Katie and Maggie.
In 1854 the abolitionist and reformer William Lloyd Garrison
described attending one of her seances:

The circle was composed of six gentlemen, and four ladies.
We sat around it in the usual manner (the hands of each
individual resting upon the table) . . . While waiting for
some demonstrations from the invisible world, we had
our right foot patted as by a human hand, and the right
leg of our pantaloons strongly pulled by some unseen
agency . . . Raps were then distinctly heard . . . The presence
of several spirits was indicated during the evening, and
satisfactory tests were made; but the most communicative
and efficient one purported to be that of Jesse Hutchinson.
It was he who had been playing bo-peep with us under the
table . . . Heavy raps were now made on the floor; and on
being requested to that effect, Jesse beat a march – it seemed

to us Washington's march – in admirable time . . .
He was then asked to beat time while the company
joined in singing several tunes . . . He then spelled out
the following communication by the alphabet: 'I am
most happy, dear friends, to be able to give you such
tangible evidence of my presence. The good time has
truly come. The gates of the New Jerusalem are open;
and the good spirits, made more pure by the change
of spheres, are knocking at the door of your souls.'

Various objects were also placed on the floor under the table
and moved about, plus the name 'Jesse' was written on a sheet of
paper placed beneath the table. Another spirit (father to one of the
women present) told them, 'the subject of Spiritualism will work
miracles in the cause of reform.'[22] Note that the word 'seance' does
not appear in Garrison's description; the event is referred to as a
'sitting'.

Early Spiritualism in England and the USA

The method of calling out letters of the alphabet and waiting for
the spirit raps to occur at the letters needed to spell out a message
had been dubbed 'spirit telegraphy', and in October 1852 this practice would be introduced in England for the first time when an
American medium named Mrs Hayden arrived there and began
to hold public sittings. Her demonstrations were met with mixed
reviews. In his periodical *Household Words*, Charles Dickens ran a
piece with the witty title 'The Ghost of the Cock Lane Ghost', in
which two of his reporters attended one of Mrs Hayden's sittings.
This account draws a comparison between the rappings produced
by the Fox Sisters and those associated with the Cock Lane Ghost
nearly a century before; it notes that the way Katie and Maggie
produced sound via their toe joints had already been revealed. Mrs

Hayden was introduced by a mesmerist and business manager, Mr Stone, who explained mediums to his two guests:

> There are some persons in whose sphere the spirits have more power. The grossness of matter commonly repels them, but there are some people whose nervous systems appear to act – you know how delicate the nervous system is – whose nervous systems appear to act as – we can only suppose, of course, we do not profess to account for these things – as conductors, as magnets, so to speak whose bodies are surrounded by an atmosphere in which the spirits freely move. In the neighbourhood of such a person, spirits manifest themselves. Such a person is a Medium.[23]

After paying one guinea each, the two gentlemen were taken to another room and seated at a table with Mrs Hayden and her husband; they were shown a large card upon which numbers and letters were printed, and were supplied with pencils that they could use to point to the card and also to transcribe messages. When one of the two reporters received word that the spirit of his mother was present, he asked for her first name, but all attempts were failures; one of the names spelt out, 'Timok', was strange enough to cause the medium to blame a lack of light. When one of the visitors wrote down a question – 'How many children shall I have?' – and left it unspoken, telling Mrs Hayden only that the question required a number for the answer, the spirits provided '136'. After two hours the guests left without having had a single question correctly answered. Their article in *Household Words* concludes by suggesting that the rage for spirit-rapping has already peaked.

How wrong they were.

In a letter dated 4 February 1853 Mrs Hayden's husband wrote to a friend in America, S. B. Brittan, of their trip thus far. He called the episode with the two gentlemen from *Household Words* one of their few failures, and listed those prominent persons they had already met with: 'the Earl of Eglinton and the Countess, Lord and Lady Naars, the Marchioness of Stafford, Sir Edward Bulwer-Lytton, Mrs. Crowe, Miss Anna Blackwell, Dr. Elliottson, Dr. Ashburner, and many others, who have expressed great satisfaction, and a full belief in its truth and reality'.[24] In another letter a few months later, Mr Hayden strikes an evangelical tone: 'The Spiritual work has fairly begun here, and is quietly progressing among the higher classes.'[25]

In 1853 Mr Hayden, inspired by the pioneering American publication the *Spiritual Telegraph*, began the first British Spiritualist paper, the *Spirit World*. These papers published a mix of editorials (chiefly railing against sceptics), news of sittings and fervent poetry devoted to the cause, like Joseph Mathews' 1853 'Hymn for a Circle':

Father of all, thy children guide
Through life's unsteady way,
And let the voice of thy true love
Each faithful soul obey.

Here let us calm our childish fears,
And tranquilize each mind;
Nor suffer worldly cares to vex
Or banish thoughts sublime.

Why do we mourn our friends sincere,
Whose sorrows now are o'er?
In regions pure they reappear,
On Canaan's blissful shore.

Their Circles we shall surely join –
If we in goodness grow –

Where harmony and joy entwine
The souls we lov'd below.

Oh, let us learn of Spirits pure
Their lessons kindly given;
Our Guardian Angels guide us sure,
Until we join in Heaven.[26]

At about the time that the Haydens were converting England's elite, a new kind of medium appeared: Emma Frances Jay was the first significant trance medium. Unlike physical mediums, who called on spirits to produce effects like levitation or rappings, trance mediums allowed the deceased to speak directly through them. Jay was often acclaimed for her vocal skills: 'Miss Jay's Mediumship consisted of speaking with extraordinary eloquence on metaphysical subjects. She also concluded her addresses by singing; both words and music being improvisations of remarkable beauty and sweetness.'[27] After a few months in England, Miss Jay returned to America, married and apparently discontinued her mediumship.

In America a community composed entirely of Spiritualists was set up in Mountain Cove, Virginia, in 1850. A Baptist minister named James L. Scott had claimed previously to have communicated with the apostle Paul via a medium, Mrs Benedict; however, Scott soon began to receive his own direct messages. Following these visions, Scott led a colony of a hundred believers to purchase 10,000 acres of land in rural Virginia (the specific area was chosen when the spirits knocked on the window of the carriage in which Scott was travelling[28]). Scott and his followers produced publications with titles like *Disclosures from the Interior and Superior Care for Mortals*, in an attempt to proselytize the good word of spirit-rappings.[29]

Michael Faraday, the brilliant physicist whose work in electromagnetic fields paved the way for the electric motor, was possibly the first to earnestly investigate the phenomena of table-tipping.

In 1853 he constructed apparatus to gauge the movement of a table which he concluded the sitters were unconsciously moving. 'The effect produced by table-turners has been referred to electricity, to magnetism, to attraction, to some unknown or hitherto unrecognized physical power able to affect inanimate bodies – to the revolution of the earth, and even to diabolical or supernatural agency.'[30] In his article 'Experimental Investigation of Table-moving', he concluded, 'Further, I have sought earnestly for cases of lifting by attraction, and indications of attraction in any form, but have gained no traces of such effects.'[31]

Faraday's cousin Cromwell Fleetwood Varley, a specialist in telegraph technology who worked at the same time as Faraday in demonstrating the movement of electric signals through deep-sea cables, conducted his own experiments at seances and as a result became a confirmed believer. He tested both Katie Fox and Florence Cook, a British medium who rose to prominence in 1872; he hooked the latter up to an electrical circuit that then remained unbroken, even as Cook's 'spirit control' (or the medium's guide and conduit to the spirit world) Katie King manifested. Varley attests to other phenomena he personally observed at seances, including experiencing a tremendous loss of energy ('I could with difficulty only support myself'), and noting that dogs 'at *séances* would howl, bark, and run under their owners' chairs when the phenomena were about to begin'.[32]

The most important and longest-running American weekly Spiritualist newspaper, *Banner of Light*, appeared in 1857, and continued publication for fifty years (although it moved to a monthly schedule in its final year). At its height it claimed to have 30,000 subscribers, although this number was likely inflated. Three times a week *Banner of Light* held free seances in the paper's 'spirit room', reporting communications obtained during these sittings in their column 'The Messenger' or 'The Message Page'; the paper would print letters from correspondents who recognized something that pertained to them in the messages. *Banner of Light* also published serialized novelettes and even addressed social issues.

A few years earlier, in 1854, driven by the growing popularity of mediums and the outpouring of devotion in the pages of the Spiritualist press, the movement tried its first foray into politics: a petition signed by 15,000 was presented to Congress to commission an investigation into Spiritualism. The petition defined the physical attributes of Spiritualism, called for action and concluded: 'It is obvious that these occult powers do influence the essential principles of health and life, of thought and action, and hence they may be destined to modify the conditions of our being, the faith and philosophy of the age, and the government of the world.' The petition was presented to the Senate in April 1854. One senator (John B. Weller, D-Calif.) suggested that the entire matter be referred to the Committee on Foreign Relations. After some laughter, the petition was tabled.[33]

The politicians may have laughed, but by 1860 Spiritualism was a major movement in America. The *Spiritualist Register* for that year lists the following figures:

> Whole number of Home and Foreign Journals, in part or wholly devoted to Spiritualism, about 30, reaching over 200,000 readers; books and pamphlets, 600; places of meetings and lectures in America, 1500; speakers reported, 408, probable number in all, 1,000; mediums reported, 303, probable number, 50,000; schools, 3, and one Collegiate Institute contemplated; several humanity movements and associations; actual believers, 1,600,000, nominal, 5,000,000.[34]

Even though most experts now believe the number of actual believers reported here is greatly inflated, the fact that three schools for mediums are listed is extraordinary in itself.

Spiritualism received a more tragic boost in the 1860s when the American Civil War claimed the lives of roughly 620,000 men, mostly young. Grieving parents, wives and spouses turned to mediums, desperate for any sign that their loved one might provide from the beyond; Spiritualism also provided solace to those who received no word about their young men's fate (a not uncommon occurrence, given the scope of the war and the difficulty of tracking down many of those who perished). Although Spiritualism had the ability to offer comfort to the bereaved, it lacked the organization to do so (and many of its younger adherents had died in the war, leaving its ranks depleted); there were, for example, no Spiritualist clinics or homes for disabled veterans.

Spiritualists claimed foreknowledge of the war, thanks to spirit communications. In her comprehensive *Modern American Spiritualism*, Emma Hardinge (later also known under her married name Emma Hardinge Britten) described a vision she'd had in 1858 in which she'd seen a great sword and a cross:

> The vision was represented, furthermore, as dual, both
> political and religious, and predicated, first a political,
> and then a religious war, which should only terminate
> when the two countries were united under the dispensation
> of the true light of heaven, Spiritualism, typified, finally,
> by the vision being presented to a spirit medium.[35]

Hardinge also notes that Spiritualists made the bravest of soldiers, because of their 'total unconcern on the subject of death',[36] and affirms that mediums saved the lives of many on the battlefield. Hardinge also suggests that Spiritualists have common ground with the newly freed African Americans, 'many who see spirits, foretell events, and recognize influences'. She recounts a discussion between a Union lieutenant and an elderly slave in which the latter talks of how many former slaves saw visions that prophesied the coming war.[37]

Britten closes her chapter on the Civil War with this: 'Invisible armies marched to the rescue of America's freedom through many mediumistic warriors ... Heaven itself, through human instrumentalities, does battle on the side of liberty and justice.'[38]

In 1870, when Britten's book was published, Spiritualism seemed to be on the decline; the war had perhaps converted some but had also injured the movement by claiming so many of its younger members. In the concluding pages of *Modern American Spiritualism* Britten seems to be already mourning its passing: 'The wonder and novelty of modern Spiritualism are alike passing away.'[39]

Fortunately for Britten, who would continue being a major figure in American Spiritualism, her spirit guides were wrong in this case.

The Davenports

Lest mediumship be thought to have been a talent confined solely to women, the period 1852–4 also saw the appearance of the first major male mediums, all of whom originated in America. The Davenport Brothers, Ira and William, began their rise to stardom in 1854 when both were still in their teens. They were essentially stage magicians and escape artists who introduced the use of the 'spirit cabinet', a large custom-built wooden enclosure into which they were both placed and bound to chairs, along with musical instruments (a violin, a guitar, tambourines, a trumpet and bells); the cabinet was placed on trestles, allowing the audience to see beneath it throughout the seance. Once the doors of the cabinet had been closed, the instruments would begin to sound and spirit hands might even be seen to emerge from the cabinet; however, whenever the doors were opened, the brothers could both be found still tied. The boys were evidently so skilled that they could escape the knots before the doors were even completely closed, at which point the audience members chosen to perform the final investigation might be playfully poked or stroked by 'spirit hands'. Within seconds of the doors being closed, the spirits would commence:

> The doors were closed and the committee took seats! Tremendous knocks were heard at the back, side, front, and top of the closet. Two hands – not ghostly and shadowy, but plainly flesh and blood, appeared out of the opening and shook the fingers. The guitar and the violin were heard, as though being tuned ... Suddenly a band of musicians seemed to be playing inside the closet. There was the violin, the guitar, and sometimes the banjo or bells. A very quick jig was struck up and continued a little time, and while it was playing, a hand came at the opening. The doors were opened quickly, and the young men were discovered sitting apparently in the meditative mood, tied fast.[40]

With their arms held captive in wooden boxes while tied to chairs, the Davenports commune with the spirits in this 1869 illustration.

The Davenports claimed that their spirit control was named Johnny King (although he was also, somewhat confusingly, said to be Sir Henry Morgan, former governor of Jamaica). They were soon travelling the country producing Johnny King and daring sceptics to find a way to tie them securely. In various cities, they were put in sacks that were nailed to the floor, were tied with wraps that were tacked or nailed down and even had long wooden boxes clamped over their arms, and yet the musical instruments continued to play. The spirits, of course, tied and untied the knots.

A Spiritualist writer who covered the Davenports suggested why the production of spirit hands required darkness:

The manifesting spirits claim that with the use of electricity, they collect particles thrown off from the mediums, and form bodies and limbs which they control with more readiness than they formerly used their own tenements of clay. But

A fight breaks out when the Davenports are accused of imposture in this 1869 illustration.

light, say they, makes it more difficult to collect and hold those particles in compact bodies.'[41]

Magician John Mulholland outlined other methods employed by the Davenports. In his 1938 book *Beware Familiar Spirits* he describes how they were tied by a single long rope, which must by necessity be slack in some places – say, at the lower back, making it easy to move a hand enough to retrieve a folded knife from a hip pocket. Another classic escapologist's trick was to hide a second, complete rope which the so-called medium could wind quickly around himself to disguise the cut pieces of the original.[42] When the magician Houdini asked Ira about reports that the musical instruments flew over the audience during seances, Ira responded: 'Strange how people imagine things in the dark! Why, the musical instruments never left our hands yet many spectators would have taken an oath that they heard them flying over their heads.'[43]

In 1865 the Davenports took their act to England, but the tour was to prove disastrous. At a performance in Liverpool, the knots were tied so firmly that William and Ira claimed they couldn't perform because the circulation to their hands was being cut off. When they refused to proceed with the evening's spectacle, the audience rioted, their cabinet was smashed and the Davenports had to flee the town.

The Davenports were most famously debunked by John Nevil Maskelyne, who, at the time, was a 25-year-old repairer of watches. While attending an evening with the Davenports, Maskelyne got a peek into the spirit cabinet and happened to see one of the brothers unbound. Determined to unmask them once and for all, Maskelyne joined forces with cabinet maker and amateur magician George Alfred Cooke. They spent three months recreating the Davenports' equipment and routine, even adding a bit in which Maskelyne was locked inside a small cube that was placed inside the cabinet; when the doors were opened, Maskelyne was seated atop the box, which was still wrapped in chains.

When Maskelyne and Cooke were ready they presented their show publicly; they showed audiences exactly how the Davenports (and other mediums) accomplished their 'spirit manifestations', making their presentation more comedic as they perfected it. They toured the show for two years, ending by establishing a residency at the Egyptian Hall in London's Piccadilly that continued for thirty years, as Maskelyne expanded his magical repertoire, gaining more fame with each new trick.

The exposure didn't significantly damage the Davenports' career, however; when they returned to America in 1868, they did so with $600,000.[44] The act ended in 1877 when William died during a tour of Australia. Ira retired to America, where he tried to resurrect the routine in 1895 with William Fay, who had collaborated with the Davenports in some of their past shows, only to have the attempt sputter out in less than a week, a dismal failure.

There has been some debate over whether the Davenports may have actually been Spiritualists, even while they were knowingly conducting fraudulent seances. Arthur Conan Doyle insisted they were, and there is some evidence to support that Ira was. In 1885 Ira was present in Lily Dale, the great Spiritualist enclave in New York, and his obituary would list him as a Spiritualist. Even more interesting, the Davenports' own scrapbook was found in a storage area in Lily Dale and put on display in the town's museum, where sceptical author Joe Nickell was given a chance to examine it. He found examples of Ira's writing throughout, including (in an obituary regarding his first wife) a reference to 'the great truths of spiritualism'.[45]

In 1911 Harry Houdini sat down to chat with Ira; he'd been an admirer of the Davenports since childhood. While touring in Australia in 1910, Houdini had sought out William's grave, which he paid to have cleaned, refurbished and planted with fresh flowers.

Ira was so touched by this that he taught Houdini some of the Davenports' secrets, including a rope-tie they'd perfected that allowed for easy escape. Ira proposed that they tour together, but he passed away shortly after the meeting.

In 1902 Georges Méliès, one of the great pioneers of early cinema, made a short film called *L'Armoire des frères Davenport* (also known by its American title *Cabinet Trick of the Davenport Brothers*). The whimsical little movie begins with the Davenports climbing into their cabinet; at first the film follows their actual routine, then – in typical Méliès fashion – the mayhem escalates until one of the mediums misplaces his own head. Ira was still alive when the film was released; it's unknown whether he saw it or not, but one can only imagine what he would have thought of seeing a new version of delightful visual trickery extending what he and his brother had engaged in for so long.

Daniel Dunglas Home

While they may have been among the most financially successful of all mediums, the fame of the Davenports pales beside that of D. D. Home, considered by most to be the greatest medium of the nineteenth century. Home is frequently referred to as the only medium who was never exposed, but Harry Houdini had a different take on him: 'He was the forerunner of the mediums whose forte is fleecing by presuming on the credulity of the subject.'[46]

Daniel Dunglas Home was born to a poor family in Edinburgh in 1833; he was adopted by an aunt who took him to America when he was nine. Home claimed to have had powers from birth; in his autobiography, he says, 'when I was a baby my cradle was frequently rocked, as if some kind guardian spirit was tending me in my slumbers.'[47] He believed that his mother possessed second sight, even informing him of her own passing four months prior to the event. In 1850, after hearing about the Fox Sisters, Home and his aunt were startled one morning by poundings in their kitchen; soon furniture was being moved about the house. Home's pious aunt accused him of calling up the Devil, but Home responded that he served God.

By 1851 the manifestations had become widely known. Home began travelling about the USA, giving seances at the houses of his friends. In February 1852 Home was staying with Rufus Elmer in Springfield, Massachusetts, when the Elmers received a visitor from New York named S. B. Brittan. Although there had been no plans to host a seance, one nonetheless took place, according to Brittan's account:

One evening Mr. Home, Mr. and Mrs. Elmer, and I were engaged in general conversation, when suddenly, and most unexpectedly to us all, Mr. Home was deeply entranced. A momentary silence ensued, when he said, 'Hannah Brittan is here.' I was surprised at the announcement; for I had not even thought of the person indicated for many days, or perhaps months, and we parted for all time when I was but a little child. I remained silent, but mentally inquired how I might be assured of her actual presence.

Immediately Mr. Home began to exhibit signs of the deepest anguish. Rising from his seat, he walked to and fro in the apartment, wringing his hands and exhibiting a wild and frantic manner and expression. He groaned audibly, and often smote his forehead and uttered incoherent words of prayer . . . Ever and anon he gave utterance to expressions like the following:–

'Oh, how dark! What dismal clouds! What a frightful chasm! Deep down – far, far down, I see the fiery flood. Save them from the pit! . . . I see no way out. There's no light! The clouds roll in upon me, the darkness deepens! My head is whirling!'

During this exciting scene, which lasted perhaps half an hour, I remained a silent spectator, Mr. Home was unconscious, and the whole was inexplicable to Mr. and Mrs. Elmer. The circumstances occurred some twelve years before the birth of Mr. Home. No person in all that region knew aught of the history of Hannah Brittan, or that such a person ever existed. But to me the scene was one of peculiar and painful significance. She was highly gifted by nature, and endowed with the tenderest sensibilities. She became insane from believing in the doctrine of endless punishment; and when I last saw her the terrible reality, so graphically depicted in the scene I have attempted to describe, was present in all its mournful details before me.

Thirty years have scarcely dimmed the recollection of the scene which was thus re-enacted to assure me of the actual presence of the spirit.[48]

This particular recollection is interesting for two reasons: it shows that Home possessed talent as both a physical medium and a trance medium (most stories of Home's seances focus on his abilities to move objects, cause rappings and so on); and S. B. Brittan was the editor of the *Spiritual Telegraph*, and was friends with the Haydens, who would be introducing Spiritualism to England just seven months after this occurrence. The connection to the Haydens becomes even more interesting: in *Beware Familiar Spirits*, John Mulholland talks about the early days of Home in America, when he had left his aunt's house and arrived in the small town of Willimantic, Connecticut: 'Here he met a Mr. and Mrs. Hayden, who had set up in business as regular mediums. They naturally took an interest in the young man, who was delicate-looking, attractive if not handsome, and of a likeable disposition . . . However we may imagine his apprenticeship to the Haydens, he was born with or somehow acquired a wisdom, a precaution which carried him far beyond them.'[49] Mulholland also notes that when Home visited England he was put up at the home of William Cox, who had formerly hosted Mrs Hayden.

It seems likely, then, that Home was acquainted with the Haydens, who may have not only tutored him in some of the finer points of mediumship, but assisted in paving the way for his arrival in England. Interestingly, Home makes no mention of the Haydens in his autobiography, perhaps to avoid any suggestion that his seance skills may have been acquired in part from other mediums.

In 1855 Home sailed to England, where he soon had more requests for sittings than he could accommodate. Within a short space of time he was travelling Europe, the darling of kings and emperors (as Cagliostro had been not quite a full century earlier). In 1857, for example, British newspapers reported on Home's sitting with Napoleon III in Paris:

Mr. Hume [*sic*] has been twice received at the Tuileries, and each time has filled the Imperial circle with awe. The apparition of the first love of the Emperor, whose hand clasped his with a firm pressure, is spoken of as one of the wonders of the *séance*. The Emperor, whose first impression was to doubt, requested the spirit-rapper to give, as proof of his power, some palpable and evident sign acting on the material world. 'Can your spirit stop that clock?' said he, the moment that the artist stepped into the room. Hume looked at the clock intently; the hands were pointing seventeen minutes past ten – both stopped on the instant – and the Emperor has ordered that they shall remain pointing at the same hour until Hume himself sets them going by another shock.[50]

Strangely, Home left Paris abruptly not long after the above gathering, creating a mystery that has caused speculation for more than a century now. Was he revealed as a fraud by an enemy (a singer named Gustave Nadaud) during a seance? Was he caught in a homosexual affair? In her book *The Spiritualists*, Ruth Brandon suggests that Home might have been gay, and that this may have influenced the generosity he was sometimes shown by male admirers.[51]

Paris wasn't the only place Home had to leave abruptly. In Stuart Cumberland's *That Other World*, he describes a story of Home in St Petersburg that was told to him by a well-known diplomat:

> He had dematerialised a splendid row of emeralds lent the 'dear spirits' for the purpose of the test; but up to the time of his departure from the seance, the emeralds, for some occult reason, had declined to materialise and thus be handed back to the confiding owner. They were, of course, in spirit land engaging the attention of the spooks, who seem to have a pretty taste for valuable jewels. But the chief of the police had not that faith in spiritual probity generally accepted at the Court, and before leaving the Palace, Home was searched, and – so the story came to me – the dematerialised emeralds were found materialising in his coat-tail pocket. They had been placed there by an evil spirit, of course. But the police chief impressed upon the medium that the climate of the Russian capital might not be good for his health – that an early departure would probably benefit it. Home took the hint and his early departure.[52]

Regardless of why he fled Paris or St Petersburg, Home's reign as Spiritualism's greatest medium continued for the next twenty years as he travelled the world. Those who witnessed a sitting with Home described everything from seeing musical instruments float above him that were playing at the time, to seeing him hold red-hot coals just removed from the hearth, to watching him elongate his body. Home's greatest feat, however, occurred in 1871 and is often referred to as 'the Ashley House levitation'. The most famous description of this feat was provided by Lord Lindsay to *The Spiritualist*, but it was so extraordinary that it ended up being reported throughout England in major newspapers. In the letter to *The Spiritualist* Lord Lindsay describes a meeting that took place with Home, during which Lord Adare and a cousin of his were also present:

> During the sitting Mr. Home went into a trance, and in that state was carried out of the room next to where we were, and was brought in at our window. The distance between the windows was about 7 ft. 6 in., and there was not the slightest foothold between them, nor was there more than a 12 in. projection to each window, which served as a ledge to put flowers on. We heard the window in the next room lifted up, and almost immediately after we saw Home floating in the air outside our window. The moon was shining full into the room; my back was to the light, and I saw the shadow on the wall above it. He remained in this position a few seconds, then raised the window and glided into the room feet foremost, and sat down. Lord Adare then went into the next room to look at the window from which he had been carried, it was raised about 18 inches, and he expressed his wonder how Mr. Home had been taken through so narrow an aperture. Home said (still in a trance), 'I will show you'; and then with his back to the window, he leaned back, and was shot out of the aperture head first with the body rigid, and then returned quite quietly. The window is about 70 feet from the ground. I very much doubt whether any skilful tightrope dancer would like to attempt a feat of this description, where

The famous
levitation of
D. D. Home.

the only means of crossing would be by a perilous leap, or
being borne across in such a manner as I have described,
placing the question of the light aside.[53]

This incident became a central part of Home's mythology.
Home also owed much of his reputation to the fact that he didn't
accept payment for his services; unlike other mediums, he neither
charged sitters attending him privately nor sold tickets to large
public performances. Home's banker joked that the medium was
'no business man', and said he had often urged Home to charge
for his seances, but Home had refused.[54]

However, Home certainly benefited in other ways. He was
treated grandly by emperors, lords and numerous Spiritualists, he

never lacked a place to stay and he was often gifted with items of great value. Probably the most substantial of these was from an elderly, wealthy widow named Jane Lyon, who first met Home in 1866; she was already a confirmed Spiritualist who claimed to have received visions from her own spirit guides, and she believed Home was a person who had been revealed to her in these visions. She astonished Home by proclaiming that she intended to adopt him as her son and bestow a substantial fortune on him, which she did, despite Home's later claims that he had tried to dissuade her. In October 1866 she transferred £24,000 to Home, who (despite his earlier objections) accepted the gift and changed his name to Home-Lyon. Mrs Lyon soon directed her solicitors to revise her will, leaving her entire fortune to Home.

A year followed during which Home claimed that, due to increasing ill health, he was forced to travel, leaving Mrs Lyon for long periods; meanwhile, she penned effusive letters to him, calling herself his 'affectionate mother', and gave him additional monetary gifts, bringing the total amount she had bestowed on him to £60,000.[55] Without Home by her side, Lyon began to regret her decision and in 1867 she sought the return of the funds. The case went to court. Home lost and was forced to return the monies to Mrs Lyon. Needless to say, he also ceased signing his name as 'Home-Lyon'.

In Home's curiously titled *Light and Shadows of Spiritualism* (curious because much of the book is devoted to prophets rather than mediums), first published in 1877, Home revealed a side of himself that didn't completely match up with his image as a respectful, sensitive gentleman (although one could argue that Home is not incorrect in his assessment of his place in the history of Spiritualism):

We hear much of 'Fathers of English Spiritualism.' If the paternity be genuine, I must needs be the grandfather, for they are, almost without exception, my converts; and thus, in a symbolical sense, my children. I must confess that I stand in the position of many parents; being heartily ashamed of some of my offspring. With me, their father, they were thorough in their investigations, and based conviction only on absolute certainty. Now, they have cast caution aside, and seem to experience an insane pleasure in being duped. Should I try to convince them of their folly they turn on me in fury; and, if unable to injure me otherwise, degrade themselves by inventing and circulating monstrous falsehoods, which they trust will damage my moral character. Truly, I am an unfortunate father.[56]

The book engages in vigorous attacks, sometimes running over numerous pages, against various members of the Spiritualist community. Although he never uses actual names, Home criticizes Henry Steel Olcott's book *People from Another World* at length (the book is 'contradictory nonsense' written by a 'pseudo-philosopher' and 'calumniator'), mediums who engage in materializations (although he admits to believing that those presented by Florence Cook were real), those who escape from being tied (probably a jab at the Davenport Brothers) and spirit photography.

Home is often referred to as the only medium who was never disproven, but this is inaccurate, because Home was frequently debunked, arrested on several occasions and even made the subject of the most notorious satirical poem in Spiritualist history.

Home's imposture was detected almost as soon as he arrived in England. In September 1855 Sir David Brewster attended a Home seance at Cox's Hotel in St James, where Home was then residing; also present that evening were Lord Brougham and William Cox. After seeing exaggerated reports of the seance in newspapers, Sir David wrote a letter to the *Morning Advertiser* in which he said that Home 'insults religion and common sense, and tampers with the most sacred feelings of his victims'.[57] He later addressed claims that spirits had moved a heavy table and levitated an accordion as it played:

It is not true, as stated, that a large dinner-table was moved about at Mr. Cox's in a most extraordinary manner. It is not true that a large accordion 'was conveyed by an invisible or any other agency into my hand.' I took it up myself, and it would not utter a sound. It is not true that the accordion was conveyed into Lord Brougham's hand. It was placed in it. It is not true that the accordion *played an air throughout* in Lord Brougham's hands. It merely squeaked. It is not true, as stated in an article referred to by Mr. Home, that Lord Brougham's 'watch was taken out of his pocket, and found in the hands of some other person in the room.' No such experiment was tried ... At Mr. Cox's house, Mr. Home, Mr. Cox, Lord Brougham, and myself, sat down to a small table, Mr. Home having previously requested us to examine if there was any machinery about his person, an examination, however, which we declined to make. When all our hands were upon the table noises were heard, – rappings in abundance; and finally, when we rose up, the table actually rose, as appeared to me, from the ground. This result I do not pretend to explain; but rather than believe that spirits made the noise, I will conjecture that the raps were produced either by Mr. Home's toes ... and rather than believe that spirits raised the table, I will conjecture that it was one by the agency of Mr. Home's feet, which were always below it.

Sir David goes on to discuss another Home seance he attended, this one in Ealing, when five handkerchiefs that had been thrown out onto the table were found tied in knots:

On one occasion the spirit gave a strong affirmative answer to a question by *three raps*, unusually loud. They proceeded from a part of the table exactly within the reach of Mr. Home's foot, and I distinctly saw three movements in his loins, perfectly simultaneous with the three raps ... Mr. Home, three or four times, gave a start, and looked wildly at the company, saying, 'Dear me, how the spirits are troubling me,' and at the same time putting down his left hand as if to push away his tormentors, or soothe the limb round which they had been clustered. He had, therefore, both his hands beneath the table for a sufficient time to tie the five marvellous knots.[58]

In addition to blaming failures on spirits, Home would often tell sitters exactly what he wanted them to believe: for example, he might state loudly that his chair was off the ground, or that he himself was floating.[59] He also likely employed a common medium's trick called 'the human-clamp': this involved a medium using their hands placed atop a table to start it rocking from side to side, until they could wedge one foot under a table leg. At that point, by placing their hand atop the table on the same side as the table leg that was now supported by the medium's foot, they created a 'clamp' that was effective enough to 'levitate' an entire table (provided it wasn't too heavy).[60]

Home's imposture was detected again in 1857. In a letter dated 25 September of that year, the physician to Napoleon iii's son, one Dr Barthez, detailed Home's imposture:

The thing is very simple. Mr. Hume wears thin shoes, easy to take off and put on; he also has, I believe, cut socks which leave the toes free. At the appropriate moment he takes off one of his shoes and with his foot pulls a dress here, a dress there, rings a bell, knocks one way and another, and, the thing done, quickly puts his shoe on again.[61]

Several of those present at this seance (which became a source of controversy) later confirmed the details, noting that Home had been caught by General Fleury, who left the room during the seance and then secretly returned to stand directly behind Home, while the medium remained unaware of his presence.[62]

Home also failed to impress the poet Robert Browning. After attending a seance with Home, Browning (whose wife Elizabeth was a believer) confided to his friend Nathaniel Hawthorne:

> Browning and his wife had both been present at a spiritual session held by Mr. Home, and had seen and felt the unearthly hands, one of which had placed a laurel wreath on Mrs. Browning's head. Browning, however, avowed his belief that these hands were affixed to the feet of Mr. Home, who lay extended in his chair, with his legs stretched far under the table.[63]

It wasn't enough for Browning to simply complain to a few friends about Home; he also wrote a 65-page poem entitled 'Mr. Sludge, the Medium', which is a devastating account of his experience with Home. The poem begins with:

> Now, don't sir! Don't expose me! Just this once!
> This was the first and only time, I'll swear, –
> Look at me, – see, I kneel, – the only time,
> I swear, I ever cheated – yes by the soul
> Of Her who hears – (your sainted mother, sir!)
> All, except this last accident, was truth –
> This little kind of slip! – and even this,
> It was your own wine, sir, the good champagne,

(I took it for Catawba, – you're so kind)
Which put the folly in my head![64]

Later on in the poem, Browning gets more specific in tipping his
hand to the real identity of 'Mr. Sludge':

Take my word,
Practise but half as much, while limbs are lithe,
To turn, shove, tilt a table, crack your joints,
Manage your feet, dispose your hands aright,
Work wires that twitch the curtains, play the glove
At the end of your slipper[65]

Home split the more scientific contingent of the Spiritualist
community. Frank Podmore, a dedicated Spiritualist who was among
the most thoughtful and rational members of the community,
studied Home and commented on how often he controlled the
situations under which he was tested:

Home – a practised conjurer, as we are entitled to assume –
was in a position to dictate the conditions of the experiment.
By the simple device of doing nothing when the conditions
were unfavourable he could ensure that the light (gas in the
present instance) was such, and so placed, the apparatus so
contrived, and the sitters so disposed, as to suit his purpose.[66]

However, one of Home's chief defenders was a man who was
possibly the most famous scientist within Spiritualism: William
Crookes, whose work led to the discovery of the electron and who
discovered the element thallium, who was knighted in 1897, added
to the Order of Merit in 1910 and served as the president of the
Royal Society from 1913 to 1915. Crookes was also an ardent believer
in Spiritualism who tested many of the most well-known mediums.

FIG. 2.

D. D. Home with cage built by William Crookes.

In 1871 Crookes tested Home extensively, concluding, 'Of all the persons endowed with a powerful development of this Psychic Force ... Mr. Daniel Douglas [*sic*] Home is the most remarkable.'[67] In a paper published in the *Quarterly Journal of Science* in 1871, Crookes laid out Home's abilities:

> Among the remarkable phenomena which occur under Mr. Home's influence, the most striking, as well as the most easily tested with scientific accuracy, are – (1) the alteration in the weight of bodies, and (2) the playing of tunes upon musical instruments (generally an accordion, for convenience of portability) without direct human intervention, under conditions rendering contact or connection with the keys impossible. Not until I had witnessed these facts some half-dozen times, and scrutinized them with all the critical acumen I possess, did I become convinced of their objective reality.[68]

In order to challenge Home, Crookes constructed several elaborate items, including a large cylindrical cage made of a wooden frame with copper wire wound around it; this cage was placed beneath Crookes's dining table, Home was seated before it and the accordion was placed into the cage. Crookes and his assistants saw the accordion moving about within the cage while it played; at some point it was removed from the cage and held by one of the assistants, yet it continued to play.

Here is one of the critical errors in Crookes's testing method: Home was not searched beforehand. Crookes notes that he had witnessed Home changing his outfit before the test, but makes no mention of having closely examined the clothing. It's now believed that many of the mediums employed music boxes to produce the otherworldly sounds of instruments during their seances – which would also explain why the tunes usually played were old standards – and it would have been easy enough for Home to have secreted a small music box in a pocket. Musician Tom Waits has suggested that mediums also used pipes (similar to those used in pipe organs) to create sound during seances: 'they would outfit the room where they would conduct the séance with this whole matrix of pipes and things they could send voices into and have come out in unusual places.'[69] This, of course, would only have been practical for professional mediums whose seances were held in their residence or parlour, not for those like Home who travelled.

Crookes also tested Home's ability to move a board balanced on a fulcrum and connected to measuring devices, and again, Crookes was completely convinced that Home was channelling some sort of spiritual energy. After running a second series of tests on Home later in the year and producing a follow-up paper, Crookes concluded: 'These experiments *confirm beyond doubt* the conclusion at which I arrived in my former paper, namely, the existence of a force associated, in some manner not yet explained, with the human organization, by which force increased weight is capable of being imparted to solid bodies without physical contact.'[70]

Home was also examined by scientists in Russia, where he'd performed favourably for the Emperor at the Winter Palace. Home ended up developing close ties with Russia, as both his first wife, Alexandria de Kroll, whom he married in 1858 and who died from tuberculosis four years later, and second wife, Julie de Gloumeline, were members of the Russian aristocracy. Home himself finally succumbed to tuberculosis in 1886; he was 53.

William Crookes and Florence Cook

While William Crookes's conclusions to his experiments with D. D. Home were remarkable, they pale in comparison to Crookes's tests of Florence Cook.

Cook is both one of the greatest and most enigmatic mediums of the nineteenth century. The exact date of her birth is unknown; it's possible that she was actually several years older than sixteen, the age she claimed when she first gained notoriety for her mediumship. In the decades that have passed since her seances with Crookes, there are those who continue to maintain that her psychic powers were as genuine as Crookes stated them to be. As the Nobel Prize-winning physiologist Charles Richet noted, 'it seems it is impossible to doubt Crookes's methodology and results in regards to Florence Cook.'[71]

When Cook's mediumship first came to notice in London in 1872, Spiritualism was moving away from the old rappings and table-turnings to materializations. It was no longer enough to produce just spirit hands; the demand was on for faces. Cook excelled at this from a young age, and the editors of *The Spiritualist*, who were already writing accounts of her seances, asked her to draft a short biography of herself:

I am sixteen years of age. From my childhood I could see spirits and hear voices, and was addicted to sitting by myself talking to what I declared to be living people. As no one else could see or hear anything, my parents tried to make me believe it was all my imagination, but I would not alter my belief, so was looked upon as a very eccentric child. In the spring of 1870 I was invited to the house of a school-friend ... She asked me if I had ever heard of spirit-rapping, adding that her father, mother, and self had sat at a table and got movements ... A séance was arranged. The sitters were Mr. and Mrs. –, their daughter, and myself. We placed our hands on a moderately large table; it soon moved about uneasily; then distinct raps were heard ... Mr. – said,– 'We have never had raps before. Florrie, it must be through you.'[72]

After returning home, Cook began to experiment with her mother, and after a few seances Florence was levitated while seated; she was also told that she was a medium. Unfortunately, things took a turn for the worse after that:

The next evening we sat at home, a table and two chairs were smashed, and a great deal of mischief done. We said we could never sit again, but we were not left in peace. Books and other articles were thrown at me, chairs walked about in the light, the table tilted violently at mealtimes, and great noises were sometimes made at night.[73]

The mayhem ceased only when Florence agreed to meet with other Spiritualists.

She soon became a protégée of Frank Herne, who had begun his mediumship in 1869 and, after partnering with Charles Williams, became one of the most successful mediums in England (Williams would suffer a particularly embarrassing exposure in 1878 when he and a different partner were caught fleeing a disastrous seance with wigs, false moustaches, muslin, a bottle of phosphoric oil and other paraphernalia that they had used to create the spirit faces[74]). After attending a few sittings with Herne and Williams, Florence found her spirit guide in 'Katie King', who she said was the daughter of the spirit 'John King' who was summoned by Herne and Williams. 'Katie King' was also known as 'Annie Morgan' and 'John King' was said to be a spirit name for Henry Morgan, the buccaneer and one-time governor of Jamaica, who, as we have seen, had also been used by the Davenports as well as other mediums; in writing about the frequent appearance of this name among Spiritualist mediums, Roger Luckhurst comments,

> An imperialist of Britain's first empire operating at the periphery, Morgan's contempt for metropolitan proprieties, combined with his abilities to command and control unruly populations with a violent hand, offer suggestive reasons for his return as a powerful spirit control in a cultural practice itself considered unruly, marginal, and semi-lawful.[75]

Apparently channelling King wasn't initially easy for the young Miss Cook: 'While she and other spirits are talking, I feel as if I cannot breathe.'[76] She finalizes her statement for *The Spiritualist* by stating, very simply, what was no doubt so appealing about the religion to most of its followers: 'I used to be afraid of death, but Spiritualism has taken away all my fears.'[77]

Florence wrote that short biographical sketch for the May 1872 issue of *The Spiritualist*, and by September the paper was reporting the production of spirit faces at her seances. 'Katie King' bore a striking resemblance to her medium, but other faces did not, including some that were 'as black as ink, sometimes chocolate colour, and sometimes white'.[78] Cook usually held her gatherings at her family's home; her younger sister Edith was frequently present, and Cook claimed that she drew power from Edith (the four-year-old was occasionally seen to have a bloody nose at the conclusion of the seances).

Just like D. D. Home, Florence didn't charge sitters; the Cooks did, however, receive a monetary windfall when a gentleman from Manchester named Charles Blackburn offered them a regular stipend to hold seances. Even though 'Katie King' did not garner universal acclaim (some of those who attended Cook's seances noted the resemblance between the medium's face and the spirit's), Blackburn was unshaken in his belief in Florence's abilities, which advanced through 1872, building to the ultimate revelation sought by Spiritualists at the time: a full-body materialization.

Herne had come close on several occasions, producing a dark-robed spirit of 'John King' that stepped out of the spirit cabinet and roamed about the sitters in semi-darkness; however, Spiritualists wanted to be able to actually *see* the materialized spirit, and – even more – to be able to touch it. Blackburn's faith in Florence and Katie was rewarded in early 1873, as he wrote to *The Spiritualist*:

When Miss Cook was in the cabinet, the light was nearly extinguished. After a short interval, a white, full length figure was dimly visible; in a few minutes we were allowed to have more light, but still to keep the gas rather low. The shawl or rug in front was then seen to be pulled back, and a white figure showed herself full length, which appeared to me to be quite two, if not three, inches taller than Miss Cook; her feet and hands were bare, and much larger than Miss Cook's. I could clearly distinguish every toe, and on my saying she was taller than Miss Cook, she stamped her foot on the ground to show she was not on tiptoe. She lifted her dress, and we saw her bare leg a few inches above the ankle. She stooped, picked up paper from the floor, and also took paper and my pencil from a table near the cabinet; then, in our presence, wrote on different pieces of paper. One was directed to me, and was as follows:–

Soon I shall be able to give this manifestation under test conditions, but for a little time I must have my own way. If I had had proper conditions, I could have done this before. – A. MORGAN.[79]

The spirit 'A. Morgan' (or Katie King) lived up to her promise: soon she was moving easily among her sitters, even touching and embracing them. On 9 December 1873 a man named William Volckman attended one of Florence's seances; when Katie King offered him her hand, Volckman grabbed both her hand and her waist and demanded that someone else look into the spirit cabinet as he detained the 'spirit'. When none of the other sitters was willing to examine the cabinet, Katie King managed to pull away from Volckman. A scuffle ensued, Volckman was ousted and Florence was discovered back in the spirit cabinet, looking alarmed but still bound. Volckman, who maintained that he'd had hold of Florence Cook in the flesh, complained to the Spiritualist press and controversy ensued, with some pointing the finger at Volckman. As a result, Charles Blackburn withdrew his financial support of the Cooks. A short time afterwards, Florence approached William Crookes about testing her.

It's likely that Florence knew of Crookes's investigation into, and verification of, the authenticity of D. D. Home's powers and hoped for the same outcome. Crookes started by attending one of Florence's seances; at this sitting, Katie King made only a brief appearance before saying that her medium was ill and not strong enough to continue the materialization. Throughout the seance, Crookes was seated near the curtain that closed off the 'spirit cabinet' (in this case, the seance was held at the house of a Mr Luxmoore, and the 'cabinet' was just another room, separated by

William Crookes
and the 'spirit'
Katie King.

a curtain), and he claimed to hear Florence moaning and sobbing even while Katie King was present.

For the next six months, Florence held private seances at Crookes's home in London. During these, Crookes didn't simply claim that he had seen Katie and her medium together – he stated that other sitters had witnessed this as well, and under well-lit conditions. Of course, none of these sitters was allowed to examine the entranced Florence up close, and critics pointed out that they likely saw Florence's discarded clothing shaped into human form.

Speculations about Florence Cook among Spiritualists provide yet another insight into just how far they were willing to bend logic to support their faith: while many simply accepted that Katie King was indeed a spirit materialized by Florence, others suggested that the spirit had assisted Florence from escaping her confining ropes, provided her with a white robe 'and sent her forth to personate a ghost'.[80]

Cromwell Varley had created an electrical device that employed a galvanometer to create a circuit around a medium, and he loaned it to Crookes in order to test Florence; if the medium were to disconnect the wires that connected her to the circuit, the break in the current would be detected immediately. During the seance, Varley *did* notice fluctuations in the electrical readings, but because the circuit was never completely broken, even when Katie King stepped out of the spirit cabinet, he pronounced Florence and Katie genuine. Had Crookes colluded with Florence prior to Varley's testing and prepared a way for her to keep the circuit intact even while she detached herself to move about as Katie King?

Crookes also photographed Katie King during the private seances of 1874. He photographed her with, 'Five complete sets of photographic apparatus ... accordingly fitted up for the purpose, consisting of five cameras, one of the whole-plate size, one half-plate, one quarter-plate, and two binocular stereoscopic cameras'. Crookes claimed to obtain 44 photographs; these were later destroyed, but not before a few had been published. Perhaps the most famous of these shows him standing next to Katie, and when he duplicated the same shot with Cook, he claimed that she was significantly shorter than Katie. Nearly fifty years later, Sir Arthur Conan Doyle would show the photo of Crookes and Katie to audiences during his lecture tour of America and call it 'the most remarkable picture in the world'.[81]

Throughout April and May of 1874, Crookes held a last series of seances with Florence Cook. For these sittings, the guests were allowed to see into the bedroom serving as the spirit cabinet, where the medium could be viewed entranced on the floor as Katie King moved among them. Charles Blackburn, Florence's off-and-on-again patron, was even allowed to go into the bedroom and touch the figure in order to confirm its reality. However, the medium's face was covered with a shawl, which Blackburn did not remove. On 21 May Katie King appeared for the last time, to a small group of sitters that included the author Florence Marryat and Florence's family. Of this farewell appearance, Crookes wrote in a letter that Katie said goodbye to each of those present, asked him to care for 'Florrie' and then invited him to join her as she returned to the medium's side:

> After closing the curtain she conversed with me for some time, and then walked across the room to where Miss Cook was lying senseless on the floor. Stooping over her, Katie touched her, and said, 'Wake up, Florrie, wake up! I must leave you now.' Miss Cook then woke and tearfully entreated Katie to stay a little time longer. 'My dear, I can't; my work is done. God bless you,' Katie replied, and then continued speaking to Miss Cook. For several minutes the two were conversing with each other, till at last Miss Cook's tears prevented her speaking. Following Katie's instructions I then came forward to support Miss Cook, who was falling on to the floor, sobbing hysterically. I looked round, but the white robed Katie had gone. As soon as Miss Cook was sufficiently calmed, a light was procured and I led her out of the cabinet.[82]

Florence Marryat also claimed to have been present with Florence when Katie said her goodbyes; in her account, the spirit was nude as she prepared to journey to the other side.

Marryat's and Crookes's accounts underscore one of the most striking aspects of both the Florence Cook case and numerous other retellings of Victorian seances: the erotic element. Crookes mentioned that he felt Katie King to determine if she was wearing stays (she wasn't), and Marryat went so far as to claim that Katie King had sometimes appeared at her home and joined her and her husband in their bed. Just as D. D. Home was rumoured to have had romantic liaisons, it's entirely possible that Crookes (and Florence Marryat) was infatuated with Florence Cook. Many of Crookes's descriptions of his interactions with Florence/Katie certainly sound far from scientific:

> photography is as inadequate to depict the perfect beauty of Katie's face, as words are powerless to describe her charms of manner. Photography may, indeed, give a map of her countenance; but how can it reproduce the brilliant purity of her complexion, or the ever-varying expression of her most mobile features, now overshadowed with sadness when relating some of the bitter experiences of her past life, now smiling with all the innocence of happy girlhood.[83]

During his work with Florence Cook, Crookes was 41, a married man with six children (his wife had borne him ten, but three had died early and one daughter had died at thirteen). At the time, his wife was pregnant with their last son.

Years later, a gentleman named Francis G. H. Anderson testified to the Society for Psychical Research that in 1893 he'd had an affair with Florence, who was then a married woman in her thirties with two daughters (Anderson was 23). He described Florence as 'very highly sexed', and said she'd admitted to him that she had had an affair with Crookes and that the seances had been a cover for that. He also said that Florence had admitted to him that her mediumship had been completely fraudulent.[84] Anderson's testimony was later backed up when a second man came forward to claim an affair with Florence, and to reiterate her claim of a romance with Crookes and his complicity in her fraudulent seances.

Throughout the investigation of Florence Cook, Crookes had a running critic in fellow Spiritualist Serjeant Edward William Cox, a barrister who had assisted Crookes with some of his earlier examinations but who maintained that Florence Cook was a fraud – which could only make Crookes a confederate. Some of Cox's letters to the Spiritualist newspapers and to friends detail the ways in which the materialization mediums operated. In a letter to D. D. Home in 1876, Cox had laid out the conditions necessary to perpetrate the fraud:

> The curtain is guarded at either end by some friend. The light is so dim that the features cannot be distinctly seen. A white veil thrown over the body from head to foot is put on and off in a moment, and gives the necessary aspect of spirituality. A white band round head and chin at once conceals the hair and disguises the face. A considerable interval precedes the appearance – just such as would be necessary for the preparations. A like interval succeeds the retirement of the form before the cabinet is permitted to be opened for inspection. This just enables the ordinary dress to be restored.
>
> While the preparation is going on behind the curtain the company are always vehemently exhorted to sing. This would conveniently conceal any sounds of motion in the act of preparation. The spectators are made to promise not to peep behind the curtain and not to grasp the form. They are solemnly told that if they were to seize the spirit they would kill the medium ... Every one of the five mediums who have been actually seized in the act of personating the spirit is now alive and well.[85]

Even more damning, though, Cox goes on to detail a letter he had glimpsed in which one medium educates another as to how the imposture is best performed:

She informs her friend that she comes to the séance prepared with a dress that is easily taken off with a little practice. She says it may be done in two or three minutes. She wears two shifts (probably for warmth). She brings a muslin veil of thin material (she gives its name which I forgot). It is carried *in her drawers!* It can be compressed into a small space, although when spread it covers the whole person. A pocket-handkerchief pinned round the head keeps back the hair. She states that she takes off all her clothes except the two shifts, and is covered by the veil. The gown is spread carefully upon the sofa over the pillows. In this array she comes out. She makes very merry with the Spiritualists whom she thus gulls, and her language about them is anything but complimentary.[86]

It's possible that the letter Cox describes was written by Florence Cook to Mary Showers, another young medium with whom she was friendly; in fact, Crookes had hosted a seance in which both mediums had produced their respective forms, who had happily paraded arm-in-arm about Crookes's rooms. Cox had also attended a seance given by Mary Showers in which she had been exposed by an onlooker who had pulled back the curtain, revealing that Mary was not, in fact, lying entranced on soft cushions, but standing and wearing the spirit's headgear. When discovered, Mary had cried out, 'You have killed my medium!'[87] Needless to say, Mary survived the discovery; her followers declared that she'd committed the imposture in a state of 'somnambulism'.

It should also be noted that the letter quoted above was written by Cox to D. D. Home, whom he obviously did *not* consider to have committed imposture. Whether this is a testament to Home's skills, or an example of nineteenth-century misogyny on Cox's part (that is, young women are likely to commit fraud, but not a gentleman), is unknown.

Throughout the rest of his life, Crookes maintained his belief in the authenticity of Florence Cook (and the other mediums); however, he rarely mentioned her in his recollections. Another individual who was left disappointed by Florence was her patron, Charles Blackburn, who had suspended his financial support when Katie King departed (it's also worth noting, however, that Florence had secretly married in April 1874, which she didn't reveal until June). Blackburn soon turned his attention to Florence's sister Kate, who had taken up mediumship, materializing a spirit named 'Lillie Gordon'. Blackburn not only once again offered the Cooks a monthly stipend, but included them in his will. When he finally passed away, he left a substantial part of his estate to Kate and to other members of the Cook family – all, in fact, except Florence.

Florence did resume holding seances, now materializing a spirit called 'Marie', but she was exposed repeatedly. She continued to hold small, private seances, but finally died of pneumonia in 1904, alone and impoverished.

William Crookes, of course, went on to knighthood and the presidency of the Society for Psychical Research. Even though he never wavered in his belief in the powers of mediums, he did shift his thinking more towards thought-transference. In his 1897 President's Address to the Society, he discussed the idea that the then newly discovered Röntgen rays might carry intelligences into the minds of 'sensitives': 'A sensitive may be one who possesses the telepathic transmitting or receiving ganglion in an advanced state of development, or who, by constant practice, is rendered more sensitive to these high-frequency waves.'[88]

The story of Crookes and Florence Cook has fascinated scholars and artists for more than a century. In 1963 Aldous Huxley was in talks to write a movie about William Crookes and the Cook family for the great film director George Cukor. Sadly, it didn't happen.[89]

Spiritualism at the End of the Nineteenth Century

Despite the glum predictions made by Emma Hardinge Britten in 1870 about the future of Spiritualism, it survived to become even more popular, especially in England.

Why in England, where there'd been no war to spur interest in contacting deceased loved ones? As Janet Oppenheim notes in her study of Spiritualism, *The Other World*, 'They were absolutely convinced that theirs was the faith that united all faiths, that reconciled religion and science, and gave man the facts to prove his immortality.'[90] Not everyone was easily converted, however: John Tyndall, the Irish physicist, believed (along with the anatomist Thomas Henry Huxley and the social philosopher Herbert Spencer) in the strict separation of religion and science. After attending a seance, he was – to put it mildly – unconvinced: 'The victims like to believe, and they do not like to be undeceived. Science is perfectly powerless in the presence of this frame of mind.'[91] In 1879 he added, 'I have been more than once among the spirits. They do not improve on acquaintance. Surely no baser delusion ever obtained dominance over the weak mind of man.'[92]

It seems likely the British renewal of interest in Spiritualism was due to two events that occurred in October 1871. First, the London Dialectical Society, which had been founded several years earlier to study Spiritualistic phenomena, released its detailed report of over four hundred pages, in which it found in favour of the supernatural. Among its assertions were that rappings and movement of furnishings occurred; that thirteen witnesses saw levitation of objects and, in some cases, men; fourteen witnesses saw and/or touched whole or partial human forms; thirteen witnesses heard music; five witnesses saw red-hot coals held without injury; three witnesses saw drawings produced faster than human agency should be capable of; six witnesses received prophecies which proved accurate; and evidence was also provided 'of trance-speaking, of healing, of automatic writing, of the production of flowers and fruit into closed rooms, of voices in the air, of visions in crystals and glasses, and of the elongation of the human body'.[93]

The second event was the arrival of Kate Fox in London. Kate's trip was paid for by her American patron Charles Livermore, which he considered 'a contribution to the cause of Spiritualism'.[94] Livermore's financial support enabled Kate to give seances free of charge, and by December the British newspaper *The Spiritualist* was calling her 'the best rapping medium now in England'.[95] Kate soon met and married Henry Jencken, a well-regarded Spiritualist and barrister, and their house became a gathering point for England's Spiritualist community, even after Kate partly retired from giving seances to devote more time to her and Henry's two sons.

During this time, the faith drew some surprising converts. In addition to scientists such as William Crookes and Alfred Russel Wallace, and writers like Elizabeth Barrett Browning and Arthur Conan Doyle, the explorer and translator Richard F. Burton created his 'Decalogue', a ten-part creed for Spiritualists, and said, 'Spiritualism, which, despite ridicule and fraud, numbers millions of converts, is virtually a new religion; it cuts itself loose from all former connection, freely accepts any cosmogony or history offered to it by science, and aspires to become the Faith of the Future.'[96]

Spiritualism wasn't only practised among the elite, however; it was equally at home with the working classes, in part because it allied itself with causes such as universal suffrage and labour reform. In fact, the labour reformer Robert Dale Owen was a fervent believer, in part because he believed that Spiritualism would bring about great moral changes. After emigrating from his native Scotland, he worked with his father Robert Owen (also a believer, and who took Dale Owen to his first seance), who had set up a socialist utopian community, New Harmony, in Indiana in 1825, and became active in politics, serving in the u.s. House of Representatives from 1843 to 1847.

Dale Owen also produced some of the best and most cogent writings on Spiritualism. He frequently contributed to the Spiritualist newspapers; in 1874 he provided *The Spiritualist at Work* with his theory regarding spirit communications, which distils the prevailing thought regarding the phenomenon into six parts:

1 There is a phase of life after the death-change, in which identity is retained; the same diversity of character being exhibited among spirits as here on earth, among men.

2 Under certain conditions the spirits of the dead have the power to communicate with the living.

3 Spirits, when in communication with earth, have the power of moving considerable weights, and of producing certain sounds; also the power of reading in the minds of some men and women, but perhaps not of all. They experience many difficulties in communicating; and partly because of this, but partly also for other reasons, their communications are often uncertain and unreliable.

4 Spirits communicate more readily when the communications happen to coincide with the thoughts or expectations of the questioner; yet they do, in many instances, declare what is unthought of and unexpected by those to whom the communications are made.

5 One of the conditions of spiritual communion is the presence of one or more of a class of persons peculiarly gifted, and who are usually called mediums.

6 This communion occurs, not through any suspension of the laws of nature, but in accordance with certain constant laws, with the operation of which we are very imperfectly acquainted.[97]

With his massive *Footfalls on the Boundary of Another World*, first published in 1860, Dale Owen supplied the then burgeoning movement with a compendium of history and information that was written more reasonably and clearly than many of the books to come after. Dale Owen, of course, affirms the existence of spirit communications, but he also offers a warning:

> Intimations from another world (supposing their reality) may be useful; they may be highly suggestive; they may supply invaluable materials for thought: just as the opinions of some wise man or the advice of some judicious friend, here upon earth, might do. But no opinion, no advice, from friend or stranger, ought to be received as infallible, or accepted as a rule of action, until Reason shall have sat in judgment upon it and decided, to the best of her ability, its truth and worth.[98]

The Spiritualists were also well organized in both Britain and the USA, with dozens of associations at both national and regional levels. In 1891 the Spiritualists' National Federation (SNF) started with 42 affiliated Spiritualist societies (in 1902 the name changed to the Spiritualists' National Union (SNU), and was now affiliated with 141 societies throughout England). The Marylebone Spiritualist Association was a typical smaller organization, founded in 1872 as a neighbourhood group, but, thanks largely to the efforts of popular Spiritualism supporter Mrs Everitt, who joined with her husband in 1890, the organization experienced a tremendous boost in membership. Today it's known as the Spiritualist Association of Great Britain, with headquarters in London, where it holds weekly services and free demonstrations of mediumship.

Mediums had their own organizations: in the U.S. mediums formed a Mutual Aid Association in 1860; in the UK the Lancashire

Johann Heinrich Füssli, *Tiresias Appears to Ulysses During the Sacrifice*, *c.* 1780, watercolour and tempera on cardboard.

John Hamilton
Mortimer, *Sextus
Pompeius Consulting
Erichtho before the
Battle of Pharsalia*,
c. 1780, oil on canvas.

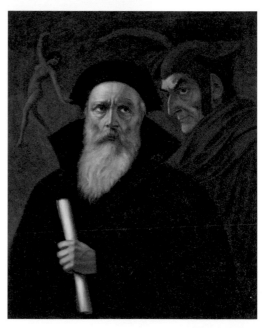

Anton Kaulbach,
Faust and Mephisto,
1900, oil on canvas.

Peter Paul Rubens, *Hercules and Cerberus*, 1636, oil on canvas.

Early drawing of a magic lantern projecting a demon, *c.* 1420, by Giovanni da Fontana.

Gilles de Rais practises sorcery on his victims in this 1862 engraving by Jean-Antoine-Valentin Foulquier.

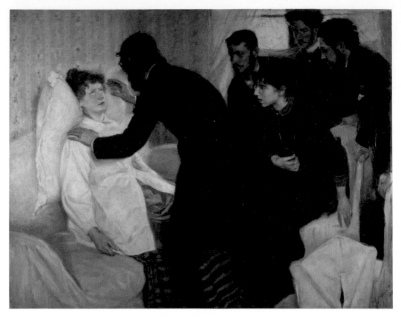

A mesmerist puts a patient into a hypnotic trance in Richard Bergh's *Hypnotic Seance*, 1887, oil on canvas.

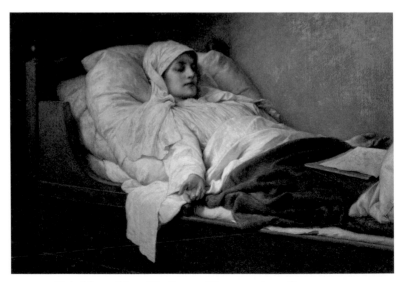

Gabriel von Max, *The Seeress of Prevorst*, 1892, oil on canvas.

Front cover of Catherine Crowe's
The Night-side of Nature (1848).

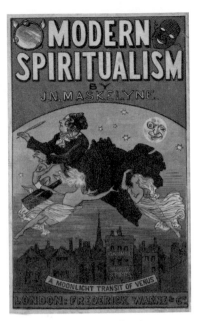

The teleportation of Mrs Guppy
adorns the cover of J. N. Maskelyne's
Modern Spiritualism (1876).

Mumler's spirit photograph of
Mrs Lincoln and Abe's ghost.

Madame Blavatsky, 1889.

The Fox cabin – and the birthplace of the seance.

Georgiana Houghton, *The Eye of God*, 1862, watercolour on paper.

Peter Lorre, Bela Lugosi and Boris Karloff in *You'll Find Out*
(dir. David Butler, 1940).

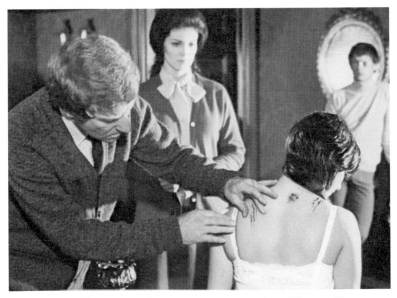

Dr Barrett (Clive Revill) examines injured medium Florence Tanner
(Pamela Franklin) while Ann (Gayle Hunnicutt) and Ben Fischer (Roddy
McDowall) look on in *The Legend of Hell House* (dir. John Hough, 1973).

Stanislawa P. emits ectoplasm during a seance on 25 January 1913.
Photo by Albert von Schrenck-Notzing.

Mediums' Union (later the British Mediums' Union) was formed in 1900.

Spiritualists had a 'capital' – Lily Dale, founded in 1879 in New York state. Lily Dale has been a destination for Spiritualists for over a century now; although it can no longer claim to contain the relocated Fox family house (that burned down in 1955), it calls itself 'the World's Largest Center for the Religion of Spiritualism' and boasts more than fifty resident mediums. Lily Dale receives over 22,000 visitors a year, all of whom pay an entrance fee to the hamlet.

The many weekly and monthly publications devoted to Spiritualism also united the believers. Among the longest-running and most successful were *Banner of Light* and *Daybreak*; at its peak, *Banner of Light* claimed to have 30,000 subscribers, although most historians believe that number was exaggerated. When it debuted in 1869 *The Spiritualist* emphasized scientific investigation; the paper would go on to become the leading British Spiritualist periodical until 1882, when it ceased publication.

In London James Burns's shop the Progressive Library and Spiritual Institution at 15 Southampton Row was a gathering place catering to Spiritualists. Meetings and seances were held there, and Burns also kept a lending library dedicated to Spiritualist books.

Spiritualists tended, like Robert Dale Owen, to be progressive and liberal. Anti-vivisectionism – what would now be known as animal rights – was also gathering steam in the nineteenth century, and references to it are frequent in the Spiritualist papers. When, for example, a new medium encountered a spirit who claimed to be an old friend who had just died, and then found out that the friend was in fact very much alive, he wrote to *Light* to ask for an explanation. One answer offered a comparison to animal experimentation:

> Or is it not just possible that it may have been an experiment conducted by some one of the many thousands who live for experimenting and stick at nothing from pinning down a

smitten butterfly to vivisecting a living dog? There must be millions of experimenters on the other side; and if they are only a tenth as willful there as they were or may have been here, they would not be particular about giving any name to produce the necessary 'shock.'[99]

Spiritualism was increasingly promoted as a sort of egalitarian belief that could be practised anywhere, by anyone, regardless of nationality, gender, economic class or previous religious background. A Boston Spiritualist newspaper set the tone by claiming that 'one or more persons possessing medial powers without knowing it are to be found in nearly every household', and went on to outline nine steps in how to hold a seance, including temperature of the room, the number of sitters ('three or five to ten'), singing (as long as it's not 'of a frivolous nature'), how only one person should respond when phenomena begin, and how to identify the best medium in a group.[100]

By 1876 London apparently boasted a thriving industry of mediums, many of whom continued to have spirit guides named King; an article in a Spiritualist newspaper from that year discusses 'the number of darkened parlours on back streets that are the scenes of frequent séances for spirit-materializations' and mentions that it was necessary to apply in advance for admittance to these establishments, with the applicant being told that his petition would be referred to 'John King'.[101] (It's also possible that one of the reasons for applying in advance at the medium's parlour was to allow a confederate of the medium to follow the applicant home, gaining information for use in the seance.[102]) In an article from an 1872 issue of *The Spiritualist*, William H. Harrison notes the prevalence of the names 'John and Katie King' among spirits, and says the name 'King' is used because it is 'symbolical of "power"'.[103] It was also said that John King's wife Katie King was the spirit in charge of all 'apports' (solid objects that abruptly appeared at a seance).[104]

In his autobiography the preacher and abolitionist Moncure Conway described attending a school for mediums in London in 1882. He encountered about twenty men and women in a large room, practising rapping, spirit communication and musical mediumship. During his visit Conway challenged the student mediums to guess the amount of money in his wallet; when one of them tried and failed, she said her powers were not yet developed enough. Conway left the school unconvinced.[105]

What Conway doesn't mention is seeing the would-be mediums trading secrets in how to commit fraud, although other writers have suggested there was a healthy industry in this part of the business as well. Fraudulent mediums needed to learn how to move tables by 'the human clamp', or how to suggest levitation by putting their shoes on their hands and letting sitters feel the floating shoes in the darkness of a seance. They needed to know how to make or where to purchase telescoping rods, which could be used to float objects over the heads of sitters, or (by attaching a pencil to one end) might make a mark on the ceiling that the medium would claim to have made while floating. They would need to know how to work with a watchmaker to make a small box that would contain the gears necessary to produce rapping sounds, and how to hide that tiny device in a cigarette box so that it wouldn't be discovered if they were searched. They should know how to use phosphorus oil, which could be mixed into a bottle of any regular fatty oil and wouldn't glow until the bottle cap was removed. Being knowledgeable in the acquisition and instruction of confederates was certainly an asset.

There were claims that some of the mediums had created documents called 'Blue Books', which would list information about the Spiritualists in a town that mediums could use when holding seances; they would, for instance, already know that a sitter's Aunt Clara had died of cholera ten years ago, or that the sitter's mother had passed on two years ago. However, although there were undoubtedly mediums who would acquire foreknowledge of Spiritualists by visiting cemeteries and newspaper offices, there's no evidence that the 'Blue Books' actually existed.

However, even without 'Blue Books', mediums were adept at gaining information for use with clients (and potential clients). In his book *A Magician among the Spirits*, Houdini says that he heard of mediums who had confederates in hotels, on trains, in brothels, working as domestics in wealthy households, in beauty parlours and even in funeral homes.[106]

Did businesses that specialized in supplying mediums with materials such as telescoping rods and special shoes really exist? In his 1938 *Beware Familiar Spirits*, John Mulholland claimed they did, and that he personally owned some of their catalogues; he also stated that he'd seen one of these dealers' client list of several thousand mediums. The catalogues offered items like a 'Spirit Rapping

A fraudulent medium is unmasked in this satirical drawing by George Cruikshank, from his *A Discovery Concerning Ghosts* (1864).

Satirical drawing by George Cruikshank mocking the Church rationale for table-lifting, from his *A Discovery Concerning Ghosts* (1864).

Table' ($50), a 'Self Playing Guitar' ($25) and even 'A Complete Spiritualistic Séance' (for the very reasonable price of $25).[107]

Sometimes the mediums were themselves the victims of hoaxes. In his autobiography, Charles Ranlett Flint – an industrialist who was an integral part of the beginning of IBM – described a hoax perpetrated by five friends that targeted the popular Boston-based newspaper *Spiritualist Scientist*. The quintet each supplied a letter from their name to create 'Hiraf'; four then created random esoteric sentences and gave them to the fifth man, who compiled the sentences into an article. The article appeared in the newspaper's 1 July 1875 issue, and although it's a nearly indecipherable mess, the paper introduced it as a 'valuable' piece.[108] Later on, the 'Hiraf' authors discovered that Madame Blavatsky had praised the work of 'Hiraf' and quoted from it, as had her second-in-command in theosophy, Annie Besant.[109]

The non-Spiritualist newspapers and magazines continued to poke fun at belief in ghosts and the abilities of mediums; the

Front cover of the programme for a Maskelyne & Cooke performance (where they are billed as 'Illusionists and Anti-Spiritualists').

Cambridge Chronicle and Journal memorably called it 'a mixture of quackery and gim-crackery',[110] the famed illustrator George Cruikshank released an entire book dedicated to such penetrating questions as wondering why ghosts should appear clothed,[111] and the humorous magazine *Punch* addressed the ubiquity of Spiritualism in an 1872 poem called 'Old Ghosts and New':

> White-sheeted Ghosts have grown mere fables.
> Instead of groaning, Ghosts rap tables:
> With smells of sulphur ne'er assail us;
> With curious perfumes oft regale us.
> They 'mediums' raise by 'levitation,'

And subject them to elongation,
And in and out of windows float them,
Two stories high, lords vow, we quote them.

. . .

Some Ghosts, do, mortal hands compelling,
Write letters in phonetic spelling.
Some others, on accordions, cunning
In music, *Home, Sweet Home*, play, punning . . .[112]

Poets and scientists weren't the only ones who took jabs at the Spiritualists; magicians John Nevil Maskelyne and George Cooke regularly debunked Spiritualist mediums and seances. As noted earlier, Maskelyne had come to fame after recreating the Davenport brothers' stunts; he would go on to be remembered as the author of the definitive work on card sharps, the creator of the levitation illusion and the inventor of the pay toilet. In 1891 Maskelyne wrote, 'There does not exist, and there never has existed, a professed "medium" of any note who has not been convicted of trickery or fraud.'[113] Some Spiritualists responded by labelling Maskelyne and Cooke mediums: 'If they are mediums, they are naturally most anxious to conceal the fact, lest their profits should diminish and themselves be scouted and vilified by the non-spiritual public, both of which results would, of course, follow their detection.'[114]

Maskelyne was frequently called on to testify in court cases involving mediums (during Dr Henry Slade's case, for example, he was brought in by the prosecution to examine a table confiscated from Slade, and he demonstrated how the bottom of it had a movable support that could be used to hold slates[115]), but in one notable case he was both plaintiff and defendant. That case involved medium Francis Ward Monck, who was mentioned in the Introduction. Monck remains conspicuous in the history of Spiritualism not for his spectacular feats or money-making prowess, but for the number of times he wound up in court after being exposed. On 23 October

1876 Monck had held a seance at a house in Huddersfield; the seance had included 'raps under the table, the moving of a musical instrument along the table by an unseen power, sounds from a musical-box covered with a wooden case, the appearance of a head at the edge of the table, writing on a slate under the table, a button being pulled off a lady's dress, and sounding the notes of a piano while a lady sat on the lid'.[116] One of the gentlemen present wasn't satisfied with Monck's performance, and the medium fled, climbing out of an upstairs window using a sheet and a water spout. In Monck's room a number of suspicious articles were discovered, including hands made from gloves, an extendable rod, paper faces and wire. Monck was arrested by Chief Constable Henry Hilton, and the resulting case of Monck v. Hilton – also known as the Huddersfield Spiritualist case – was in the papers for months. After he was found guilty, Monck appealed on the grounds that what he did shouldn't be covered by the Vagrancy Act, but his conviction and sentencing were upheld and he served three months in prison.

An Anglican reverend named Thomas Colley was an enthusiastic supporter of Spiritualism who repeatedly defended Monck; after the medium was arrested in Monck v. Hilton, Colley claimed the magic equipment found in Monck's residence was his. In 1905 Colley wagered £1,000 that no magician could recreate Monck's spirit materialization; Maskelyne took up the challenge and succeeded. However, Colley claimed that Maskelyne had not, in fact, perfectly reproduced Monck's effects, and refused to pay. Maskelyne consequently published a pamphlet entitled *The History of a Thousand Pounds Challenge: An Object Lesson for Spiritualists*, in which he claimed that Colley was not an archdeacon. Colley sued for libel and the case went to court on 24 April 1907, with Maskelyne counterclaiming that Colley owed him the £1,000 from the challenge. During the trial, Alfred Russel Wallace testified to having witnessed Monck perform a spirit materialization:

Dr. Monck stood up, and appeared to go into a trance. I have no doubt he was in a trance. Then, after a short time, on the left side of his coat there appeared a very faint white patch, which increased in density and moved up and down and seemed to flicker, spread out a little and flickered still more, and at last grew up to the height of his shoulder and down to the ground, and then there was a separation from the part that seemed to come out of his coat and connect itself with his body. After a few minutes more the separation was quite distinct, and he then said to us 'Look!' and put his hand through the space. Then the white cloud or figure moved away till it was at least six feet from him, and it seemed as it moved to grow more distinct and to become the outline of a woman in flowing white draperies, allowing the face to be seen. Then he looked towards it and said 'Look!' and put up his hands and clapped them. The figure imitated the medium's movements and put out its two hands, and we all heard them. Then he stood still, and the figure moved slowly backwards and sideways and drew up to his side and began to diminish in brightness. Then the waving motion began again, and it went back into his body in precisely the same way as it had come out.[117]

During the trial, the jury was even taken to see one of Maskelyne's performances, but unfortunately they agreed with Colley and Monck that Maskelyne had failed to recreate all of Monck's materialization phenomenon, because Maskelyne's bogus spirit form had not returned into his body at the act's conclusion. Maskelyne was found guilty of libel and ordered to pay Colley £75 in damages; he also lost the counter-claim and was not awarded £1,000.

As the decade progressed, so did the variety of mediums and the miracles the spirits demonstrated. For a time in the 1870s apports were all the rage. At Mrs Guppy's seances, fifteen to twenty sitters would sometimes ask in turn that the spirits bring each of them 'specimens of fruit which they named. Each sitter usually had the particular kind of fruit he asked for put into his hands directly he made the request.'[118] Mediums at this time used spirits to apport everything from snow to potted plants to live eels. One of the greatest apports took place on 3 June 1871 during a seance held by Herne and Williams:

> Before the séance began, the doors communicating with the passage outside were locked. The proccedings began, at the request of the mediums, with prayer. Then spirit lights, like small stars, were seen moving about, after which a conversation between the spirits John King and Katie King, was heard. John said, 'Katie, you can't do it.' Katie replied, 'I will, I tell you I will.' John said, 'I tell you you can't.' She answered, 'I will.' Mr. Harrison then said, 'Can you bring Mrs. Guppy?' There was no reply but a member of the circle urged that the attempt should not be made. Within three minutes after Katie had said, 'I will,' a single heavy sound was heard for an instant on the centre of the table. Mr. Edwards put out his hand and said, 'There is a dress here.' A light was instantly struck, and Mrs. Guppy was found standing motionless on the centre of the table, trembling all over . . .' The badly-shaken Mrs. Guppy claimed that she had been sitting at home, working on household accounts when she'd suddenly found herself in Herne and Williams's séance room; the observers all affirmed that the doors were still locked, and there was nowhere in the room Mrs. Guppy could have concealed herself.[119]

This apport became famous, with some believers noting that Mrs Guppy was a large woman who would seemingly have had difficulty climbing onto a table in the dark. Maskelyne even parodied the whole thing on the cover of his book *Modern Spiritualism*, which showed a cartoonish drawing of Mrs Guppy soaring over London, with the caption 'A Moonlight Transit of Venus'.

Guppy would be involved in one more controversy: it was claimed by some that she had attempted to conspire to hurl sulphuric acid into the face of Florence Cook, who was her chief rival in mediumship. Although this is disputed, what cannot be argued is that Mrs Guppy would marry William Volckman two years after his famous attempt to unmask the materialized spirit 'Katie King' at one of Florence Cook's seances.

Mrs Guppy was resurrected in 2018 when she served as the central figure in a haunted theatrical experience, 'Séance', produced by the London Dungeons.[120]

Some mediums promoted themselves as healers. For example, in an advertisement in an 1875 issue of *The Spiritualist*, a Professor Redan calls himself a 'psychopathic healer', who

wishes to make known, by desire of his Spirit Physicians, who cure through him, in his normal state, that having been developed by them into a powerful healing medium, and at the same time, by a course of deep study, acquiring a practical knowledge of the philosophy of disease, and its *rationale* of cure, he is now prepared to examine, treat, and cure patients, suffering from all kinds of acute, chronic, nervous, and organic disease of long years' standing.[121]

Cora Lavinia Victoria Scott Hatch Daniels Tappan Richmond – usually known as Mrs Cora L. V. Richmond – was an American medium noted for spirit guides who used her to speak at length to gatherings. She might channel an ancient astronomer to talk about celestial sciences, a spirit guide named 'Ouina' to deliver sermons, or even – on the occasion of his birthday – Abraham Lincoln. Richmond – or, rather, her spirit guides – produced such a vast quantity of material that she was able to produce a 'Weekly Discourse' for subscribers, and a collection of lectures that ran to nearly eight hundred pages.

Dr William Stainton Moses also offered spiritual sermons, via the spirit guide 'Imperator'. Moses was a priest in the Church of England who discovered Spiritualism in 1872, and almost immediately began to practise as a medium – five months later, in fact, he claimed to experience levitation. Like Cora Richmond, Moses produced an astonishing amount of written material, often writing under the name 'M. A. Oxon'; his work was usually produced via automatic writing while he was in a trance state. He also served as an officer in the early days of the Society for Psychical Research, founded the London Spiritualist Alliance and was generally held in high regard by his fellow Spiritualists. 'Imperator' offered regular advice in *The Spiritualist*, often preaching moderation:

> You would be well advised to prepare yourself always, both mentally and bodily, for communion. As we have before said that we cannot operate when the body is overloaded with food, so now we say, that a system depressed and weak is not favourable for our purposes. We do not advocate the depression of the vital powers by neglect of due food any more than we countenance gluttony and drunkenness. We preach the mean in all things where it is knowable.[122]

When Moses died in 1892 (at the age of 53 – the cause of death was the lingering effects of influenza he had contracted two years earlier), his obituary in the *Pall Mall Gazette* noted, 'It is perhaps not too much to say that he gradually raised Spiritualism in England from what was fast becoming a debasing superstition to a position in which it has become a prime factor in the intellectual and moral activity of the age.'[123] The name of Moses's spirit guide – 'Imperator' – also became an enduring name within Spiritualism, frequently mentioned over the years and applied as a name to groups and other spirit guides.

Far less highly regarded than Moses but still a popular figure in Spiritualist circles was Dr Henry Slade, he whose trick table was exposed by John Nevil Maskelyne. Slade specialized in 'slate writing', which involved two slates screwed together, their surfaces facing inwards, with a small stub of pencil inserted between them. The slate would then be held by the medium in his or her lap, under the table (and thus out of sight) until the medium signalled that the message had been received. Slade was skilled in producing other phenomena as well; an 1878 article mentions that, while touring Russia, scientists were impressed by his ability to turn the needle on one compass while another sat near it, motionless, 'thus destroying the theory that it was turned by a concealed magnet, which must affect both in the same manner'.[124] Curiously, this is less than two years after Slade was arrested, tried and convicted in a British court for 'endeavouring to obtain sums of money under the pretence of being able to communicate with the spirits of the departed'. During the case, Slade's slate-writing methods were demonstrated in court, as were his table-rapping and movement tricks.[125] Slade was sentenced to three months' imprisonment with hard labour, but filed an appeal on a technicality and fled the country. Slade was also dismissed as fraudulent in 1884 by the Seybert Commission, whom we shall encounter later.

Mediums also sometimes alleged fraud against each other, the most famous perhaps being D. D. Home, who devoted a considerable amount of his written works to accusations levelled against fellow practitioners. A case from 1875 between two women mediums, however, demonstrates again how entrenched the Spiritualists were in their beliefs: in late 1875 a Boston medium named Mrs Carpenter claimed to be able to prove that renowned medium Annie Fay was a fake. Fay's abilities were so completely accepted as real that not only was Carpenter roundly denounced, it was claimed that the only way to reproduce Fay's manifestations would be to *also* produce real manifestations, meaning that Carpenter would be lying about both Fay's mediumship and her own.[126]

By the 1880s the Spiritualists sought physical proof, proof that was tangible, that could be touched and captured, and so they moved from rappings and materializations to ectoplasm. The word – derived from the Greek *ektos*, meaning 'outside', and 'plasma', something that can be formed or moulded – was originally created for studying cell biology, but in 1895 the French doctor Charles Richet applied it to what the medium Eusapia Palladino was producing: a filmy white substance that was believed to be the very stuff of spirits. Palladino would prove to be the greatest of all materialization mediums; originally an Italian peasant who was illiterate but moved among Europe's aristocracy thanks to her skills, she eventually wound up being tested by Richet, who sat with her two hundred times. When Richet called his friends from England down to his residence in the south of France, they were also impressed by Palladino, and in 1895 they brought her to Cambridge for further testing. During their first sitting with Palladino, a friend of Richet called Sidgwick held her feet while Frederic Myers, co-founder of the Society for Psychical Research, grasped her hands, and yet her control spirit John King (yet again) made the table jump, moved the sitters' chairs while they were in them and materialized white shapes. Palladino, however, was soon exposed by the Society for Psychical Research; even then, some of the society's members tried to assert that the medium possessed genuine abilities alongside her penchant for trickery.

One of the last mediums to emerge in the nineteenth century was Hélène Smith (the pseudonym of Catherine-Elise Müller), whose familiar spirit was 'Léopold' (and thankfully not another 'John King'). Léopold took her back through her previous incarnations, including a fifteenth-century Indian princess who spoke in 'Hindu'. She had also been Marie Antoinette, and Léopold had been Cagliostro as they had an affair. Most incredible of all, however, was an incarnation as a resident of the planet Mars; when visiting this life, Smith spoke Martian and produced Martian writing (unreadable to Earth mortals, sadly). She was studied by a Swiss doctor named Théodore Flournoy, whose 1899 book *Des Indes à la planète Mars: Étude sur un cas de Somnambulisme* (From India to the Planet Mars: Study of a Case of Somnambulism) became a massive seller. Flournoy made no attempt to investigate scientifically, however; instead, he engaged the various spirit incarnations in conversation.

Spirit Photography

In 1859 a debate ran through several issues of *The Spiritual Telegraph and Fireside Preacher* about the possibility of spirits being captured in a photograph: after photographing a newly deceased man (a common practice then), the female photographer discovered two other figures, a man and a woman, posed behind the corpse.[127] Soon after that, a photographer (or daguerreotypist) wrote to the paper explaining that he had created such images by accident – the photographic plates then in use had to be cleaned after each image had been taken and printed, and if the cleaning was imperfect ghostly remnants might appear on the next print obtained from that plate. The paper contacted the photographer, who noted that the plate used for that photograph had been brand new and that the dress of the woman caught in the image was long out of date; however, she also noted that none of the deceased man's family recognized either of the spirits seen in the image.[128]

Despite a few early incidences of spirit photography such as the one described above, it wasn't until 1862 that an amateur photographer named William Mumler attempted a self-portrait, only to discover that he was not alone in the final photograph – the camera had captured the ghostly apparition of a woman seated in a chair. Photography was still a relatively new art – Samuel Morse had taken the first portrait photograph just 22 years earlier – and Mumler, an engraver by profession, was the first to admit that he might have made a mistake in processing the plate. He did assert that the female spectre in the photo was his cousin, who had passed away twelve years before.

Mumler soon discovered that his photographs regularly revealed spirits. Other photographers paid visits to him, certain that they could ferret out his secrets; Mumler invited them to witness all parts of the procedure, from setting up the studio to developing the plate, and they all left baffled. When Mumler wed Hannah Stuart, a war widow who owned the studio he'd been using and who was also a medium, he began to produce spirit photographs as a business. At the beginning, Mumler warned clients that the spirits didn't always materialize, but within a few years he was offering to sell photographs of deceased spirits via mail order (a photograph of a dead loved one's spirit could be had for $7.50). Unfortunately for Mumler, purchasers of his photographs began to recognize some of the 'spirits' as persons still living, all of whom had had their photographs taken at Mrs Stuart's studio. Mumler was discredited, even by the same Spiritualist newspapers that had earlier supported him.

Mumler continued, finding fresh success when he and Hannah relocated from Boston to New York. There, he had business cards made up in which he called himself a 'spirit photographic medium', and he created a booklet that he gave to potential customers extolling the comforts of his service:

What joy to the troubled heart! What balm to the aching breast! What peace and comfort to the weary soul! To know that our friends who have passed away can return and give us unmistakable evidence of a life hereafter – that they are with us and seize with avidity every opportunity to make themselves known; but alas, in many instances, that old door of sectarianism has closed against them, and prevents their entering once more the portals of the loved ones and be identified. But, thank God, the old door is fast going to decay; it begins to squeak on its rusty and time worn hinges; its panels are penetrated by the worm holes of many ages, through which the bright, effulgent rays of the spiritual sun begin to shine, and in a short time it will totter and tumble to the earth.[129]

Mumler's success in New York was fleeting; in 1869 he was arrested on fraud charges. The case was a test for Spiritualism, filling the newspapers. Witnesses included the great showman P. T. Barnum, who testified against Mumler even though a number of his spirit photographs were displayed in Barnum's American Museum. After three weeks, the judge ruled that the prosecution had failed to make its case – no one could definitively show how Mumler had created the spirit photographs – and Mumler was freed. The Photographic Section of the American Institute used the Mumler trial to issue a definitive statement against spirit photography; at their 4 May 1869 meeting, they unanimously voted two resolutions, the first of which ran: 'That the Photographic Section of the American Institute take the earliest opportunity to condemn all such methods of working upon the credulous and uninitiated, and that they receive with wonder and amazement the decision of the justice.'[130]

Mumler returned to Boston, where, in 1872, he would produce the most famous of all spirit photographs: a portrait of Mary Todd Lincoln with her late husband Abraham's spirit bent over her, seemingly consoling her. Legend has it that Mrs Lincoln arrived at Mumler's studio under a fake name with her face hidden beneath a black bonnet; Hannah claimed to discern her identity from seeing her husband's spirit with her.

In the mid-1870s Mumler created a process for transferring images directly from photographs to newsprint, thus eliminating the need for an engraver; he spent his last seven years serving as treasurer of the Photo-Electrotype Company of Boston. When he died in 1884, at the age of 51, his obituaries took little notice of his spirit photography.

A British man named Frederick Hudson produced the first British spirit photographs in 1872. When *The Spiritualist* exposed Hudson's double-exposure technique, other Spiritualist papers rushed to his defence. However, *The Spiritualist* (and other publications) continued to defend the overall practice. Alfred Russel Wallace wrote:

> We now approach a subject which cannot be omitted in any impartial sketch of the evidences of Spiritualism, since it is that which furnishes perhaps the most unassailable demonstration it is possible to obtain of the objective reality of spiritual forms, and also of the truthful nature of the evidence furnished by seers when they describe figures visible to themselves alone.[131]

Wallace goes on to discuss how sitters at a seance may all have differing reports about the spirits they have witnessed, but '*they can be photographed*' (the italics are Wallace's). Wallace next describes in depth the ways in which spirit photographs can be judged:

> 1. If a person with a knowledge of photography takes his own glass plates, examines the camera used and all the accessories, and watches the whole process of taking a picture, then, if any definite form appears on the negative beside the sitter, it is a proof that some object was present capable of reflecting or emitting the actinic rays, although invisible to those present.
> 2. If an unmistakable likeness appears of a deceased person

totally unknown to the photographer. 3. If the figures appear on the negative having a definite relation to the figure of the sitter, who chooses his own position, attitude, and accompaniments, it is a proof that invisible figures were really there. 4. If a figure appears draped in white, and partly behind the dark body of the sitter without in the least showing through, it is a proof that the white figure was there at the same time, because the dark parts of the negative are transparent, and any white picture in any way superposed would show through. 5. Even should none of these tests be applied, yet if a medium, quite independent of the photographer, sees and describes a figure during the sitting, and an exactly corresponding figure appears on the plate, it is a proof that such a figure was there.[132]

Wallace was eventually accompanied by the medium Mrs Guppy and taken to see Hudson, whose recent photographs had included one of Guppy and the medium-artist Georgiana Houghton (who worked for Hudson), along with a third woman; in the photograph of the three women, they are partly obscured by a strange, ghostly vapour.

After Wallace sat for Hudson, three photographs were produced, two of which showed Wallace and his late mother. Wallace was completely convinced of the authenticity of the photographs; unfortunately, Hudson was debunked soon after, and even other Spiritualists scoffed at Wallace's credulity. It seems likely that Mrs Guppy, whom Wallace believed in completely, was aware of, and likely a participant in, Hudson's fraud.

At the same time that Hudson was photographing Wallace and his spirit mother, a French photographer named Édouard Isidore Buguet was busily shooting ghosts in Paris. Buguet had partnered with Pierre-Gaëtan Leymarie, editor of the leading French Spiritualist periodical *La Revue spirite*, to offer photographic prints for sale in the magazine. They were very successful until April 1875, when an undercover policeman paid a visit to Buguet's studios and discovered props and trickery. Buguet and Leymarie were both arrested, as was an American medium, Alfred-Henri Firman, who had also participated in the fraud. All three men were convicted, although Buguet escaped before serving any time. After they were released from prison, Leymarie and Firman returned to successful careers in Spiritualism.[133] Believers attributed the whole thing to a conspiracy on the part of the Roman Catholic Church, suggesting that Buguet was actually an authentic medium who had been bribed in an effort to discredit Spiritualism.[134] One Spiritualist newspaper called Leymarie 'the first martyr of distinction that the cause has supplied'.[135]

Spiritualism in Literature and the Arts

Spiritualism counted many well-known writers among its ranks. Even before Sir Arthur Conan Doyle, the creator of Sherlock Holmes, was sparring with Houdini over Spiritualism, the Brownings, Charles Dickens, Marie Corelli (whose 1886 novel *A Romance of Two Worlds* was a major best-seller), Henry James and H. G. Wells all tackled the subject.

Florence Marryat was not only the daughter of a renowned author (Frederick Marryat) and a prolific writer herself, she was an ardent Spiritualist who wrote both fiction and non-fiction (and believed that Florence Cook's spirit guide Katie King had visited her bedroom). Her 1883 short story 'A Midsummer's Nightmare; or, The Amateur Detective' offers a more playful view of Spiritualism than most of the other fictional depictions of the time. It follows the titular amateur detective, who has been dispatched to a small village in search of a missing man. After taking an apartment in the village, he hears strange sounds – footsteps, thumps, arguments, groans – coming from the floor above, and urges the landlord to hold a seance. The landlord and his wife (who are unfamiliar with the word 'Spiritualism') reluctantly agree, and the narrator describes his preparations for the evening:

> I was really going to hold a séance, under my own direction and the most favourable circumstances with a large haunted house at my command, and no one to be any the wiser for my dabbling in the necromantic art. I took out an old number of the 'Spiritualist', and referred to the directions for forming circles at home. I prepared the paper, pencils, and speaking tubes, and symmetrically arranged the table and chairs.[136]

The resulting seance seems uneventful until a 'spirit' manifests, but is instead revealed to be the missing young man (an actor who has been rehearsing in the upstairs room).

Perhaps more than any other author, Elizabeth Stuart Phelps captured Spiritualism in a way that assured readers its belief aligned with Scripture. Her novels, which include *The Gates Ajar* (1868), *Beyond the Gates* (1883) and *The Gates Between* (1887), and her short stories, especially 'Since I Died', remain well regarded by critics and studied by scholars.

Some writers and artists used mediums and their spirit messages for inspiration. W. B. Yeats, for one, sought out mediums, one of whom – Bessie Radcliffe – channelled an exotic figure named 'Leo Africanus' with whom Yeats held long discussions, and who was attributed with breaking Yeats out of his writer's block.[137]

Art produced by Spiritualist mediums who claimed to commune with great artists of the past (including Titian and Correggio) has recently been re-evaluated for its importance in leading to later schools of abstract art. In 1861 Georgiana Houghton – who was 47 at the time – took up both mediumship and the watercolour brush and, over the next decade, produced hundreds of works. During Houghton's life, her works were denounced by critics disdainful of Spiritualism, but a 2016 gallery show of her forty remaining paintings generated fresh appreciation for her colourful, sweeping, distinctive images. Similarly, the Swedish painter Hilma af Klint generated large, bright canvases that preceded the work of Mondrian and Kandinsky; between 1906 and 1915, af Klint produced a series called *The Paintings for the Temple*, all inspired by Spiritualism and theosophy, that were rediscovered in the 1980s with showings at the Guggenheim and the Los Angeles County Museum of Art.

The Spirits and God

Throughout the nineteenth century, the Catholic Church addressed the growing interest in magnetism and Spiritualism, beginning in 1840 when the Congregation of the Inquisition ruled that 'the application of purely physical principles and means to things or effects that are really supernatural, in order to explain these on physical grounds, is nothing else than unlawful and heretical deception.'[138] The Church added a further decree on 30 July 1856, which exhorted bishops to put forth every effort for the suppression of these Spiritualistic practices 'in order that the flock of the Lord may be protected against the enemy, the deposit of faith safeguarded, and the faithful preserved from moral corruption'. The Second Plenary Council of Baltimore (1866), while recognizing that fraud often occurred in Spiritualism, warned against attending seances since spirits might actually be Satanic. A decree of the Holy Office on 30 March 1898 condemned Spiritualism, even when seeking to communicate only with good spirits.

The Catholic Church sometimes refers to Spiritualism as 'spiritism', which it defines as 'the name properly given to the belief that the living can and do communicate with the spirits of the departed and to the various practices by which such communication is attempted'. However, the Church also draws a distinction between spiritism and Spiritualism, defining the latter as 'the philosophical doctrine which holds in general that there is a spiritual order of beings no less real than the material and in particular that the soul of man is a spiritual substance'.[139] The entry on 'Spiritism' in *The Catholic Encyclopedia* concludes: 'In all these documents the distinction is clearly drawn between legitimate scientific investigation and superstitious abuses. What the Church condemns in Spiritism is superstition with its evil consequences for religion and morality.'[140]

In his study of post-First World War supernatural beliefs, Owen Davies suggests that Spiritualism was confined largely to regions where the Catholic Church was not dominant: 'Deemed incompatible with the Catholic faith, spiritualism as a religion did not gain the same foothold in Catholic Europe as it did in Protestant Britain

This 1865 anti-Spiritualism flyer puts a demon in both the story of Saul and the Witch of Endor and a Spiritualist seance.

and America.'[141] Even in America, though, Spiritualism was often condemned by religious groups: in 1856 a church in Chillicothe, Ohio, suspended two members who were found to be engaged in spirit rapping, and issued the following warning:

> Resolved, That the practice of Spirit Rappings, (so called) as it prevails in many parts, is, in view of this Presbytery, a revival of the old abomination of necromancy, so decidedly condemned in the word of God.[142]

Although the biblical prohibitions against necromancy were undoubtedly behind much of the Christian condemnation of Spiritualism, this resolution is one of the few times when Spiritualism and necromancy are clearly conflated.

John Godfrey Raupert was a former Anglican priest who converted to Catholicism and became one of the Church's staunchest warriors in the battle against Spiritualism. Raupert's *The Dangers of Spiritualism* was first published in 1901, but would go on to be reprinted multiple times. He argued that the intelligences contacted via mediums were 'all of a low and evil type and influence' and that even scientific investigation was dangerous: 'It is yet to be proved that, so far as Spiritualism is concerned, the results attained stand in anything like reasonable proportion to the perils incurred and to the mischief done.'[143] After the Ouija board became popular in the 1910s, Pope Pius x commissioned Raupert to write a book outlining the board's dangers; that book, *The New Black Magic and the Truth about the Ouija-board*, published in 1919, was largely responsible for establishing the Ouija board's reputation as a gateway to occult forces.

Much of the Christian antipathy towards Spiritualism was founded on the belief that Christians should be seeking communication only with God. In a letter quoted in Spiritualist newspapers from 1893 (and argued by the editors), the Archbishop of Canterbury wrote, 'It is a bold hypothesis which at once says "this is the work of spiritual beings," and it is quite unproved.'[144] The Bishop of Durham voiced similar thoughts:

> Many years ago I had occasion to investigate 'spiritualistic'
> phenomena with some care, and I came to a clear conclusion,
> which I feel bound to express in answer to your circular.
> It appears to me that in this, as in all spiritual questions,
> Holy Scripture is our supreme guide. I observe, then, that
> while spiritual ministries are constantly recorded in the
> Bible, there is not the faintest encouragement to seek them.
> The case, indeed, is far otherwise. I cannot, therefore, but
> regard every voluntary approach to beings such as those
> who are supposed to hold communication with men through
> mediums as unlawful and perilous.[145]

The Spiritualist newspaper *Light*, in printing this letter, introduced it as 'an excellent example of what the orthodox Christian believes, when his beliefs and thoughts are regulated by a book'.[146] That same issue of *Light* also published this statement from the Bishop of London, who sought to dismiss Spiritualism on the grounds of a lack of evidence:

> To me it seems that before such an investigation can be
> commenced with any hope of result, a *primá-facie* case
> ought to be made out for believing that there is something
> to investigate. I have come across no such *primá-facie* case.
> Hitherto, the only result of the investigations has been,
> in my judgment, to show the extreme probability that the
> investigators will be self-deluded, and tempted to consciously
> delude others. To this temptation many of them have yielded.
> But these conclusions of mine cannot be of much use to
> those who are already convinced that there is something
> to investigate.[147]

The Spiritualists themselves were divided along religious lines, with many believing that Spiritualism aligned perfectly with Christianity. The writings of William Stainton Moses, who is now sometimes referred to as 'the father of Christian Spiritualism', frequently discuss how Spiritualism serves Christianity. Moses's *Spirit Teachings* (1883) opens with this paragraph:

> Special efforts are being made now to spread a knowledge of progressive truth: efforts by the messengers of God, which are resisted, now as ever, by the hosts of the adversaries. The history of the world has been the story of the struggle between the evil and the good; between God and goodness on the one side, and ignorance, vice, and evil – spiritual, mental, and corporeal – on the other side. At certain times, of which this is one, extraordinary efforts are made. The army of the messengers of God is massed in greater force: men are influenced: knowledge is spread: and the end draws nigh. Fear for the deserters, the half-hearted, the temporizers, the merely curious. Fear for them: but fear not for the cause of God's truth.[148]

There were also anti-Christian Spiritualists, led by bookshop owner James Burns. Many believers came to Spiritualism from atheism, as often enticed by Spiritualism's alliance with progressive political causes as by its promise to provide proof of life after death.

Mind and Spirit

During the growth of Spiritualism, psychology was also a nascent study. The German philosopher Christian Wolff had first suggested psychology as a science in 1732; by the 1830s psychology (which was sometimes tied to phrenology) was exploring questions of sensory perception and involuntary responses. In 1890 William James published *The Principles of Psychology*, establishing 'psychology' as the name of the science devoted to exploring human mental processes. Prior to James, 'psychology' had frequently been applied to very different studies, especially in Spiritualism. 'When spiritualists called séance manifestations "psychological" phenomena,' notes Janet Oppenheim, 'they used the adjective to indicate the presence of psyche, not to suggest that a medium's accomplishments existed only in the minds of the audience.'[149]

Note, for example, this description of the Liverpool Psychological Society, formed in 1875:

> The object of this Association is the discovery of truth in connection with Psychology. The Society seeks to attain its object by the following measures, or such of them as from time to time are found to be practicable.
>
> 1 By frequent meetings of its members for conference, inquiry, instruction, mental improvement, spiritual culture, social intercourse, and healthful recreation,
> 2 By engaging in the education of children and others, for the purpose of developing their physical, mental, and spiritual powers.
> 3 By the dissemination of knowledge by means of public instruction, lectures, reading-rooms, the press, and spirit communion.[150]

Within a few years, though, the word 'psychology' started to skew away from spirit communion and more towards the study of the human mind. In an 1879 essay entitled 'The New Psychology', William L. Courtney prophesied the future of the new science:

> If ... we ... ask to which side will tend the future speculations of English Psychology, the answer is hardly doubtful. For many

reasons it seems likely that the ultimate victory in England will rest with the side which lays its stress on Science and Experience. It is ordinarily supposed, indeed, that the so-called Spiritualistic hypothesis has a strong ally in the religious feelings of the community; but even were such the case, the strength of the religious forces is gradually decreasing.[151]

By the time psychology was well established in the early twentieth century, it would have its own criticisms of spirit communication, with the word 'neurotic' increasingly applied by both psychologists and enemies of Spiritualism.

Spiritism and Theosophy

Spiritualism wasn't the only belief system investigating communication with spirits to be birthed in the nineteenth century. Arriving just a few years after Spiritualism were the similar doctrines of theosophy and spiritism.

Helena Petrovna Blavatsky claimed to be a Russian born in 1831 who grew up with mediumistic powers. She fled a teenage marriage to a much older man, Nikifor Vassilyevich Blavatsky, to travel to Tibet, where she said she studied with the Mahatmas for seven years (she also supposedly journeyed to New Orleans around 1850, where she claimed to study voodoo); while her years in Tibet have been the study of considerable debate, there's no question that she travelled to Europe, where she learned hypnosis and mediumship. In 1858 she met D. D. Home in Paris; Home would later assert that he had converted her to Spiritualism. Much of Blavatsky's philosophy rested on the claim that in Tibet she was allowed to visit a subterranean library where she viewed the mysterious 'Book of Dzyan'; this provided the basis for theosophy, the belief system Blavatsky laid out in books such as *Isis Unveiled* (1877) and *The Secret Doctrine* (1888). Theosophy includes such Eastern concepts as reincarnation and karma, and centres on mysterious 'Masters' who possess great occult knowledge and power. Blavatsky's borrowing of concepts from Eastern philosophy combined with her dense language make her a true antecedent of modern gurus such as Bhagwan Shree Rajneesh (also known as Osho). They each engage in language 'constructed to impress upon the reader some sense of profundity at the expense of a clear exposition of meaning or truth'.[152]

Prior to starting the Theosophical Society in 1875, Blavatsky worked as a Spiritualist medium, especially in America. In his book *The Fraud of Modern 'Theosophy' Exposed*, John Nevil Maskelyne calls Theosophy 'the greatest fraud of the present day' and cites examples when Blavatsky's mediumship was exposed.[153] 'At one of her séances, a stuffed glove that she had used for a spirit hand was found, with other contrivances, in the back of the cabinet. The enraged audience nearly killed her,' Maskelyne notes of a failed 1871 seance in Cairo.[154] After this, Blavatsky arrived in America in 1873, where she attended seances by other mediums, scrutinizing their techniques. She was working with a husband and wife who channelled a spirit named (yes) Katey King when they were exposed. Maskelyne suggests that a failed career as a medium, attempted while Spiritualism was suffering severe setbacks from the exposure of many mediums, prompted her to create the Theosophical Society in New York.

Although theosophy quickly became popular, drawing thousands of listeners to lectures given by Blavatsky and, after her death in 1891, her protégée Annie Besant, it had no place for conversing with the spirits of the dead. In a letter from 1877, Blavatsky says:

> I emphatically deny that the spirits of the dead can show
> or manifest themselves objectively in any way or manner . . .
> I do not believe in the so-called materializations of our dead
> ones. But I believe that the astral souls (erroneously called
> spirits) within a living body have the same powers or faculties
> as those who have forced themselves from their earthly

presence. Therefore I believe in some of the manifestations produced by mediums, but hold that pretty nearly all such phenomena are the results of the freaks of the spirits of the mediums themselves, unconscious to themselves, and are often helped by the 'elementary,' or those disembodied men and women who, having parted forever from their immortal spirits, vegetate within the atmosphere of the earth, which alone attracts them, and use the organs of weak mediums to lead through them a fictitious life, and cheat annihilation for a short time yet . . . Why wonder and attribute the phenomena to the agency of disembodied spirits when they are simply due to the invisible and real self of the medium? Thus, as I do not believe what your Spiritualists teach, I am not a Spiritualist.[155]

She also held a position strangely similar to the Catholic Church when she stated that participating in a seance

opens the door to a swarm of 'spooks', good, bad and indifferent, to which the medium becomes a slave for life. It is against such promiscuous mediumship and intercourse with goblins that I raise my voice, not against spiritual mysticism . . . all this dealing with the dead is *necromancy*, and a most dangerous practice. For ages before Moses such raising of the dead was regarded by all the intelligent nations as sinful and cruel, inasmuch as it disturbs the rest of the souls and interferes with their evolutionary development into higher states.[156]

Spiritualists, of course, responded by claiming Blavatsky as one of their own: 'But on carefully examining the details of the facts . . . it seems to us that they strongly point in the direction of Madame Blavatsky being but a strong physical medium, mistaken or hallucinated in her theory.'[157]

Spiritism (not to be confused with the Catholic use of the word) was the creation of Allan Kardec (the pen name of Hippolyte Léon Denizard Rivail) that – unlike Spiritualism but akin to theosophy – promoted a doctrine of reincarnation, and – unlike theosophy but akin to Spiritualism – held that spirits can interact with the earthly realm as they linger between physical bodies. Spiritism, which Kardec created after putting a series of questions to a number of different mediums, continues as a belief system into the present day, with Kardec revered as 'the codifier' and his five books compiling the Spiritist Codification. *La Revue spirite,* the leading journal of nineteenth-century French Spiritualism, was founded in 1858 by Kardec, and after his death in 1869, Pierre-Gaëtan Leymarie took over as editor. Leymarie would later be accused of using the respected journal to advertise and promote his fraudulent spirit photographs.

The Society for Psychical Research

William F. Barrett was an English physicist who developed an interest in, first, mesmerism, then Spiritualism. Barrett investigated, beginning in 1881, five sisters – Mary, Alice, Emily, Maud and Kathleen Creery – who claimed to have telepathic abilities. The initial investigations yielded extraordinary results. However, in 1887 an investigation caught the sisters using visual and audio codes; the imposture was a severe setback for Barrett (who maintained that some of the results had been genuine). As with other scientists who were also believers investigating occult phenomena, Barrett – who made several significant discoveries concerning the properties of metals – displayed a curious inattention to proper scientific methods when it came to testing the psychically 'gifted'.

In 1882 Barrett's interest in researching these phenomena led him to launch the Society for Psychical Research (SPR); William James started the society's American counterpart in 1884. Along with Barrett, the principal founding members were Henry Sidgwick, who held the Knightsbridge Chair of Moral Philosophy at Cambridge and specialized in ethics; and his wife Eleanor, a mathematician. Henry became the SPR's first president, and Eleanor would prove to be one of its finest, most keen-eyed investigators. Psychologist and psychical researcher Edmund Gurney and poet and philologist Frederic Myers were also founders, and the biologist Alfred Russel Wallace was an early supporter. During the first few decades, other illustrious members of the SPR included Arthur Conan Doyle, Andrew Lang, Henri Bergson, Charles Dodgson (Lewis Carroll), Lord Tennyson and Henry Morton Stanley.

Initially, the SPR was as interested in proving as it was in disproving psychic phenomena, and they were most keenly interested in thought-transference (which Barrett had already been investigating for several years). In 1882 Frederic Myers coined the word 'telepathy' to replace the clumsier 'thought-transference', and so gave substance to a debate that would obsess parapsychologists for the next hundred years: were mediums actually calling up spirits, or were they reading the minds of the living? Writing in 1924, forty years after the SPR started weighing spirit communication against thought-transference, *Scientific American* associate editor J. Malcolm Bird noted, 'The choice between telepathy and the spirit . . . represents the major problem of psychical research,'[158] and it would be one of J. B. Rhine's chief questions when he set up the Duke Parapsychology Laboratory in 1927. Even while they were testing mediums, the SPR was producing works like *Phantasms of the Living* (1886), their first publication; it's a massive, two-volume study of the possibilities of telepathy, chiefly put together by Edmund Gurney, but with considerable editorial assistance provided by Myers and Frank Podmore. Even Freud theorized about a 'psychical counterpart to wireless telegraphy', unknowingly reiterating a description that had (when Freud wrote those words in 1920) been used seventy years earlier to describe the spirit-rappings generated around the

Fox Sisters. Myers would also go on to produce *Human Personality and Its Survival of Bodily Death* (published after his death in 1903), a complex work that combines a variety of dogmas to suggest that mediums might be experiencing multiple streams of consciousness and subconscious memories.

The SPR's 1886 investigation of the medium William Eglinton proved that they were not interested in blindly following Spiritualism. They examined Eglinton's slate-writing abilities, undertaking the investigation partly because Spiritualists in the society were dissatisfied with the emphasis on thought-transference and other mental abilities. A series of reports in the SPR's *Proceedings* published during 1886–7 proved the deception behind Eglinton's slates; chief investigator H. Carvill Lewis noted a series of points in Eglinton's deception, including the fact that the writing on the slates always occurred under the table and covered only the part of the slate that Eglinton could reach, and that the writing produced by the 'spirit' matched Eglinton's. Lewis's reporting also cited other exposures of Eglinton, including one from 1882 when 'Eglinton co-operated with the notorious Madame Blavatsky.'[159] A few devoted Spiritualists left the organization after this, but there was no mass exodus.

In 1888 the SPR issued 'The Sidgwick Report on the Census of Hallucinations'. The project, which was five years in the making, involved surveying the public on instances of telepathy and incidences of knowing (within twelve hours) when the death of a distant loved one occurred. The SPR received 17,000 responses to their questions, and when tallied they believed that the report offered proof of the existence of telepathy. William James was among those who praised Mrs Sidgwick's work on this labour-intensive project, which he called 'extraordinarily thorough and accurate'.[160]

The SPR did continue to test mediums. In 1894 the Sidgwicks and several other members of the society travelled to southern France to attend seances given by Eusapia Palladino, the Italian peasant-cum-medium who was generating tremendous excitement over the phenomena produced during her sittings. After being impressed with her performances in France, in 1895 the SPR invited her to visit England, but an investigation there found her guilty of fraud. She continued working in Europe, however, and in 1908 the SPR sent three examiners to Naples, including the American Hereward Carrington. Carrington was so convinced that he wrote an entire book about the medium (1909's *Eusapia Palladino and Her Phenomena*); he sat with her for numerous seances, during which he reported floating objects, being touched and table levitations (he even provides a photograph of the last). He also admits catching Palladino engaged in fraud at one point, but rationalizes:

> I believe ... that this phenomenon was merely to test us, and to see if she could rely upon deceiving us during the future séances. Finding that she could not, she made up her mind that to attempt fraud was useless, and thenceforth consented

Eusapia Palladino causes a table to levitate at the home of astronomer Camille Flammarion in France on 25 November 1898.

to our most rigorous control and made no further attempt to produce phenomena by fraudulent means.[161]

Carrington ended up working as Palladino's manager, bringing her to America, but she was only there for a short time before she was exposed (she was repeatedly caught freeing her foot from her shoe to levitate the table). She died in 1918.

Writing in 1914, Barrett summed up one of the SPR's continuing frustrations with mediums, which was their inability to convey truly useful information:

> One of the most perplexing and provoking matters connected with all communications from the unseen, whether through automatic writing or otherwise, is the vagueness of the information given as to the conditions of life on the other side, and the evasion of any direct answers to questions on this subject. It may be due to the difficulty of translating their experience into terms of our experience, or it may be due to the statements they make being merely a *rechauffé* of the ideas of the medium or of those present at the sitting.[162]

The SPR continues to operate as a registered charity, with headquarters in London. They produce both a quarterly *Journal* (which publishes more scientifically oriented work) and a quarterly *Paranormal Review*.

The Fox Sisters, Part 2

After essentially creating the seance and Spiritualism, the evolution of the careers of the Fox Sisters offers a capsule summary of nineteenth-century Spiritualism.

By the 1850s Leah, Maggie and Kate Fox had become world-famous; their immense popularity brought with it fame, money, imitation and doubt. Mediums began to appear by the hundreds throughout the eastern United States, especially in cities where the sisters had performed. In 1857 Leah and Kate participated in a challenge to test their veracity; the *Boston Courier* offered a reward of $500 to any medium who could provide a demonstration that couldn't be disproven by a committee of Harvard professors and reporters. That committee's report, entitled *Spiritism Shown as It Is!*, includes (in the second edition) a preface referring to the entire movement as a 'miserable delusion'.[163] Leah and Kate were unable to produce distinct rappings, although an assistant to one of the professors was able to do so and explained that 'the taps are produced by the bones of the feet, which some have the power to employ in this way.'[164] The tested mediums – who included both the Fox Sisters and the famed Davenport brothers – so failed to impress the committee that the author of the report concluded, rather dramatically:

> I really expected, inexperienced in these matters as I was, to see something which it might be difficult to understand and account for. This expectation soon vanished and was replaced by astonishment that persons reputed intelligent could be imposed upon by operations so trickish, so trustless, so shallow . . . at once childish and ridiculous; debasing the intellect; demoralizing every honest sentiment; periling the soul; reducing all things, human and divine, to the paltry standard of pigmies and automatons.[165]

The committee's report did little to dampen the ardour of the believers, but by 1861 Leah and Maggie had both retired from the business of public seances, Leah since her marriage and Maggie because of a tragic romance that had ended when her beloved, famous Arctic explorer Elisha Kent Kane, passed away after asking her to give up her mediumship. Kate, however, continued to practise, and that year she held what many thought were the most spectacular sittings of her career. Working with Charles Livermore, the wealthy young industrialist who was grieving from the recent loss of his wife Estelle, Kate produced full-body manifestations of the late wife so realistic that Charles claimed to be able to feel his wife's long hair on his face and her hands on him. At one point during the dozens of sittings, they also viewed the spirit of Benjamin Franklin, who seems to have been frequently encountered at seances of the time, probably due to his association with early experiments in electricity.

Kate and Maggie both suffered from addiction to spirits of another kind: their father, John Fox, had been an alcoholic, and they fought the disease as well. Kate found a few years of happiness in England as the wife of Henry Jencken, a barrister, whom she married in 1872; she became a focal point of British Spiritualist society and was pronounced genuine by William Crookes after he tested her. Sadly, Jencken died of a stroke in 1881, leaving Kate with two young sons. Upon returning to America, Kate's drinking worsened and on 5 May 1888 her children were taken from her after she was arrested for neglect. The papers called her 'one of the once-noted Fox sisters', and claimed that she had been found drunk in her apartment with the boys. The article also notes that Kate had been holding seances in the apartment, but 'the spiritual business proved very unremunerative.'[166]

When Maggie read about her sister in the newspapers, she was furious, in part because she believed that Leah may have been behind the arrest, a notion that Kate shared (and made plain in a newspaper interview she gave in October 1888, when she spoke of Leah and said, 'I think she was the one who caused my arrest last spring'[167]). On 14 May, Maggie fired back with a letter to the *New York Herald* that marked the first salvo in her battle to bring down Spiritualism. The letter appeared under the headline 'The Curse of Spiritualism'; in it, Maggie attempted to defend what she and Kate had done as mediums while condemning others who engaged in the vocation:

I read in the *Herald* of Saturday, May 5, an account of the sad misfortune that has befallen my dear sister Katie . . . The sad news has nearly killed me. My sister's two beautiful boys referred to are her idols.

Spiritualism is a curse. God has set His seal against it! I call it a curse, for . . . the vilest miscreants make use of it to cloak their evil doings. Fanatics . . . ignore the 'rappings' (which is the only part of the phenomena that is worthy of notice) and rush madly after the glaring humbugs that flood New York. But a harmless 'message' that is given through the 'rappings' is of little account to them; they want the 'spirit' to come to them in full form, to walk before them, talk to them, to embrace them, and all such nonsense, and what is the result? . . . They become crazed, and at the direction of their fraud 'mediums' they are induced to part with all their worldly possessions as well as their common sense, which God intended they should hold sacred . . .

No matter in what form Spiritualism may be presented, it is, has been and always will be a curse and a snare to all who meddle with it. No right minded man or woman can think otherwise.

I have found that fanatics are as plentiful among 'inferior men and women' as they are among the more learned. They are all alike. They cannot hold their fanaticism in check, and it increases as their years increase. All they will ever achieve for their foolish fanaticism will be loss of money, softening of the brain and a lingering death.[168]

A few months later, Maggie gave an interview to the papers that was more specifically critical of Leah, whom she called 'my damnable enemy'; she also referred to her mother as 'a silly woman' and 'a fanatic'. Maggie went on to explain how she and Kate created the rappings using the bones in their feet ('the power of doing this can only be acquired by practice begun in early youth'), and intimated that she had more revelations to come.

Spiritualists, including Leah's husband Daniel, responded by suggesting that she wasn't 'in her right mind'.[169] Indeed, the description of her behaviour by the reporter who had interviewed her was suggestive of someone dealing with a personality disorder: 'In intervals of her talk, when she had risen from her chair, and paced the room, or had covered her face with her hands and almost sobbed with emotion, she would seat herself suddenly at a piano and pour forth fitful floods of wild, incoherent melody.'[170]

However, in October 1888 Kate joined forces with Maggie, giving an interview in which she described Spiritualism as 'the greatest humbug of the century'.[171] She also blamed Leah and Spiritualism for an unhappy life: 'Many a time have I wept because when I was young and innocent I was brought into such a life.'[172] Maggie also condemned Spiritualism on the basis of immorality: 'There are other séances, where none but the most tried and trusted are admitted, and where there are shameless goings on that vie with the secret Saturnalia of the Romans. I could not describe these things to you because I would not.'[173]

Maggie saved her greatest condemnation for a public speech she delivered at the Academy of Music in New York on 21 October. Near the beginning of the evening she announced, 'I am here tonight as one of the founders of Spiritualism, to denounce it as an absolute falsehood from beginning to end, as the flimsiest of superstitions, the most wicked blasphemy known to the world.' Although Kate didn't speak, she was in the audience to provide support. The speeches and interviews were collected into a book that came out late in 1888 called *The Death-blow to Spiritualism: Being the True Story of the Fox Sisters, as Revealed by Authority of Margaret Fox Kane and Catherine Fox Jencken*. The book's credited author is Reuben Briggs Davenport, but the book includes an official approval signed by Maggie and Kate.

Leah died on 1 November 1890; her age was listed as 72, but was likelier 77 or 78. Kate died in 1892, aged 53 or 55; Maggie died in 1893, aged 59. Both Maggie and Kate succumbed to alcoholism; Maggie also died in poverty.

Spiritualism Wanes

In 1884 a group of academics from the University of Pennsylvania formed what has become known as the Seybert Commission; Henry Seybert was a devoted Spiritualist who, shortly before his death, had left an endowment to the university to investigate 'all systems of Morals, Religion, or Philosophy which assume to represent the Truth, and particularly of Modern Spiritualism'.[174] If Seybert had been hoping his funds would provide the final evidence in support of Spiritualism, his spirit was undoubtedly sorely disappointed. The commission, composed of ten esteemed doctors and professors, started by investigating slate-writing, which had become popular among mediums in the 1870s. The commission first investigated a medium named Mrs S. E. Patterson, but unfortunately her test was a complete failure – after an hour and a half of the slate being held by her, nothing materialized (especially unfortunate, since in previous sittings with others she'd produced messages from Henry Seybert himself). On a succeeding evening a few nearly unintelligible words were found scrawled on one of the slates, but the screw was also found to have been obviously loosened. The commission next examined Dr Henry Slade, perhaps the most famous slate-writing medium of his time, and this time the fraud was even more apparent:

> In our investigations with this Medium we early discovered the character of the writing to be twofold, and the difference between the two styles to be striking. In one case the communication written on the slate by the Spirits was

general in its tone, legible in its chirography, and usually
covered much of the surface of the slate, punctuation
being attended to, the *i*'s dotted, and the *t*'s crossed.
In the second, when the communication was in answer
to a question addressed to a Spirit the writing was clumsy,
rude, scarcely legible, abrupt in terms, and sometimes very
vague in substance. In short, one bore the marks
of deliberation and the other of haste.[175]

Obviously, the well-written (and 'general') messages had been prepared in advance on a hidden slate, while Slade wrote the others
with his right hand beneath the table. Slade also demonstrated a
few other examples of the spirits at work, such as an accordion that
played when moved beneath the table; the commission found these
other 'little tricks ... almost puerile in the simplicity of their legerdemain'.[176] The commission encountered similarly fraudulent results
with a medium who was known for materializing a spirit hand
while clasping the arm of a sitter underneath a cloth with both of
his hands (the trick involved clasping the observer's arm with just
one hand, but spreading out the fingers in such a way as to suggest
two hands). The commission concluded that Spiritualism 'presents
the melancholy spectacle of gross fraud'.[177]

It would be 1888, though, when Spiritualism received its hardest
knocks. Throughout the USA, popular mediums were exposed: Eva
Fay in Boston; Lizzie and May Bangs in Chicago; and Mrs Tobias
T. Stryker, Mme Stoddard Gray and Eliza A. Wells in New York.[178]

One of the most bizarre cases that year involved a medium who
called herself 'Madame Diss Debar', although she had used (and
would continue to use) many other names. Debar had convinced
wealthy attorney Luther Marsh that she could call on the spirits
of history's greatest artists to produce works for him. Diss Debar
had first come to Marsh's attention by channelling both the spirit
of his recently departed wife and that of deceased actress Adelaide

Neilson, with whom Marsh had developed an obsession. When Marsh tried to show reporters some of the remarkable canvases the spirit artists – who included Raphael, Rembrandt and the classical artist Apelles – had painted for him, they asked to meet the medium behind the spirits. The reporters and friends of Marsh soon discovered more than the paintings' poor brushwork: Marsh had signed the deed of his New York town house over to Debar, with the stipulation that she run a 'Temple of Truth' there. Newspapers began to speculate on Marsh's ability to serve on the New York Parks Commission; they quipped about how Marsh's 'lonely old age is being enlivened by an experience different from that of other less superstitious dupes'.[179] It wasn't long before detectives appeared at the townhouse to arrest Diss Debar and three confederates on charges of conspiracy. The resulting trial captivated New York for weeks. During the trial, Debar, who admitted she was born Ann Salomon, claimed to have learned her abilities while attending a convent in France, where she saw the Mother Superior levitate, and 'I thought if she could rise so could I.'[180] She received a sentence of six months. Diss Debar's case was influential in convincing Maggie and Kate Fox to come out against Spiritualism.

Spiritualism also waned as infant mortality rates dropped, women found more interesting work outside the home, electric lighting became widespread and morphine and opium (which may have led to visions of occult phenomena) were made illegal.

While the Fox Sisters may have believed – with many others – that they had dealt 'the death blow to spiritualism', belief in spirit communication was far from dying. In fact, the next century would find the faith receiving a tremendous boost from two unlikely allies: war and a parlour game.

5

WARS AND OUIJA: SPIRITUALISM IN THE TWENTIETH CENTURY

At the dawn of the twentieth century, the meteoric rise of the popularity of seances was halted, fifty years after Katie and Maggie Fox had cracked their toes to rap with spirits. The superstar mediums were all dead or disgraced; some of those who had received extraordinary gifts from emperors, kings and lords had died in poverty. Many of the true believers had grown disenchanted as the mediums had been consistently exposed. Scientists, bored with deception, had moved on; even the Society for Psychical Research was more interested in telepathy and haunted houses than spirit communication.

The world had changed in other ways, too. Some of the social causes that had bonded the Spiritualists had actually come to pass. It was no longer necessary to rap out Morse code to communicate; now telephones enabled direct voice communication. 'The world is disenchanted,' said philosopher Max Weber. 'One need no longer have recourse to magical means in order to master or implore the spirits, as did the savage, for whom such mysterious powers existed. Technical means and calculations perform the service.'[1] In Russia, seances were a game for the aristocracy, one more sign of their decadence. 'We adored séances,' said popular actress Vera Leonidovna of the Russian court at the turn of the century, 'we sniffed cocaine.'[2]

Yet Spiritualism did not completely die out. It fumbled along, kept alive by the eternal quest for proof of life after death. William

James, 'the father of American psychology' (and brother to Henry James, author of the brilliant ghost story *The Turn of the Screw*), saw the new century as a chance to revive scientific investigations into the occult:

> Any one with a healthy sense for evidence, a sense
> not blunted by the sectarianism of 'Science,' ought
> now, it seems to me, to feel that exalted sensibilities
> and memories, veridical phantasms, haunted houses,
> trances with supernormal faculty, and even experimental
> thought-transference, are natural kinds of phenomena
> which ought, just like other natural events, to be followed
> up with scientific curiosity.[3]

Other early psychologists, however, saw Spiritualism as an opportunity to discuss newly named disorders. G. Stanley Hall wrote about the case of 'Annie', a young woman who had recently discovered mediumistic talents (urged on by her mother) and claimed to be the mouthpiece for a number of spirits, including Lucifer (whom she referred to as 'Zezy'). When Hall happened to play host to both Freud and Jung during a lecture tour, they viewed Annie and diagnosed 'possible incipient dementia praecox' (an earlier term for schizophrenia).[4]

Ectoplasm

That scientific curiosity lauded by James turned once more to the production by mediums of ectoplasm, a carry-over from the previous century. The Society for Psychical Research (SPR) and other investigators produced photos of mediums covered in what looked far more like wet laundry than the stuff of ghosts. Psychic investigator Harry Price mocked 'those infatuated people who worship strips of cheese-cloth when these are served up with hymns, garnished with prayers, and dangled before their eyes in the dim, religious light of the séance-room'.[5] A Harvard graduate student named S. F. Damon was lauded by Sir Arthur Conan Doyle for suggesting that ectoplasm was actually the 'first matter' that the alchemists of the past had sought.[6] Doyle also claimed that he had handled ectoplasm, which he called 'the connecting link between the material and spiritual worlds'.[7] Investigators had even managed to obtain samples of ectoplasm, but they barely shrugged when the white lengths were identified as either chewed paper or cheesecloth. When the SPR investigated the French medium Eva Carrière in 1920, the ectoplasm was produced from her nose and mouth, and described as looking like 'a heavy froth'.[8]

The fortunes of spirit photography, which had given up on producing misty images of dead relatives, transformed in the twentieth century into a method of recording mediums producing ectoplasm. The German psychologist and psychic researcher Albert von Schrenck-Notzing studied and photographed materialization mediums from 1909 to 1913. Working mostly with Carrière, Schrenck-Notzing documented ectoplasm emerging from heads, necks, mouths and ears, occasionally a spirit face can be seen in the midst of the whitish ectoplasm. In Schrenck-Notzing's photographs, the ectoplasm looks alarmingly like lengths of tattered cheesecloth with an occasional paper face pasted in. Schrenck-Notzing, however, claimed to have personally witnessed the ectoplasm being extruded and then pulled back into the mediums' bodies.

In his book *Phenomena of Materialisation*, Schrenck-Notzing summarizes the large amount of literature (much of it German) regarding the investigation of mediums, with particular emphasis on ectoplasm. He lays out procedures that will help produce the best results (noting that ectoplasm doesn't form in the presence of bright light, and can best be viewed against dark backgrounds), and reviews the mediums he has investigated (Eva Carrière, Eusapia Palladino and others). Schrenck-Notzing sides with certain other contemporaneous investigators in believing that ectoplasm (or, as he refers to it, 'teleplasm') is not the result of contact with spirits, but a psychic ability on the part of the medium to convert matter. 'The author believes that the spirit hypothesis not only fails to explain the slightest detail of these occurrences, but that it impedes and hinders in every way serious scientific investigation.'[9]

Mina 'Margery' Crandon, an American medium known as 'the Blonde Witch of Lime Street' who started by operating under the name 'Psyche', also produced ectoplasm. Margery, whose seances contained more than a whiff of eroticism – she would perform 'entirely disrobed except for a bath robe and stockings'[10] – was examined at length by the SPR and J. B. Rhine. Eric J. Dingwall of the SPR sat with Margery in June 1926, and was astonished by what he saw, as he told Schrenck-Notzing in a letter:

> It is the most beautiful case of teleplasmic telekinesis with which I am acquainted. We can freely touch the teleplasm. The materialised hands are joined by cords to the medium's body; they seize objects and move them. The teleplasmic masses are visible and tangible upon the table in excellent red light. I held the medium's hands; I saw (teleplasmic) fingers and felt them in good light. The 'control' is irreproachable.[11]

The SPR also captured Margery exuding ectoplasm in a number of photographs; however, after the material was examined (and unfortunately for Dingwall's enthusiasm), it was pronounced to be animal tissue (specifically, one spirit hand was made from the lung of a cow or pig). In 1925 Harvard researcher Grant Code said Margery was caught 'drawing from the region of the vulva two or three objects which were exhibited on the table as [her deceased brother] Walter's hands and terminals'.[12] In 1926 Margery tried a stunt involving hot wax and Walter's thumbprint impressed therein.

The Crandons had all of their friends' thumbprints taken, but none matched that left in the wax. Six years later, though, an investigator discovered that the print matched that of the Crandons' dentist.[13]Afterwards, Mina's celebrity waned. She died of cirrhosis of the liver in 1941, at the age of 52.

The British medium Helen Duncan was also photographed producing ectoplasm and her spirit control 'Peggy', who was a child. Once again, the photos are now likely to provoke laughter, not awe. Marina Warner suggests that the photos fail because they don't capture the experience of actually being in the room with these mediums: 'Many such photographs were taken, and they evidently do not catch the communal experience that led so many participants to feel that they had been in touch with the other world, seen their loved ones again, and been consoled and enriched.'[14]

The famous 'Brown Lady of Raynham Hall' photograph.

In 1920 Dr Ellis T. Powell offered a different explanation of why spirit photography (which he calls 'a fact of science') often has a flat quality about it, as if it is 'a picture of a picture': 'In spirit photography the unseen intelligences project the figure onto a psychic screen, and it is *this* which is photographed. That is to say, we photograph the spirit film picture, not the person represented on the film.'[15]

In 1939 spirit photography took another turn as cameras became instruments that might accidentally capture ghosts on film, when photographers shooting the interiors of Britain's Raynham Hall for *Country Life* magazine witnessed and photographed an apparition descending the stairs. 'The Brown Lady of Raynham Hall' has become perhaps the most famous ghost photograph of all time, and has never been completely debunked.

First World War

On 28 June 1914 Archduke Franz Ferdinand was assassinated; by July, the great powers of Europe had taken sides, later to be joined by Russia, Japan and the United States. By the end of the war in November 1918, estimates of the numbers killed included nine million soldiers and seven million civilians, with fifty to a hundred million soon to follow from genocides and a flu pandemic. Families were devastated; many lost sons, brothers or spouses. Sir Arthur Conan Doyle was not exceptional in losing eleven members of his extended family.

As had happened fifty years earlier with the American Civil War, grief-stricken mourners turned to mediums anxious for any sign that their lost soldier had survived death. In the opening editorial for the May 1918 issue of the *Journal of Educational Psychology*, J. Carleton Bell bemoaned the reinvigoration of Spiritualism as a result of the horrors of the war:

With the increasing losses of friends and relatives and the general gloom occasioned by the war, there is a quickening of religious feeling, and a readiness to lend a willing ear to stories of communication with the spirit world. This credulity is especially difficult to combat because of the impossibility of proving the negative, because of the strong emotional bias in its favour, and because of its agreement with the tenor of religious dogmas implicitly believed from childhood.

Bell finishes the piece by urging schools to educate against this 'antiquated medievalism'.[16] Others noted the increase in post-war spiritual beliefs in a somewhat more poetic sense: 'Strange that where death is busiest the evidence of life beyond and above it all should abound.'[17]

Spiritualists offered more than just the hope of communicating with a dead spirit; they assured young warriors that they had nothing to fear since they could demonstrate the existence of life everlasting, and they told bereaved kin that their loved ones continued on, ecstatic in the Summer-Land. The Spiritualist Hereward Carrington wrote of the solace the faith could offer:

What a difference it would make in the lives of countless thousands of bereaved ones if they could only realize that these statements are literally true – that their heroic fathers, husbands, sons, are no more dead than when they wore the robe of mortality, that they are, in fact, more alive than ever, that they are rejoicing in the fruits of sacrifice, and are often at the front performing deeds of mercy![18]

Carrington goes so far as to suggest that to not seek spirit communication with deceased boys lost in the war is an act of unkindness towards them:

It is not a matter of 'calling up' a somnolent soul, who is popularly supposed to be 'asleep within the tomb.' There is no 'calling up' about it. These 'boys' are very much alive, and are eagerly awaiting an opportunity to assure their desponding relatives and friends that 'All is well.' They are, in fact, far more anxious to communicate than those they have left behind are to go to a medium to hear what they have to say.[19]

Mediums during the First World War conveyed positive messages to soldiers:

The soldier need not 'dread' the temporary suspension of his personal consciousness, should he fall in battle, because there is in the experience no pain – only a confusion for a moment, a surprise of an instant's duration, as though the whole world had burst into countless atoms, succeeded by a flash of universal light which reveals a vast darkness, and then – indifference, rest, happiness, slumber.[20]

Another soldier spoke through a medium of trying to communicate with his bereaved family:

Their unbelief has been one of my hardest burdens to bear, for if they would only open the door of their hearts and let me in, it would be so comforting to us all. The family would then become reunited through the bonds of spirit-communication.[21]

This young spirit found great happiness when he discovered that he could take possession of a medium and communicate via her. Spiritualists would even place the word 'killed' in apostrophes, so assured was their belief in the continuation of the soul after the death of the body.[22]

British writer and Spiritualist Estelle Stead noted that many of the communications received via mediums were relatively short, and suggested that the massive amount of newly dead was the chief of three reasons: '1. The numbers passing over. 2. The conditions around the earth plane. 3. The mental condition of receivers here.'[23] Hereward Carrington wrote that many of those who passed over in the confusion of war arrived on the other side without even knowing they had died, so they were unable to communicate immediately with loved ones. Carrington also quoted a story of a seance in which a Ouija board connected with the spirit of a dead Canadian soldier who didn't realize he was dead, and kept offering the message 'bayonet still in me'. The spirit was relieved when one of the sitters held his hand out and moved it upward, imitating the act of removing a bayonet.[24]

Speaking about the war in a 1914 talk, the medium Mrs Wallis discussed how many spirits of dead soldiers were confused at finding themselves on the other side, how other spirits were disturbed by the strife and turmoil of the war and needed the assistance of mediums in understanding, and how spirit doctors and nurses were present administering to soldiers in need (using a method she called 'ensphering'). Mrs Wallis also confirmed the existence of clinics in the Summer-land: 'There were institutions – sanatoria – somewhat similar to hospitals on earth, where the wounded were ministered to.'[25]

The rise of Spiritualism after the First World War was reflected in the arts as well. For example, J. M. Barrie's one-act play *A Well-remembered Voice* is about a woman overseeing a seance to contact her son, who has died in the war. Although it was extremely well received at its premiere on 28 June 1918, it wasn't performed again until 2014, when it was revived at the University of Hertfordshire as part of a series of forgotten First World War plays. Sir Arthur Conan Doyle's *The Land of Mist* (1926), one of the books in his Professor Challenger series, was not so well reviewed, with critics dismissing it as 'a treatise on Spiritualism in the outward form of a novel'.[26]

No book related to the war, though, was as immensely successful as Sir Oliver Lodge's *Raymond; or, Life and Death*. This non-fiction title, published while the war was ongoing in 1916, was still on best-seller lists three years later, and would be reissued in a new edition with additional material in 1922. The original advert from the Spiritualist journal *Light* aptly delineates the book's mix of heartbreaking family story and metaphysical journal:

This very remarkable book is the record by a distinguished father of a brave soldier son. Raymond Lodge was killed in Flanders in 1915; but Sir Oliver Lodge claims to have had

Raymond, from
Oliver Lodge's book
of the same name.

communication with him since, and in the hope that other
bereaved relatives and friends may have their grief similarly
softened and their loss alleviated, he has consented to the
publication of this very intimate record of séances. It tells
the story of Raymond Lodge's young life and of his death.
It then gives full details of the communications which
his friends received from him in the spirit world, and this
is done in order that such a narrative may give hope and
comfort to mourners.[27]

Along with Conan Doyle's book *The New Revelation* (which
started as a letter to *Light* in 1916 and received major u.s. and British
publication in 1918), *Raymond* is often credited as an important
factor in the upsurge of Spiritualism after the First World War.
The book begins with a section of letters illustrating Raymond's
life, then moves into seances in which the medium Mrs Leonard,
acting under her spirit control Feda, produces a number of messages
from Raymond. The first starts with:

He finds it difficult, he says, but he has got so many kind
friends helping him. He didn't think when he waked up first
that he was going to be happy, but now he is, and he says he
is going to be happier. He knows that as soon as he is a little
more ready he has got a great deal of work to do.[28]

During sittings with two mediums, Raymond indicates the
existence of a group photo taken during the war which the Lodges
have never seen, but which arrives after the seances. Sir Oliver
takes the existence of the photograph as proof that the communications from Raymond were spiritual and not examples of telepathy.
Throughout the sittings, Lodge receives enough intimate knowledge
to confirm that he is indeed speaking to his son.

Harry Houdini and Sir Arthur Conan Doyle

In the entire history of seances, there's no relationship as famous or as fascinating as the friendship between Harry Houdini and Sir Arthur Conan Doyle.

In many respects, the two men represented flip sides of the Spiritualism debate: Houdini was the legendary magician who had started as a believer (at eighteen, he went so far as selling his watch to pay for attempts to contact his recently deceased father) and had even worked as a medium until he could no longer tolerate the fraudulent nature of the act; he then began his campaign to expose Spiritualism. Conan Doyle, on the other hand, started as the doubting man of reason and medicine who in 1887 attended a seance at which he received a spirit message he couldn't explain (a written warning about a book he was planning on reading), and became one of the movement's most ardent supporters. In a debate on Spiritualism from 1919, Conan Doyle said of his conversion:

> The same forces that brought me out of Orthodoxy
> into Materialism are the very forces which have brought
> me out of Materialism into Spiritualism. In each case
> I followed the evidence, and I tried to obey what my reason
> told me was true. I found that Materialism was not, as
> I thought, a terminus, but that it was a junction at which
> one changed from the line of faith on to the line of
> experience.[29]

Conan Doyle's 1916 letters to the periodical *Light* were even credited with reviving Spiritualism in the 1920s; in one from November, he first pointed out his long history with *Light*, the SPR and Spiritualism before noting, 'In spite of occasional fraud and wild imaginings, there remains a solid core in this whole spiritual movement which

Harry Houdini demonstrates the art of making a fake spirit hand
from paraffin.

is infinitely nearer to positive proof than any other religious
development with which I am acquainted.'[30]

When Houdini's 'sainted mother' Cecilia died in 1913, Houdini
returned to Spiritualism, hoping to make contact, but once again
mediums failed him. Angered by the fraud, in 1924 he published his

book *A Magician among the Spirits*, a comprehensive and detailed exposé of trickery used by mediums. When a copy was presented to Conan Doyle, he read it and scrawled, 'A malicious book' across the title page.

However, their first meeting in 1920 was friendly, as Houdini had lunch with Conan Doyle and his family at their home in Windlesham in Surrey. After seeing one of Houdini's performances, Conan Doyle expressed his belief that the magician could actually de- and re-materialize himself; he wrote, 'Mrs Guppy could dematerialize, and so could many people in Holy Writ, and I do honestly believe that you can also.'[31] Houdini wrote to fellow magician Harry Kellar, '[Conan Doyle] saw my performance Friday Night. He was so much impressed, that there is little wonder in his believing in Spiritualism so strongly.'[32]

Their relationship may have started with Conan Doyle's desire to convert Houdini, and Houdini's pride in having a friend who was a great author (Houdini kept Conan Doyle's letters to him in a special satin-lined box), but they soon sincerely bonded over their mutual love for books (Houdini had a renowned library, including many volumes on Spiritualism). Houdini also asked Conan Doyle for recommendations of impressive mediums, several of whom the magician sat with. He found them all unconvincing and silly. When the SPR brought Eva Carrière over from France for testing, Houdini sat in on a number of the seances, watching the medium produce ectoplasm. Publicly, he told Conan Doyle that Eva Carrière was convincing, but privately (in his diary) he commented on her sleight-of-hand abilities.

In 1922 Conan Doyle went to the United States for a lecture tour to advance the cause of Spiritualism. During his stop in New York, he visited Houdini's house in Harlem; Houdini took great pride in giving the great author a tour of his library, and during lunch the magician declared that what united the two men was greater than what divided them. They were not above playing pranks on each other: when Houdini invited Conan Doyle to attend a magicians' banquet which would include a display of mediumistic tricks, Conan Doyle initially refused, but finally gave in and attended – only to interrupt the banquet by showing a reel of film from *The Lost World* that used early special effects to create an image of dinosaurs roaming the earth. Houdini had to admire the amount of newspaper ink Conan Doyle's stunt pulled in.

In June 1922 Bess and Harry Houdini joined Conan Doyle and his family for a weekend getaway at the Ambassador Hotel in Atlantic City. On Sunday afternoon Conan Doyle invited Houdini to join him for a seance conducted by Lady Doyle, who had been practising as a medium for about a year; Houdini's wife had secretly told him that she and Lady Doyle had discussed Houdini's mother at length on the previous day, so Houdini knew it was possible that his mother might be a subject during the seance. Lady Doyle specialized in automatic writing; after sitting down in a darkened room with her husband and Houdini, she entered a trance state. Houdini later wrote about that day, saying that he approached it with an open heart:

> I was *willing* to believe, even *wanted* to believe. It was
> weird to me and with a beating heart I waited, hoping that
> I might feel once more the presence of my beloved Mother.
> If there ever was a son who idolized and worshipped his
> Mother, whose every thought was for her happiness and
> comfort, that son was myself. My Mother meant my life,
> her happiness was synonymous with my peace of mind.
> For that reason, if no other, I wanted to give my very deepest
> attention to what was going on. It meant to me an easing
> of all pain that I had in my heart. I especially wanted to
> speak to my Mother, because that day, *June 17*, 1922, was
> her birthday.[33]

Lady Doyle soon began to write furiously, filling page after page with messages purportedly from Houdini's beloved mother. Conan Doyle wrote of that afternoon,

> It was a singular scene, my wife with her hand flying wildly, beating the table while she scribbled at a furious rate, I sitting opposite and tearing sheet after sheet from the block as it was filled up, and tossing each across to Houdini, while he sat silent, looking grimmer and paler every moment.'[34]

Again, Houdini kept one public face for his friend while expressing something else at home, where he wondered why his mother, who spoke no English and was Jewish, had returned after the medium had made the sign of the Cross and spoke perfect English.

On 30 October of that same year the *New York Sun* printed a letter from Houdini in which he not only challenged any medium to produce genuine psychic phenomena (he offered $10,000), but stated,

> I don't know of any medium who has not at some time been detected in some fraud. Spiritualists admit that mediums do cheat sometimes. This to my way of thinking is like catching a pickpocket with his hand in your pocket, but if you don't catch him, he is not a pickpocket; a queer type of Spiritualistic logic. When not stealing he is perfectly honest and should be trusted, even respected.[35]

Conan Doyle was very upset, since he believed that Houdini was deliberately calling Lady Doyle a fraud. The friendship was over.

The rift between the two former friends was widened later that same year when *Scientific American* offered a cash prize to anyone who could produce an authentic psychic manifestation, and Houdini served on the panel of five judges. Conan Doyle wrote to *Scientific*

American, expressing his belief that the judges were biased and the contest would draw only frauds to enter; he also wrote a private letter to Houdini, admonishing him for serving on the panel. When the committee of judges began investigating Margery Crandon, accusations flew between Houdini and Conan Doyle. The writer vigorously defended Margery, and the magician denounced her trickery, even suggesting that her doctor-husband had surgically enlarged her vagina to allow her to hide 'ectoplasm' there.

Over the next few years, both Houdini and Conan Doyle gave lecture tours. In 1926 Houdini told friends that he was sure he would die at the hands of an angry medium, but on 31 October – Halloween – he succumbed to peritonitis, likely brought about after he'd allowed a young man to come backstage and test his ability to take a punch. His wife, Bess, offered some of his books to his former friend Conan Doyle.

Bess and Harry had exchanged a code that she would recognize as proof that her late husband had contacted her from beyond the grave. Bess began working with a young medium named Arthur Ford, who, in 1929, used the code phrase – 'Rosabelle, believe'. However, in 1928 the code had been published in a biography of Houdini that Ford had likely read.

Bess continued to try to contact Houdini every Halloween until 1936, when she held the last seance on the roof of the Knickerbocker Hotel in Hollywood. The tradition was carried on by Houdini's brother Hardeen, followed by Hardeen's protégé Sid Radner. After Sid died in 2011 the tradition was continued by his son Bill and his friend Tom Boldt. In 2012 they opened the seance to the public, and tickets may now be purchased every Halloween. Additionally, the Magic Castle in Hollywood offers regular performances of the 'Houdini Seances', a Victorian-themed display of magic and mediumship.

Sir Arthur Conan Doyle survived Houdini by almost four years. He spent the last years of his life listening to 'Pheneas', a spirit guide with whom his wife Jean routinely communicated and who predicted the coming approach of the end times. After Conan Doyle died in 1930, his funeral, which was attended by thousands, included an appearance by the medium Estelle Roberts, who went into a trance state, pointed to an empty chair and screamed, 'He is here!'

In 2016 ITV and Sony Pictures Television debuted a series called *Houdini and Doyle*, which paired the sceptical Houdini (Michael Weston) with true believer Conan Doyle (Stephen Mangan) to investigate strange crimes, à la *The X-Files*. The series received mediocre reviews, however, and lasted for only one season.

The Rise of Trance Mediums

The war had another effect on the history of mediumship: physical mediums, with their tricks for producing rappings and ectoplasm, were now out of fashion, replaced by the newfound popularity of trance mediums. An article from a 1947 issue of *Light* laid out the way mediumship had evolved over the last century:

> Nearly one hundred years ago the general trend of objective manifestation was in the direction of the heavier physical phenomena: materializations, movement of objects, apports, direct writing. As time went on, these became rarified; and more recently there has been development of Direct Voice mediumship, mostly with the trumpet. Now there are signs of an effort to discard the trumpet altogether, and it seems possible that, in some quarters, even this form of independent Direct Voice may merge into a more etherealized method still, one in which we shall be able to dispense entirely with darkness, cabinets, trumpets (and the doubts clinging thereto), one which will provide a clearer channel for the true creative mentality and Spiritual Whole of the communicators.

And that, conceivably, would be as great a cause for satisfaction among certain pioneer workers on the Other Side as it would be for us here.[36]

While trance mediums had certainly been present in the nineteenth century, they now dominated a world in which most of those who sought their services were more interested in receiving a reassuring message from a dead loved one than proving the existence of after-death spirits. The renowned psychologist and psychic investigator C. D. Broad described trance mediumship:

When a trance-medium is about to give a sitting to a client, she generally begins by shutting her eyes while resting quietly in her chair. Soon after this she begins to breathe deeply, to groan slightly and to struggle, and in general to behave like a person who is profoundly but restlessly asleep and is suffering from a rather distressing dream. In a few minutes, as a rule, she becomes calmer, and one often hears a kind of whispering going on.[37]

This is the point at which, according to Broad, the personality of the medium's spirit control emerges. After the sitting concludes, the medium will awaken with no memory of what occurred during her trance state.

In the early twentieth century spirit controls named John or Katie King were replaced by spirits that were often children, or at least childlike (like Helen Duncan's 'Peggy'). They were also often reported to be of a different race from the medium. Broad notes that these spirit controls tended to speak in broken English and seemed to know little about their own purported culture: 'I have been asked for "the key of my *wigwam*" by a control who professed to be an African Negro child.'[38] Broad suggests that Spiritualism may have become mixed up with theosophy, thus accounting for the number of spirit controls who were said to be Egyptian, Hindu or of Asian heritage.

The personality of the spirit control will typically yield to that of the deceased loved one sought by the sitter. Some of the early trance mediums were distinguished by their startling ability to produce voices that bore little resemblance to either their own speaking voices or the voice of the spirit control.

Given the intimate, personal nature of a typical seance with a trance medium – that is, a grieving parent, spouse or sibling desperate to receive word from a dead loved one – sittings rarely involved large groups. They no longer demanded the singing of hymns and might not even require holding hands around a table.

Trance mediumship also offered another advantage for mediums: it was far more difficult to expose someone who produced little more than strange voices.

One of the most famous of the early twentieth-century trance mediums was Mrs Osborne Leonard, who undoubtedly rose to stardom after being featured in Sir Oliver Lodge's book *Raymond*. Mrs Leonard's spirit control Feda was a young girl from India, who had supposedly been forced to marry early and died during childbirth at thirteen or fourteen years of age. Mrs Leonard claimed that the first time she encountered Feda was when, at the age of 25, she was working at the London Palladium; this was 1913, and Feda warned her of the coming world war. Before the war, Leonard – who charged a shilling to attend one of her seances – and her husband were so impoverished that they could move all of their belongings in a hand cart. By the end of the war, business boomed and Leonard raised the charge to her sitters. The medium saw clients in her home, usually singly, sometimes in groups; the sitter was seated at a small table with a shaded lamp, while Mrs Leonard sat at some distance, partly obscured by darkness. A few minutes after entering a trance state, the shrill, rapid voice of Feda would sound, sometimes for as long as two hours. Spirits communicated with Feda, and the control would then announce their messages to the sitters. Feda would present messages from a number of other spirits, who normally announced their identities only with initials. Mrs Leonard's clients often reported hearing two voices at once – one that whispered to them while Feda continued to speak – but when *Scientific American* Associate Editor J. Malcolm Bird sat with Mrs Leonard, he was not impressed:

> The most rabid spiritist will grant that, in this sitting, there is no evidence of survival. In view of the very large amount of irrelevant material – visitors whom I fail to recognize after the most elaborate description, incidents which mean literally nothing to me, etc. – I am not at all sure that the possibility of interpreting two of my communicants as relatives would give any standing to the séance.[39]

Despite Bird's poor review, Mrs Leonard worked successfully as a medium for 45 years.

Bird also sat with Welsh medium Evan Powell. Like Mrs Leonard, Powell's control was a spirit from a culture far removed from his own: Black Hawk was a Native American with an acerbic sense of humour (he would ask sitters during his seances to consider the possibility that they were experiencing a collective hallucination). Powell was a cross between an old-fashioned Spiritualist medium and one of the newer trance mediums. He began his seances by stripping and asking one of the sitters to search him and his clothing; he was tied at the beginning of the gathering, and seated with sitters holding his hands and feet. The lights were extinguished, a hymn was sung and then Black Hawk greeted all of the sitters. Black Hawk soon brought other spirits through, some of whom reacted angrily if not recognized by a particular sitter. He also caused musical instruments to play, flowers to be plucked from a vase and spirit hands to touch the sitters.[40]

Mother Leafy Anderson and the Spiritual Church Movement

While nineteenth-century Spiritualism had embraced abolition-ism, by the twentieth century American Spiritualist churches sometimes denied admittance to African Americans. Seeking a way to practise the Spiritualist religion as a black woman, in 1913 the Wisconsin-born Leafy Anderson (soon to be known as Mother Leafy Anderson) founded the Eternal Life Christian Spiritualist Association. In 1920 Mother Anderson headed south to New Orleans, where Creoles had not only practised Spiritualism in the 1850s but had corresponded with other Spiritualist groups. In New Orleans she founded her first Spiritualist church, the Church of Eternal Life. Mother Anderson's Spiritualism lived in tension alongside the area's history of voodoo, hoodoo and Marie Laveau, the nineteenth-century 'Voodoo Queen' and spiritual leader; although Anderson didn't approve of voodoo, some of her followers practised it. The Church of Eternal Life grew quickly, providing the model for the spiritual church movement and the spread of black Spiritualist churches across the u.s.

After operating out of rented halls and her own home, Mother Anderson finally acquired a three-storey building on Amelia Street, where she offered services, 'readings' (popular with both black and white guests) and training in church leadership. Acquiring the charter for her church had come with its own set of difficulties: she was supposedly jailed after reports that she was engaging in 'hoodoo, witchcraft, or fortune telling', and gained her release by telling a judge things about himself that she could not have known.[41] Mother Anderson's services included messages from her spirit guide, the Native American Black Hawk (yes, another), and hymns played by jazz bands.

Mother Anderson tragically passed away in 1927 aged only forty, but her church and organization continued under new leadership. Visitors that year included a Spiritualist minister from Lily Dale and the writer Zora Neale Hurston. Hurston described her visit to the church:

> At 'The Eternal Life' church on Monday nights there is a meeting presided over by a woman, which the spirit of Mother Anderson (now dead) attends. One can get there a small vial of 'Spirit oil' for fifty cents. The oil is used to anoint one's body against various illnesses and troubles. Mother Anderson's followers are not allowed to call the name of Jesus. The reason given is that Jesus as a man was not important – he was merely the earthly body of a nameless 'Spirit' by which name the deity is always addressed.[42]

By the 1940s the New Orleans churches had all moved to using 'spiritual' in place of 'Spiritualist' in their names; by the 1990s 'ministers and members emphatically dissociate[d] themselves from [spiritualism]', which they perceived as 'occult'.[43] However, Black Hawk – the Native American hero who led the Sauk people in the Black Hawk War that eventually brought freedom for his people – remained popular in spiritual churches. 'Black Hawk stands for righteousness,' said New Orleans reverend Jules Anderson, explaining why his parishioners still call on the legendary warrior.[44] Sadly, Hurricane Katrina decimated the spiritual churches, many of which still operated out of houses in the Lower 9th Ward.[45]

Moving Planchettes and Unseen Guests

On 10 February 1891 the U.S. Patent Office granted Patent No. 446054 to inventor Elijah J. Bond of Baltimore. The second paragraph of the patent laid out the basics:

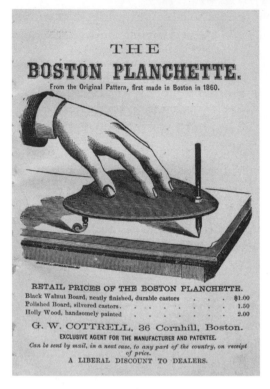

An early planchette with casters and pencil.

Improvements in toys or games, which I designate as an 'Ouija or Egyptian luck-board'; and the objects of the invention are to produce a toy or game by which two or more persons can amuse themselves by asking questions of any kind and having them answered by the device used and operated by the touch of the hand, so that the answers are designated by letters on a board.[46]

The unusual name was supplied by Bond's sister-in-law, medium Helen Peters, who asked the board for a name and watched as it spelled O-U-I-J-A (although there's also been speculation that the name is a combination of the French and German words for 'yes'). Nowhere in that patent is there even the slightest whiff of spirit communication. In fact, 'the touch of the hand' is the only mention of what's powering the device.

Bond's patent was filed as an 'improvement', and indeed 'witch boards' or 'talking boards' had already been in use in Spiritualistic circles for around thirty years. Although the writer Lewis Spence would claim in his 1920 *Encyclopedia of Occultism* that Pythagoras had used a device similar to a Ouija board about 540 BC, this appears to have been a fiction created by Spence to lend classicism to the board's history (Spence also claimed the planchette – 'little plank' – was named after a well-known French Spiritualist).[47]

In reality the first popular mention of a similar device came in 1868, when a book called *Planchette's Diary* was published. While no author is credited, an editor named Kate Field is given on the title page. The book describes the adventures of a young lady who purchases a 'planchette', 'a little board of varnished wood, fashioned in the shape of a heart, seven inches long and five inches wide, that formed a sort of table by means of two pentagraph wheels at the broad end of the heart, and a lead-pencil inserted in a socket, one inch and a quarter from the point of the heart'.[48] When the planchette is placed on paper and has a suitably magnetic operator, it writes messages from the spirit world (the narrator of the book initially chalks the messages up to unconscious impulses, but she's soon convinced otherwise).

In his 1899 seances with the patient S.W., Carl Jung employed a primitive version of the board, a 'psychograph': it consisted of letters written on slips of paper laid out in a circle on a table, with two fingers of the right hand placed atop an overturned tumbler set in the circle's centre. Jung said the glass 'moved with lightning speed from letter to letter'.[49]

Other similar methods would be used over the next few decades, but many involved paraphernalia that was too clunky and complicated either to be used easily or to be of interest to all but the most dedicated Spiritualists. Planchettes were produced by a number of companies and were popular, but the scrawled messages were frequently difficult to read. Elegantly designed talking boards, with letters already neatly laid out in a printed board, were introduced in the late 1880s, immediately supplanting the clumsy planchette. When Bond patented his board in 1891 there had been a few similar devices produced, but it was the Ouija that would take off. In 1897 William Fuld acquired control of what had by then become the Ouija Novelty Company; he ran the company for 26 years, acquiring in the process the title of 'the father of the Ouija board'. Fuld died in an accidental fall in 1927, leaving his children to run the company until 1966, when it was sold to Parker Brothers.

For the first two decades of its existence, the Ouija board was considered essentially a parlour game (albeit a very popular one). Spiritualists didn't seem to be immediately taken with it; an 1898 guide to mediumship notes that better results will likely be achieved by automatic writing.[50] That all changed, though, on the evening of 8 July 1913 when a thirty-year-old St Louis housewife named Pearl Curran and her friend Emily Grant Hutchings received a visitation via the Ouija board from a seventeenth-century British woman named Patience Worth. Patience, it seemed, was a writer who'd been looking for the perfect medium for nearly three centuries, and over the next 24 years, Patience – via Pearl and Pearl's husband John, who transcribed as Pearl dictated – would produce nearly four million words of novels, poems and plays. Patience 'wrote' seven novels in seventeenth-century English, with words that John had to sometimes look up in a dictionary (Pearl had dropped out of school at thirteen). Her first novel, *The Sorry Tale*, released in 1917, received rave reviews, and Pearl/Patience became a celebrity, composing spontaneous poems in front of large groups of the curious. Psychologists (with whom Pearl refused to cooperate) suggested multiple personalities; Spiritualists wrote books about Patience and went to England searching for any hint of the spirit's earthly existence, finding only places that matched descriptions Patience had provided but nothing more concrete.

After her husband John died, Pearl toured the country, offering visits with Patience via her board. She finally settled in Los Angeles, where she died from pneumonia in 1937, only a week after her last communication from Patience.[51]

In 1920 Harper & Brothers published an extraordinary book called *Our Unseen Guest*. The book was released anonymously, and follows a married couple named Darby and Joan as they experiment with a Ouija board they discover in 1916 after a Halloween party. The couple is startled to receive communications from an American serviceman who was killed by an exploding shell in the First World War; the young man suggests that those who die suddenly are lost in the afterlife, with no one waiting to meet them. 'Stephen', the spirit, has thus made it his after-death mission to greet those who have died unexpectedly in battle.

Joan and Darby become so interested in these messages that they buy their own Ouija board (noting that it's the larger of two sizes then available) and hide it when not in use. Stephen tells them about both his life and his death: 'owing to the vast slaughter of the war, so much of consciousness still close to earth is on my plane.'[52]

Darby and Joan use clues Stephen's messages provide to research him, and his story is corroborated in a history of the war. They try other tests, like allowing a friend to blindfold them, but the planchette continues to move across the board in answer to questions. Eventually Joan is able to pass the messages from Stephen without the use of the Ouija board. Darby and Joan even have Stephen play the piano via Joan's hands, but ultimately they decide to desist:

'Tests that are worth while,' I said to Joan, 'must come unsought!'

'And even then,' she answered, 'one can always find some plausible theory by which they can be explained away. Also, one test creates an appetite for another. The thing becomes an endless search.'[53]

Stephen also suggests that erroneous messages are the result of something he calls 'colouring', or subconscious memories on the part of the medium (or 'receiving station', his preferred term for one who channels spirit communications). Stephen also repeatedly tells Darby and Joan that there are certain things he cannot explain because they'd be incapable of comprehending them.

Darby and Joan also encounter other spirits. One, a less comfortable entity named Armand Dupont, had been blown apart during the war and his consciousness was apparently also somewhat fractured. Another, 'Fred Q', had been Darby's friend and room-mate, and appears to Joan as a full-body apparition who tells her that another popular book of the time, Margaret Cameron's *The Seven Purposes*, is also about him (a fact which Darby claims was affirmed by Cameron).

Although presented as non-fiction, *Our Unseen Guest* reads like a metaphysically themed novel, complete with plot twists, side characters and conflicts. It incorporates discussions about God, faith, evolution and the afterlife; it lays out concepts such as 'colouring' and 'quality of consciousness' (or 'magnetic consciousness'). It concludes with a summary of Stephen's philosophies and two emotional letters dictated by the discarnate spirit.

The identity of 'Darby and Joan' remained secret until 1990, when they were revealed to be Ruth and Emmet Finley (who passed away in 1955 and 1950, respectively). Ruth and Emmet were both newspaper reporters who didn't want their Spiritualism to be known in their work circles; in addition, Ruth was an acclaimed expert on quilting.[54]

Sceptics accused the Ouija board of operating purely as a result of ideomotor response. The theory that unconscious movement lay behind certain occult phenomena was first advanced in 1852 by

William B. Carpenter, who was studying the practice of dowsing. It became readily apparent that this same response – which could be created even by the most doubtful – could be applied to explain other occurrences in seances, including table movements and planchettes.

But ideomotor response is only part of the rational answer to Ouija boards. A 2019 study used virtual reality and small devices that produced tactile (or haptic) cues in subjects' fingers. The study determined that not only did visual and tactile cues generate ideomotor response, so too did the presence of other subjects.[55] In other words, when using a Ouija board, we unconsciously respond to each other.

The Church Strikes Back

As post-war interest in Spiritualism, the occult and Ouija boards grew, the Roman Catholic Church became concerned (in part because it was losing members to Spiritualism). Pope Pius x found an anti-Spiritualism crusader in J. Godfrey Raupert, a one-time Spiritualist and member of the SPR who renounced Spiritualism when he converted to Catholicism. Spiritualism, though, continued to serve the newly Catholic Raupert well, as he wrote books like *The Dangers of Spiritualism* and toured giving anti-Spiritualism lectures. In 1911 Pius x made Raupert a Knight of St Gregory in recognition of his anti-Spiritualist services to the Church.

Although it's unclear whether Pius x actually commissioned the book or not, in 1919 Raupert published an anti-Ouija board book called *The New Black Magic*. The most frequently quoted line from the book is, 'The spirits are ready enough to come but they do not go away quite so readily,' although what follows is seldom shared: 'the invading spirit ultimately paralyzes the normal thinking powers, dominates the will and the sensory organism, until the mental and moral powers of the subject decay and he becomes an imbecile.'[56] Raupert also describes mediums as suffering from 'mind-passivity', and refers to the early Christians who believed that ghosts were demons in disguise: *'impersonation of the dead by deceiving spirits is a well-known frequent and admitted phenomenon in connection with spirit-manifestations'* (the italics are Raupert's).[57] But the really damning part in regards to the Ouija board comes near the end of the book (suggesting that perhaps this might have been a late addition due to the Ouija board's growing popularity after the Patience Worth books):

> Persons habitually and systematically using the ouija or planchette board, or similar automatic devices for obtaining spirit messages, experience, after a time, a peculiar condition of lassitude and exhaustion – in many instances accompanied by severe pain at the top of the spine and gradually spreading over the entire brain. This state of prostration is due to the now well-established fact that, in order to obtain the movements of the board, vital or nerve-energy is withdrawn from the organism of the experimenter, often out of all proportion to the physical health and constitution.[58]

Raupert's condemnation set the tone for decades of argument against the use of the Ouija board.

A year later, an even more vitriolic attack against Spiritualism in general appeared in Elliot O'Donnell's *The Menace of Spiritualism*. In the foreword to that book, Bernard Vaughan, SJ, argues in favour of deceptive demons – and more:

> Firstly, let me remind you that no one attending a séance in which spirits from the vast deep make themselves heard or seen can prove that their spirit visitants are the creatures they claim to be. How can any one disprove them to be satanic

spirits? You may be sure that evil spirits can quite as cleverly personate the dead as music-hall artists do the living.

Secondly, let me ask you, what have spirits, after thousands of years practice, revealed to mankind calculated to be of any practical service to humanity? As yet they have not even solved the problem as to what is a sardine, or what a new-laid egg.[59]

Vaughan's argument might make the reader wonder how many mediums queried spirits about sardines, especially given what a 'practical service to humanity' that would have been.

O'Donnell goes on to suggest that Spiritualists are largely elderly, childish, neurotic, ugly and epileptic.[60] He explains the involvement of such distinguished figures as Sir Arthur Conan Doyle and Sir Oliver Lodge as proof of the abnormality of genius, and suggests that insanity was a frequent end result of practising Spiritualism (this claim was often applied by Spiritualism's opponents). O'Donnell – a ghosthunter – justifies belief in the appearance of apparitions at haunted houses by noting that they are frequently observed by multiple witnesses, while claiming that the phenomena manifested at seances 'are usually experienced only by the medium, or, at the most, by one or two of the sitters'.[61]

O'Donnell also notes how many women are mediums or Spiritualists, and opines that these women frequently form societies devoted to men-hating and anti-marriage. The kind of love they pursue is condemned by the Bible, and, 'It is free lance, anarchical love that, if once permitted and encouraged, would soon lead to utter social chaos, and eventually to the hopeless, wholesale destruction of the race'[62] (a curious statement coming from someone writing two years after the end of a world war). O'Donnell continues his misogynistic musings with,

Though, no doubt, it owes its origin to some extent, at least, to jealousy and unsatisfied cravings for motherhood, as well as to other more or less natural causes, it also receives much inspiration and obtains considerable impetus from Spiritualism and Spiritualism's kindred cults – Theosophy and Christian Science.[63]

The Christians had at least one unlikely ally in warning against use of the Ouija board: Aleister Crowley, the famed occultist also known as 'the Great Beast'. In his magical studies Crowley experimented with nearly every type of spirit communication; while working with automatic writing (produced while under the control of a spirit called Aiwass), Crowley produced *Liber AL vel Legis* (also known as *The Book of the Law*), the text that establishes his frequently quoted credo, 'Do what thou wilt shall be the whole of the Law.' Crowley wrote of the dangers attendant in summoning spirits, which could be elementals, creatures that feed on life-essence. He believed that those who hadn't studied magic and prepared appropriately could be in danger when using the board. In writing about Crowley's own use of the board, J. Edward Cornelius summed up Crowley's feelings toward the uninitiated: 'When beginning any Ouija ritual, you should consider yourself a pathfinder who is sailing off into uncharted waters: the realm of the astral. This is no child's game.'[64] Crowley's student Frater Achad (Charles Stansfeld Jones) experimented with the board to summon angels, rather than elementals. In a 1917 letter, Crowley told Jones, 'Your Ouija board experiment is rather fun. You see how very satisfactory it is, but I believe things improve greatly with practice. I think you should keep to one angel, and make the magical preparations more elaborate.'[65]

Seances between the World Wars

From 1918 to 1939 Spiritualism continued to be practised, and was often mentioned in attention-grabbing newspaper articles. In 1928, for example, a trial known as 'the Spiritualist case' made headlines when a medium named Mrs Cantlon was accused of having 'professed to tell fortunes', and Mercy Phillimore, secretary of the London Spiritualist Alliance, was charged with 'aiding and abetting, counselling, and procuring'. Testifying on behalf of the accused were Sir Oliver Lodge and Sir Arthur Conan Doyle. Conan Doyle, who at the time was president of the London Spiritualist Alliance, verified that the Alliance was non-profit, and that it existed to 'strengthen what we regard as the central core of religion, which is that man carries on after death'. However, when the prosecution asked Sir Arthur why a medium wouldn't know if police spies were present at a seance, he responded 'that the laws governing such things were very much beyond our comprehension'. In the end the charges against both defendants were dismissed.[66]

Another sensational story from 1928 involved a gardener-turned-medium named Blaise whose materialized spirit 'Madeleine' was abruptly revealed during a seance when two French journalists leapt from their chairs and tore the material away. The medium responded by raining blows on the interlopers, and – rather than being restrained by the others assembled – was joined by the remaining sitters, who called out, 'Kill the spies!' The incident occurred in a house in Mantes in north-central France that was owned by a medium named Madame Alexandre, who possessed an album of testimonials from a variety of important personages, including a former president of the Portuguese Republic. When Blaise was arrested on swindling charges after the beating of the journalists, Madame claimed that 'the spirits maltreated them for revenge', and, because it couldn't be proven that Blaise had collected money for his services, the swindling charges were dismissed.[67]

A 1931 case from Sunderland in the UK offered the unusual situation of both a medium and her client's family claiming fraud. The medium, Cissie Wall, was the plaintiff in a case against Mrs Harriet Isabella Silverthorne, widow of the late Luther Silverthorne, who had apparently rewritten his will in Wall's favour the day before his death. The widow's solicitor claimed that the signature on the will was a forgery, and that 'Miss Wall had used spiritualistic influence on Mr Silverthorne.' A witness claimed that Silverthorne had told him that Wall was his 'spiritual wife', to which the witness had responded, 'Do not talk rubbish. She has got to you again.' Wall claimed that she didn't know Silverthorne was married until after his death, that she loved him (their relationship was 'of the spiritualistic kind'), that they'd held seances in the bathroom and that 'she loved him to bathe her.'[68] The jury decided the will was indeed a forgery and found in favour of the widow.

Police attended seances undercover. In 1940 a Cardiff gentleman named Austin Fred Hatcher was found guilty of deception and fined £10. Police had purchased tickets to one of Hatcher's seances, and when 'Sister Agnes' materialized, one of the police officers turned his torch on her, revealing Hatcher. In court Hatcher denied that he'd engaged in any form of fraud, while an assistant, Emily Little, who was also found guilty and fined, maintained that she had never shaken a tambourine in the dark.[69] When the persistent Hatcher and Little were brought up on charges again two years later, their defence solicitor assumed the unique tactic of claiming that he'd attended one of their seances and been converted to a belief in psychic phenomena.[70]

There were still physical mediums who impressed, like Willy and Rudi Schneider, two young Austrian mediums who investigator Harry Price thought were the most genuinely gifted that he ever examined. The brothers had started demonstrating mediumistic abilities when still children and were tested by many researchers; some claimed that they experienced no phenomena under controlled circumstances, and others claimed that the brothers used confederates.[71] Rudi was generally acknowledged to be the more powerful of the two; there were also claims that Rudi had orgasms during seances.[72] When Price visited the family in their home town of Braünaü in 1925, Rudi was seventeen and Willy was twenty-three;

Willy's spirit guide was a half-German, half-Italian man named 'Otto Bauer'. Price sat through two evenings with them, both seances being held in the Schneiders' modest second-floor apartment, which was redressed with a 'cabinet', or curtained-off area. Price arranged stringent controls, which included a red light, special paper on the floor and visibility of all sitters. During the first session, he observed violent shaking of the curtains forming the cabinet, glowing spirit hands, tilting furniture and cold breezes, all while he held the medium's wrists. At the end of the seance (which lasted just under two hours), the temperature in the room had dropped.

However, the following evening was even more spectacular. Willy again acted as medium (Rudi was ill and bedridden with a serious leg infection), and this time sitters saw multiple hands and tendrils and felt more cold breezes, lights flickered violently, a handkerchief was tied into a knot in mid-air and that same article danced in time to a song the sitters sang. In concluding his report on his two nights with the Schneiders, Price noted, 'that not one of the phenomena we saw during our stay could have been produced normally with the severe control I imposed'.[73]

Helen Duncan

The most spectacular medium trial of the twentieth century (or, arguably, ever) took place in 1944, when medium Helen Duncan and four others stood trial in a case that made British newspaper headlines for weeks. Duncan was a Scottish medium who divided her time between Edinburgh, where she had six children, and Portsmouth, where her services were much in demand. Duncan had realized her gifts early on, earning the nickname 'Hellish Nell' in her small Highland village. As an adult, her spirit guide was the jocular 'Albert Stewart', who might blurt out something like, 'I don't think much of my medium; she's too fat.'[74] Duncan, who was said to be able to produce 'ectoplasm' or 'teleplasm', was tested in

Helen Duncan, photographed with 'ectoplasm' (actually, cheesecloth and a face cut from a magazine).

investigator Harry Price's laboratory in 1931, and Price announced her a fraud – the 'teleplasm' (a white substance suspended in a jar of water) turned out to be the white of an egg, and she failed to produce ectoplasm after Price bound her to a chair (Albert claimed that the tape used to bind Mrs Duncan had cut off her circulation[75]). One scheduled test with Duncan went awry when she refused to submit to an x-ray and ran screaming into the street. In a later seance, teleplasm was obtained from Duncan's mouth and proved to be toilet paper; the oral production confirmed Price's theory that Duncan possessed the ability to regurgitate at will, and he pronounced her a complete fraud. In 1933, when Duncan held a seance in Edinburgh and materialized the spirit of a little girl named 'Peggy', the 'spirit' was seized by an onlooker and proved to be a woman's vest. Duncan was arrested, convicted and sentenced to a fine of £10 and one month's imprisonment. As a result of the conviction, the Spiritualists' National Union re-evaluated Mrs Duncan, of whom they had previously issued official approval, and the vote of confidence in her abilities was 57 to two.[76] Mrs Duncan's popularity continued unabated, and she made enough money to keep her large family going as well as indulge in luxury items such as a fur coat for herself.

On 24 May 1941 she gave a seance at the upper-class home of a Mrs Waymark in Edinburgh (entering through the service entrance, as lower-class mediums were required to do[77]) in which Albert provided information about a British battleship that had just sunk. Unknown to Helen (or, apparently, Albert), one of those present – a gentleman known by the locals as Brigadier Roy Firebrace – was actually Chief of Military Intelligence for Scotland. When Firebrace checked on information provided by Albert during the seance, he discovered that the British had indeed just lost a major battleship and the information was supposed to be top secret. British intelligence opened a file on Duncan, and in 1944, when a detective working for Portsmouth's chief constable Arthur Charles West mentioned hearing that Duncan had swindled another detective, West saw a potentially easy way to take care of an intelligence leak by apprehending Duncan for fraud. After a seance in January 1944 Duncan was arrested on the minor charge of telling false fortunes. When the case arrived in court a month later, the charge had been moved up to a criminal offence – conspiracy – and Helen had three co-defendants: Ernest and Elizabeth Homer, who ran the Spiritualist temple where the seance had taken place, and Frances Brown, Helen's assistant. The case, which many felt put the entire religion of Spiritualism on trial, was sent to the highest criminal court in England and Wales, the Old Bailey. The prosecution lacked any material evidence, and Helen was tried under the antiquated Witchcraft Act of 1735. In the opening remarks for the prosecution, John Maude drew on the war to provoke the seven jurors: 'These people caused money to be paid for false pretences, for the pretence that Helen Duncan was in a position to bring about the appearance of spirits of the dead. At this time, in wartime, when the dead are anxiously sought by persons who have lost their boys, such conduct is a false and hollow lie.'[78] The defence followed by noting both the absurdity of the obsolete Witchcraft Act and suggesting that the jury consider the possibility that the spirit world was real. When the defence solicitor (a canny man named Charles Loseby) urged the judge, His Lordship Sir Gerald Dodson, to approve allowing Albert to testify (in other words, allowing the jury to witness Helen's talents as a medium), Dodson denied the request. Loseby instead brought forth a parade of witnesses who testified to seeing Duncan's skills amply demonstrated; many affirmed that they'd viewed the spirits of lost loved ones who came through Helen, and that she'd given them comfort and happiness. One of the most interesting of the defence witnesses was Hannen Swaffer, a famed theatre critic who was also a Spiritualist and who, twelve years earlier, had been involved in a test of Mrs Duncan with four magicians:

> The professionals tied Mrs. Duncan with 40 yards of sashcord, she was handcuffed with regulation police handcuffs, her thumbs being tied tightly together with eight yards of thread, so tightly that it cut into the flesh.
>
> It took eight minutes to tie her up, but she was free in three minutes. Even Houdini did not do that. There was ectoplasm, but no one appeared. Obviously she had been released by Albert, the spirit guide.

Swaffer described the ectoplasm as looking 'like living snow', a far cry from the cheap fabric that the prosecution had displayed as an example of what they claimed Helen used as ectoplasm.[79]

At the conclusion of the case, the jury found all four defendants guilty. His Lordship Gerald Dodson sentenced Helen to the maximum time of nine months in prison, while Mrs Brown received four months and the Homers were released.

It wasn't just Helen's supporters and Spiritualists who were outraged by the case: the prime minister himself, Winston Churchill,

was disturbed enough by the daily newspaper accounts of the trial
– accounts that sometimes seemed to take precedence over reporting on a world war – to draft a note to the home secretary. 'Let me
have a report on why the Witchcraft Act of 1735 was used in a
modern Court of Justice,' the note began, and went on to call the
whole affair 'obsolete tomfoolery'.[80]

Two months later, the Supreme Court heard the case on appeal.
Much of the presentation centred around the exact meaning of the
old Witchcraft Act: did it proscribe only against dealing with *evil*
spirits? What was the exact meaning of 'conjuration' or 'witchcraft'?
In the end, the court upheld Helen's conviction and sentence.

In 1951 Parliament finally revoked the Witchcraft Act of 1735
(and Section 4 of the Vagrancy Act of 1824), replacing it with the
Fraudulent Mediums Act; interestingly, the new law pertained
specifically to 'Spiritualistic mediums'.[81] The home secretary at the
time, Chuter Ede, saw the bill as a positive advance for Spiritualists:
'By having their mediums subject to the Vagrancy Act, Spiritualists
feel that they are placed in a category that people who hold firm
religious views sincerely ought not to be placed in.'[82] The secretary
is undoubtedly referring to the bill's specific language regarding
a medium who 'acts for reward'. The first use of the law was in
February 1952, when a gentleman named Charles Basham was
arrested under a warrant that stated 'he did on November 23, in
purporting to act as a spiritualistic medium, unlawfully use a certain
fraudulent device, namely a length of cheese cloth.'[83]

On 11 November 1956 Helen Duncan was caught acting as a
medium when police raided a seance in Nottinghamshire. The shock
sent Helen to hospital. She died six weeks later.

Duncan may have joined Albert on the other side, but her fame
lives on in this world: there are multiple books about her, she has
numerous web pages dedicated to her and the Stirling Smith Art
Gallery hosts a bronze bust of her. There have also been several
unsuccessful petitions to have her pardoned.

A situation that made headlines in 1956 provides clues as to how mediums operated in Great Britain after the passage of the Fraudulent Medium Act: after a Middlesex resident named Ray Densham lost his 32-year-old wife following surgery, he turned to Spiritualism for answers. He and his late wife Edna had engaged in seances before, including one that predicted Edna's death. The seances were held with a woman, Doris Pollard, who is described as 'a friend of the family', and who had moved in with Ray after Edna's hospitalization.[84] To conduct the sittings, Ray and Doris positioned small pieces of paper around the edges of a table and each placed two fingers on an overturned wine glass. During the second seance, when Ray asked 'Edna' if they should continue, the glass gave a confusing answer and Ray angrily smashed it, announcing that he would hold no more seances. Ray ended up gaining permission for Edna's body to be exhumed and a new autopsy performed, since the seances led him to suspect foul play, but the death was again ruled due to natural causes. It's worth noting that nowhere in the coverage of this story does the word 'medium' appear, and Doris never charged for her services.[85]

The story of Ray Densham is one of the few interesting seance tales to emerge from the post-Second World War period. After the war, Spiritualism faded (without ever completely dying out), and seances became novelties of the past, suitable only for tabloid headlines or mildly spooky mysteries. Why didn't spirit calling see the same resurgence after the Second World War that it had after the American Civil War and the First World War?

The answer to that question can only be considered owing to a complex mesh of factors: first, the women who had largely made up Spiritualism's corps of mediums had been put to work in the 1940s for war production and emerged from the war anxious to continue working. A century of exposing fraudulent tricksters had finally led to stricter laws, making the environment for mediums less friendly. And the world had a new threat that was almost more terrifying than death: the atomic bomb.

Perhaps it was simply too difficult to give thought to dead spirits when the entire planet was, for the first time, suffering a global anxiety attack.

The Channellers

In the 1970s Western culture experienced a number of counter-culture movements, birthed by the fervour of the '60s. Among these ascendant movements was the 'New Age' (or, as its practitioners sometimes call it, 'Mind/Body/Spirit'), which brought doctrines like magnetism and theosophy back into the spotlight.

Under the New Age, a fresh variety of trance medium appeared: channellers. Channelling is comparable to mediumship in that both involve entering a trance state to invoke a visit by a spirit who speaks through the medium. Channelling, however, is distinct from the seance in both its form – it doesn't involve a group – and its goals, which are not to bring forth the spirits of deceased loved ones, but rather to call up past masters who offer mystical teachings. The teachings derived from channelling often refer – just as theosophy did – to Eastern religions such as Buddhism, Hinduism and Vedanta; and, as with Spiritualism, the channelled spirits react against materialism, focusing instead on positive messages of love and enlightenment. 'The new cosmology', says Suzanne Riordan in her essay 'Channeling: A New Revelation', 'posits a friendlier universe than that of the Fundamentalist and one with a great deal more soul than that of the scientist.'[86]

The first major channeller of the New Age was Jane Roberts; her instructive spirit was Seth. Seth first appeared to Roberts one evening when she sat down to write; he soon revealed his name when Roberts and her husband experimented with a Ouija board. By early 1964 Roberts no longer required the board – Seth spoke directly through her as her husband transcribed the words. Although she had published earlier books, including one on extrasensory perception (ESP), Roberts's authorial breakthrough came in 1972 with *Seth Speaks*, which not only achieved best-seller status but influenced a generation of New Age thinkers, including Marianne Williamson, Deepak Chopra and Dan Millman.[87] At the online Seth Learning Center, Seth – who authored the phrase 'You create your own reality'– is credited with launching the New Age movement.[88]

Second only to Roberts and Seth – and perhaps following in their footsteps – is J. Z. Knight and Ramtha. Ramtha, a warrior who lived more than 35,000 years ago, first appeared to Knight in 1977. Since then, Knight has built Ramtha into a media empire, with books, videos, events and a school (Ramtha's School of Enlightenment). 'I have the fortitude and the power to change the moon into gold, but that would pale if I could change people into Gods, and that is my mission,' says Ramtha at the School's website.[89] One of Ramtha's most notable fans was actress and New Age icon Shirley MacLaine, who once believed she was Ramtha's brother in a past life. Knight has been involved in a number of very earthly court disputes with other psychics who have also claimed to channel Ramtha and former students who have violated non-disclosure agreements to post videos of Knight online that cast the medium in an unpleasant light.[90]

An argument frequently put forth in favour of channellers is that the messages they produce contain material that demonstrates a higher intellect than that possessed by the medium, but psychologist Graham Reed argues: 'The reiterativeness, diffuse structure, and trite content of these statements place them well within the intellectual capacity of any fluent but uninhibited individual, without any assistance from occult or other sources.'[91]

The Seance on Film and Stage

Right from the beginning of cinema, films depicting the calling up of spirits were popular (note, for example, the previously mentioned Georges Méliès film *L'Armoire des frères Davenport* (1902)). George Albert Smith's *Photographing a Ghost* (1898) playfully took on spirit photography, as it showed a photographer's attempts to take a spirit picture. Some of the silent shockers, like 1921's *The Phantom Carriage*, in which a man must redeem himself by driving death's soul-collecting wagon, presented frightening depictions of spirits, while others (Buster Keaton's 1921 *The Haunted House*) intermingled slapstick and ghoulish images. One of the more revealing films from this period is *The Medium Exposed? or, A Modern Spiritualistic Séance*, produced in 1906 by the R. W. Paul Company, which specialized in 'trick' films. In this seven-minute gem a group assembles for a seance; after tying the medium to a chair, the lights are dimmed and strange phenomena – a jangling tambourine, spirit hands, a flying skull – are glimpsed in the darkness. One of the sitters abruptly brings the lights back up, revealing the medium's confederate standing behind them with the objects dangling from a telescopic rod. The confederate flees and the outraged sitters throw the bound medium, chair and all, into a trunk, which they take from the house. After hurling the trunk down a hill, it opens, revealing the stunned (and still tied) medium, who is carried off by police.

Stories of mediums and seances became more popular in the late 1930s and early '40s, when mysteries made use of a murder at a seance: *The Thirteenth Chair* (1937), *At the Villa Rose* (1940, although it was based on a 1910 novel and had received three previous film adaptations), *Mrs Pym of Scotland Yard* (1940) and *Miracles for Sale* (1939) all mixed Spiritualism and murder. One of the more unusual (and entertaining) entries in this subgenre is 1940's *You'll Find Out*, which features big-band leader Kay Kyser and horror stars Boris Karloff, Bela Lugosi and Peter Lorre in a musical-horror-comedy-mystery about a group of young people who are trapped in a spooky, isolated mansion for the weekend with a dotty Spiritualist, her medium (Lugosi, in a turban), her crooked lawyer (Karloff) and a sardonic psychic investigator (Lorre). The film's seance scenes are genuinely unnerving and among the best from this era.

In 1941 a curiosity called *Spellbound* (not to be confused with the Hitchcock film of the same name, released four years later) was released. Also known as *Ghost Story*, *Passing Clouds* and *The Spell of Amy Nugent*, the film tells the story of a wealthy young student, Laurie, whose fiancée Amy dies, leaving the young man understandably devastated. When his mother's friend introduces him to a Spiritualist medium named Mr Vincent, Laurie becomes obsessed with trying to contact Amy. Vincent, who calls Spiritualism 'natural law', channels Amy's voice, but promises a full materialization of her; meanwhile, a professor of theology, Cathcart, tries to warn Laurie of the dangers of Spiritualism. Laurie is warned not to touch Amy's spirit when it appears, but he is unable to resist reaching out to her. Touching the spirit transforms Laurie into a madman, although Cathcart pronounces him possessed of something evil. When Cathcart fails in an exorcism, Laurie's lifelong friend Diana saves him through the power of love.

Spellbound, which was directed by John Harlow, may lack pacing and real chills, but its depiction of Spiritualism is fascinating: at a time when most films enjoyed playing on fake mediums and fraudulent seances, *Spellbound* presents its spirits as completely real. At first banned by the British censors, who thought it would be offensive to Spiritualists, the film's distributors went to one of the leading Spiritualists of the day: Hannen Swaffer, the acid-penned theatre critic who had also tested Helen Duncan and testified on her behalf during her trial. With the addition of a spoken prologue by Swaffer, the film was approved for release; unfortunately, it has become scarce, and there are no prints known to exist that include Swaffer's prologue.[92]

Although the genre cinema of the 1950s reflected the public's atomic fears, focusing mainly on stories of irradiated men and monsters, one horror film from the decade is worth mentioning: Jacques Tourneur's *Night of the Demon* (1957, also known as *Curse of the Demon*), based on M. R. James's classic short story 'Casting the Runes'. Although the story features mainly occultism and demonology, there is one significant scene in which the American psychologist and sceptic Dr John Holden (Dana Andrews) attends a seance with a trance medium at a wealthy English country manor.

The films of the 1960s and '70s reflected the shifting perspective on spirit-calling: mediums were depicted as unbalanced, and more emphasis was placed on paranormal investigation. In Bryan Forbes's 1964 thriller *Séance on a Wet Afternoon*, medium Myra Savage (Kim Stanley) engineers the abduction of a child so she can go to the police and report the child as found (she and her husband also demand a £25,000 ransom). Myra is unravelling, however, and tries to tell her husband (Richard Attenborough) to kill the child. The film was a critical success, with Stanley winning or being nominated for numerous awards; it also inspired a 2009 opera of the same name.

The Haunting of Hill House, Shirley Jackson's brilliant 1959 novel of a paranormal investigation, also centres on an unstable protagonist, although in this case it's not the medium, Theodora, but the meek Eleanor who has a history of being around poltergeist activity, and who unravels when she accepts the invitation of a psychic investigator to stay at the notoriously haunted Hill House. In 1963 Robert Wise directed the first film adaptation, starring Julie Harris as Eleanor and Claire Bloom as Theodora. The film is now considered one of the greatest horror films of all time, with its scenes of breathing walls and deafening poundings. Jackson's book also inspired one other notable adaptation, Mike Flanagan's critically acclaimed 2018 Netflix series. Although this adaptation kept the title and the key element of the house, it focused on a family who try to remodel the house and who instead end up being haunted by it throughout their lives.

Richard Matheson's 1971 novel *Hell House* also concerned the paranormal investigation of a haunted house, but upped the ante considerably in terms of sex and violence. The book was adapted (by Matheson) into the 1973 film *The Legend of Hell House*, directed by John Hough and starring Pamela Franklin as medium Florence Tanner, Roddy McDowall as medium (and sole survivor of a previous investigation of the house) Ben Fischer and Clive Revill as Dr Lionel Barrett, leader of the investigation. Although the film adaptation is tepid by comparison to the source novel, it is interesting for depicting a scene of a medium (Franklin) producing ectoplasm during a seance.

The final film directed by Alfred Hitchcock, 1976's *Family Plot*, is a mystery that features a fake psychic (played by Barbara Harris) who is hired to help find a man. Part of the plot hinges on the question of whether the psychic possesses real abilities or not.

After the explosion of horror cinema in the 1970s, seances and Ouija boards became common devices in horror films. Some, like Peter Medak's *The Changeling* (1980) or James Wan's *The Conjuring* (2013), included seances or paranormal investigations as pivotal plot elements; others, like the low-budget *Witchboard* films (1986–93), centred on spirit communications via talking boards.

These films loaned many of their visuals and shock effects to a new industry that exploded around 2000: haunted attractions. In 1969 Disneyland opened a long-planned ride called the Haunted Mansion, which placed guests in 'Doom Buggies' that took them through a seance that opened the way to a haunted house and graveyard. The seance scene, in which the head of medium Madame Leota floats within a crystal ball as musical instruments and other objects levitate overhead, is one of the best-known and most influential depictions of a fictional seance. The Haunted Mansion (which borrows elements from Robert Wise's *The Haunting* as well as referring back to Spiritualist seances and haunted house folklore) inspired the modern haunted attractions industry and has been copied innumerable times since, in both professional attractions like Orange County, California's Sinister Pointe, whose attraction 'Séance' offers 'a fully theatrical look into the afterlife',[93] and amateur yard haunts, some of which – like the now-closed Los Angeles-based Hallowed Haunting Ground – recreated the Haunted Mansion's head in a crystal ball effect.

On the theatrical stage, seances and Spiritualism have often served as fodder for comedic material. Written in five days during the height of the Second World War, Noël Coward's *Blithe Spirit* (1941) is probably the most famous comedy written around Spiritualism. The plot centres upon a flamboyant medium named Madame Arcati, who calls up the spirit of widower Charles Condomine's first wife. Coward was said to have been partly inspired by an experience he had at the age of eleven, when his mother took him to the London Coliseum to see the medium Annie Eva Fay. During the performance, Coward's mother asked the famed medium if she'd done the right thing in recently hiring out her son to perform in a play. Fay's answer: 'Keep him where he is! He is a great talent and will have a wonderful career!'[94]

Moss Hart and George S. Kaufman's *You Can't Take It with You* (1936) is another now-classic comedy that lampooned Spiritualism, this time in the character of Mrs Kirby, one of the play's many supporting characters and both a snob and an ardent Spiritualist. The play (which opened with Virginia Hammond playing Mrs Kirby) won the Pulitzer Prize for Drama, and the 1938 film adaptation (with Mary Forbes in the role), directed by Frank Capra, won the Academy Award for Best Picture.

Seances also figured in Gian Carlo Menotti's 1946 opera *The Medium*. Menotti was inspired by his own experience attending a seance:

The idea of *The Medium* first occurred to me in 1936 in the little Austrian town of St. Wolfgang near Salzburg. I had been invited by the neighbors to attend a séance in their house. I readily accepted their invitation but, I must confess, with my tongue in my cheek. However, as the séance unfolded, I began to be somewhat troubled. Although I was unaware of anything unusual, it gradually became clear to me that my hosts, in their pathetic desire to believe, actually saw and heard their dead daughter . . . it was I, not they, who felt cheated. The creative power of their faith and conviction made me examine my own cynicism and led me to wonder at the multiple texture of reality.[95]

The Medium debuted in New York on 8 May 1946. The entire short two-act story takes place in the parlour of a Spiritualist medium known as Madame Flora (or Baba). As the opera begins, her daughter and her assistant Toby are preparing for a seance involving the middle-aged Gobineaus, who have lost their child and come to Madame Flora to talk to their dead daughter (who is imitated by Madame Flora's daughter, hidden behind a curtain). Madame Flora eventually tries to tell the Gobineaus that she has defrauded them, but they refuse to listen, or even accept the return of their money. *The Medium* was a hit, and was also the first American opera to be shown commercially in cinemas.

The Return of the Ouija Board

Although interest in Ouija boards continued from the 1920s onwards, it rose exponentially after one movie exploded like a cultural bombshell in 1973: *The Exorcist*. That landmark film (based on William Peter Blatty's novel of the same name) is the story of a film star's daughter who is possessed by the ancient demon Pazuzu, but it's her seemingly innocent dabbling with a Ouija board that opens

A display of Ouija-themed merchandise in 2019.

the gateway to evil. In the scene that offers the first supernatural occurrence, the girl, Regan, tells her mother that she's contacted 'Captain Howdy' via the board and the planchette suddenly slides across the board on its own.

The resulting furore brought both the Roman Catholic ritual of exorcism and the use of Ouija boards back into the spotlight. Although the film plainly sides with the Church's condemnation of the board, sales rose and within a few years the Ouija board would be adopted by New Age groups as a useful tool for self-exploration. In her 1979 *The Ouija Book*, Gina Covina suggests that 'using the Ouija board automatically brings our beliefs and the ways they affect our world into sharper focus'.[96]

By the twenty-first century, Ouija boards had been culturally enshrined as collectibles, with websites like the Museum of Talking Boards and non-profit organizations such as the Talking Board Historical Society serving to gather and archive their history.

The look of the classic Ouija board – the quaintly lettered board – has also become a source of considerable merchandizing. There are Ouija boards themed after popular properties like the Netflix series *Stranger Things*, Ouija T-shirts can be purchased at Hot Topic clothing stores and the Spirit Halloween stores feature an entire selection of Ouija-branded items, including candles, coasters and place mats. In 2014 Hasbro – the company that currently manufactures the Ouija board – joined forces with horror specialists Blumhouse Productions and Platinum Dunes to produce the feature film *Ouija*; directed by Stiles White, the low-budget shocker proved financially successful although it was critically panned. A 2016 follow-up, *Ouija: Origin of Evil*, directed and co-written by Mike Flanagan, received largely excellent reviews and also performed well at the box office.

Merchandising and movies prove that spirit communications have been commodified in the twenty-first century.

6

HOW UNIVERSAL IS THE SEANCE?

W hile belief in some form of existence after death, be it as a
soul in a heavenly realm or an earthbound spirit, is found in
virtually every region and period of human existence, the form,
methods and goals of the Spiritualist seance are confined largely
to Western culture. That peculiar, distinctive ritual of a group of
people who gather around a medium – who may or may not be
trying to deceive them, and who has likely had no special training
– in order to communicate with the dead and prove their existence
is confined largely to Europe, Russia, the British Isles and the
USA from 1848 on. While a comprehensive study of global ways of
communicating with spirits is outside the scope of this book, a few
instances will help to clarify how the Western-style seance differs
from, and resembles, other methods.

In most religions that offer a form of talking to the dead (not all
do), reaching out to the spirits is typically performed by a shaman or
priest, in a ritual which may or may not be open to all members of
the community. Among, for example, the Akawaio – a small, indigenous people found in Guyana – a settlement's shaman, or *piai'chang*,
enters a trance state in the evening (which is achieved through fasting and smoking), and stages a theatrical performance in which the
spirits are invoked to assist with healing or judging disputes.[1]

In some parts of the world dead spirits were kept in material
form. The Andean Incas, for example, mummified their dead, who

retained their possessions and would be brought out of their after-death homes – usually either caves or special burial towers called *chullpas* – for celebrations or more solemn events. The mummies were also consulted (by family members who acted as interpreters of their unspoken wishes) if questions arose regarding distribution of any part of their wealth.[2]

One of the most macabre methods of communicating with spirits contained in a physical form is found in Thailand, where belief in the protective powers of the *kuman thong* ('golden boy') was once prevalent and can still be found today. The creation of a *kuman thong* involves roasting a human embryo until it becomes a dried husk, then applying lacquer and gold leaf to create a tiny ghost guardian; the owner of a *kuman thong* must treat the idol like a real child, feeding it and (if necessary) disciplining it. Although modern-day *kuman thong* are wood or ceramic reproductions (and may be easily purchased online), news stories of discoveries of

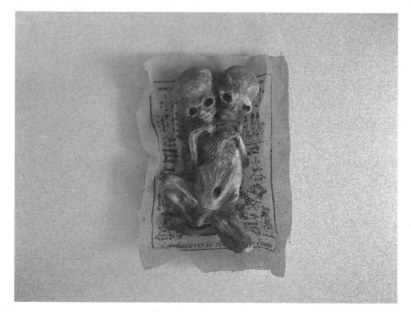

A replica *kuman thong*.

Fu ji automatic writing shown in an early engraving.

aborted foetuses intended for conversion into *kuman thong* still surface.[3] Malaysia also believes in these spirit-possessed embryos, although they call them *toyol*; they are created by shamans called *bomohs*, and they are powerful enough to steal or murder for their owner.

In China, especially among practitioners of Daoism, there's a form of automatic writing that is still performed. Called *fu ji* or *fu chi*, this practice relates back to the end of the Southern Song Dynasty (AD 1279); in the past it involved a sieve turned upside down with a stick inserted through it, but now it uses a pair of sticks (suitably called a 'planchette') held above sand. In 1923 six members of the staff of the Arts and Theological Schools of the Shantung Christian University visited the Tao Yüan and observed a demonstration of *fu ji*:

The planchette stick was held at either end by men standing one at each side of the table. Near by stood another, whose duty it was to call out the characters as they were written in the sand, while on the opposite side, at a small desk, stood one with pen and ink ready – to write down the characters upon yellow paper. At first the planchette merely made circles, first slowly, then at a great rate. One of the writers held a piece of wood in his free hand, with which he smoothed out the sand again, and immediately the first character appeared. Character followed character at a surprising rate.[4]

In *fu ji* the spirit guiding the planchette is thought to be divine rather than human; the planchette is moved by the god or goddess and the medium together. The practice may be descended from a tradition called 'the invitation of Tzu-ku', in which the goddess Tzu-ku was summoned on the fifteenth night of the first month; Tzu-ku sometimes assisted with writing or composition. The earlier form of *fu ji*, involving a sieve or basket upended in sand or ashes, is similar to other practices involving sieves found in India and parts of Europe. In Confucianism spirit-writing was said to have originally involved the numinous luanbird.

The training of new mediums is dictated by the gods. If new mediums are called for, the training lasts 49 days, involving meditation, a vegetarian diet and two instructors: a human medium (*renshi*) and an immortal teacher (*xianshi*) who will become the medium's spirit control.[5]

In the mid-nineteenth century spirit-writing cults sprang up throughout China and Taiwan which continue today. These cults believe that the writings obtained via *fu ji* will assist the members in achieving deity status themselves after death. These 'phoenix halls' also publish and sell the divine messages received during their *fu ji* seances.

While spirit-writing mediums are called *wenji*, there is a second kind of medium found in China: *wuji*, or 'martial mediums'. *Wuji* are considered to be of lesser trustworthiness and importance than *wenji*; they travel the world offering immediate relief rather than being the agent of moral texts from the gods. Even the gods that are channelled via martial mediums are thought to be of lower rank.

In Buddhism all ghosts are thought to be malignant, with the worst being the *preta*, or hungry ghost; these spirits, said to be the ghosts of greedy people, are especially dangerous. This is why what is referred to as 'necromancy' in Buddhism is designed to exorcise or banish ghosts rather than summon them. Similarly, Hindus may encounter a ghost called a *bhoot* (although they appear as very human, they can be identified by their feet, which point backwards), and the Hindu rituals regarding *bhoots* are designed for exorcism, not invocation.

In modern Japan an *ogamiya* is similar to a Western psychic: they consult with clients about healing, fortune telling or contacting spirits. Unlike psychics, however, they usually urge those who have benefited from their services to pursue religion.

Although the word 'voodoo' has been commercialized and used in everything from alcohol to horror movies, vodou (which has a variety of spellings and is called simply 'the religion' by its New Orleans adherents) is a complex religion found in both Haiti and New Orleans (it varies slightly between the two regions). Vodou resulted when West Africans were taken in the slave trade, brought to the New World and forced into Catholicism, which they syncretized with their own beliefs. Vodou therefore combines African and Catholic influences into a distinctive religion that is deeply dependent on spirit communication (in Haiti, followers of vodou describe their religion by saying, 'I serve the spirits'[6]). The principal spirits, *lwa* (or *loa*), were created by Bondye or *Le Grand Maître* (God) to act as intermediaries between the Grand Master and humans. There are hundreds of *lwa* (just as there are hundreds of Catholic saints); one of the most well-known is Baron Samedi, the skull-faced and top-hatted ruler of the dead who helps spirits pass over. To call upon the *lwa*, a service will be held in the open space at the front of the peristyle (temple), and will include songs, dancing, drumming, prayer, sacrifice and the creation of *vèvè*, or spiritual symbols (each *lwa* has its own distinctive *vèvè*). The *lwa* will possess

Vodou *vèvè* for the *lwa* Baron Samedi.

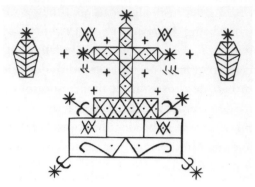

or 'ride' a *chwal* ('horse') or an entranced worshipper during a service; Haitians believe that only indigenous people can be ridden since families have multi-generational relationships with particular *lwa*. During the time that an *lwa* rides, it may be questioned or have favours requested.

As with Spiritualism, vodou is aligned with certain progressive movements, especially LGBTQ. Elizabeth McAlister of Wesleyan University has commented on how vodou provides a welcoming community for LGBTQ people: 'There is an idea that Vodou spirits that are thought to be gay "adopt" and protect young adults who then become gay.'[7] *Lwa* may also ride members of the opposite gender.

Vodou holds that each human possesses two spirits, the *ti-bon-ange* ('little good angel') and the *gros-bon-ange* ('big good angel'). The *ti-bon-ange* is the individual personality, and is what leaves the body when an *lwa* rides; the *gros-bon-ange* is roughly equivalent to the Western idea of the soul, and it is what will eventually argue the person's case before Bondye. After death, the *gros-bon-ange* first travels to the waters of Ginen in the ancestral world; however, one year and one day after death, the family of the deceased must recall the *gros-bon-ange*. The spirit will be kept in a *govi*, an earthenware bottle, and must be propitiated with food and sacrifices; however, it will also give advice and answers when consulted. After several generations, the *gros-bon-ange* will be returned to the Ginen.

Similar to vodou's *lwa* are the kachinas of the Hopi and Pueblo cultures in the American southwest. The kachinas are spirits that may be the personification of some part of the natural world or they may be ancestors. They are invoked by dancers who wear masks that identify them as particular kachinas; when the dancers descend into underground kivas, the kachina spirits enter their bodies. The kachinas are also represented in carved and painted dolls, traditionally passed out to girls during the dancing ceremony. The Hopi Kachina cult dates back to about AD 1100 and may have been Aztec in origin.[8]

The pre-Christian people of the Huon Gulf region of Papua New Guinea also believed that the soul of the deceased could be conjured into an object. The movements of the object holding the spirit could be read: the spirit, for example, might be conjured into an eel, with the eel's writhing interpreted to answer questions.

In Polynesia the shamans (kahunas or tahungas) can see and capture spirits, which they say are much smaller than men and come at night; it may be the spirit of a sleeping man that's left his body as he dreams. The kahunas capture spirits by enticing them to drink, then squeeze the spirit between their hands until its few drops of blood are forced out; what's left is a small, flat shape.

In Santeria the priests/priestesses channel spirits during *misas* (seances). The spirits give the mediums abilities that they haven't previously possessed, such as being able to drink a great deal of rum without getting drunk. A California *santera* (priestess) named Sonia Gastelum has several spirit guides, including Michaela, an elderly African American woman who died on an antebellum plantation (and who resides in a doll), and Congo, an African who was taken from his home and made a slave in Cuba.[9]

Note throughout this brief world survey that in no other religious system but Spiritualism are spirits invoked by small groups who desire only some proof of their existence. The dead are usually approached with reverence or caution. Spirit invocation is typically considered difficult or dangerous; these ghosts, often ancestral, are either sought for protection or advice, or to be aided in their own transmigration. While there are some similarities in these rituals to both the oracles of the ancient world and the necromancers of the Middle Ages, nothing closely resembles the seance as created by the Spiritualists. The seance has neither the solemnity of *fu ji* nor the wild ecstasy of vodou; it's neither approached as an obligation to one's deceased kin nor a frightful encounter.

Only in the Western seance are the dead sought out by untrained (and possibly fraudulent) mediums to engage in conversation or minor magical demonstrations in polite settings.

7

THE MODERN SEANCE

The seance as inaugurated by the nineteenth-century Spiritualists was centred around two principal goals: first, to communicate with spirits of the dead; and second, to prove that such communication occurred. Although certainly the seance performed other functions – a reaction to materialism, creating a group that reinforced spiritual beliefs and allied to pursue progressive causes, even simple entertainment – it existed first and foremost to promote these dual objectives.

If the seance seemed to fade into near-oblivion between the two world wars, it might be more accurate to suggest that its two goals split the form apart. The desire to converse with the dead – or, more specifically, dead loved ones – led directly through the early twentieth-century trance mediums to the psychics of the latter part of the century; and the need to scientifically prove the existence of life after death ran from the formation of the Society for Psychical Research in 1882 to university-based laboratories and finally to the paranormal investigation.

Put more simply, Spiritualism has led us to John Edward and James Van Praagh on one hand, and reality paranormal television shows and K-II meters on the other.

In the twenty-first century belief in the existence of ghosts continues. A recent survey of Americans revealed that nearly half believed in ghosts or demons, over a third said they had personally felt the presence of a ghost or spirit and 13 per cent said they had directly communicated with a ghost or spirit.[1] Compare this with the rise of 'superstar' psychics: in the u.s. James Van Praagh has an estimated worth in 2020 of $23 million,[2] and John Edward's net worth is placed at $1 to 5 million.[3] On the other side of the seance split, paranormal investigator Zak Bagans (executive producer and lead investigator of the television series *Ghost Adventures*) is worth an estimated $69 million,[4] and Yvette Fielding, host and co-producer of the long-running British series *Most Haunted* (and nicknamed 'the first lady of the paranormal') has amassed enough wealth to indulge her passion for luxury cars.[5] The psychics offer comfort and the reassurance that our loved ones continue; the paranormal investigators create miniature horror movies that are presented as documentaries. If net worth is any indicator, in the twenty-first century we want to have our fears stoked, not quieted.

The College Labs

While William Crookes, Cromwell Fleetwood Varley and Oliver Lodge were unquestionably geniuses within their own scientific fields, and the Society for Psychical Research (SPR) had been undeniably important in advancing early analysis of psychic happenings when it came to their investigations of seance phenomena, twentieth-century scientists found serious flaws with their methodologies.

Among the most obvious was their reliance on the reports of those who attended seances. Hereward Carrington, himself a believer, was nonetheless critical of the over-dependence on first-hand reports:

> The majority of sitters who attend seances are entirely unfitted either to judge the value of the evidence presented or to distinguish fraudulent from genuine phenomena – and this is in no sense an insult to their intelligence.

It is utterly *impossible*, as a rule, for the sitter – no matter how sceptical he may be – to detect many of these tricks, without aknowledge of the *actual methods employed*; for they are practically undetectable. Only a wide general knowledge of legerdemain and the psychology of deception will render this possible. The methods of trickery are so numerous and so clever, the daring and the ingenuity of the pseudo-medium are so remarkable, that it is small wonder that the average sitter fails to detect the *modus operandi*; and hence comes away convinced that he has, in truth, seen genuine 'phenomena,' whereas he has seen but clever tricks and blatant fraud.[6]

The Seybert Commission that investigated mediums in the 1880s suggested two reasons why the report of Spiritualists themselves could not be trusted:

The first reason is to be found in the mental condition of the observer; if he be excited or deeply moved his account cannot but be affected, and essential details will surely be distorted.

For a second reason, note how hard it is to give a truthful account of any common, everyday occurrence. The difficulty is increased a hundred-fold, when what we would tell, partakes of the wonderful. Who can truthfully describe a juggler's trick?[7]

Nor should the sheer number of Spiritualist seance reports support their scientific validity. As David Marks and Richard Kammann noted in their influential study *The Psychology of the Psychic*, 'it is not the *quantity* of evidence that makes an idea correct, but the *quality* of the evidence.'[8]

Obviously, something more rigorous than anecdotal reports from seance sitters was called for.

In May 1922 a 26-year-old botanist named Joseph Banks (J. B.) Rhine and his wife Louisa attended a lecture given by Sir Arthur Conan Doyle about the virtues of Spiritualism. Rhine was impressed, and a few years later he signed up for psychology courses at Harvard University, studying under Professor William McDougall. McDougall was already a renowned figure in paranormal research; he was the first to lecture seriously at a university (Clark University) about psychical research. He contributed a paper, 'Psychical Research as University Study', to the book *The Case For and Against Psychical Belief.* In that paper, he noted that a key reason he was in favour of studying psychic phenomena at a university level was because 'guidance of public opinion' was sorely needed.[9] Although he counted Harry Houdini as a close friend, McDougall was convinced that telepathy was a real possibility and he was open to belief in the existence of ghosts and clairvoyance.

In 1928 McDougall left Harvard to head the Psychology Department at Duke University in Durham, North Carolina. McDougall had already urged Rhine to also relocate to Durham, and in 1929 he brought Rhine into Duke's Psychology Department, where he would assist McDougall in establishing the first university-based Parapsychology Laboratory.

Rhine was certainly on board. In 1926 he'd researched 'Margery', aka Mina Crandon, the popular Boston medium whose spirit guide was her gruff, vulgar brother Walter, deceased fifteen years earlier. Margery also produced ectoplasm that had once taken the form of Walter. An investigating committee from *Scientific American* that included Hereward Carrington and Harry Houdini had been split in their verdict, with four votes against and one in favour.

J. B. and Louise sat with Margery on 1 July 1926, but she failed to impress them. The American Society of Psychical Research's board of trustees had supported Margery, and Rhine wrote to them about his own experience: 'I am disgusted, not only with the Case but with the attitude our *Journal* has taken on it, sponsoring it before the scientific world. The whole case is sure to crash some of these days and where will our reputations be then? We will be the laughing stock of the world for years to come.'[10]

The Duke Psychology Laboratory started with Rhine spending six months studying the case of a man named John Thomas who had tried to communicate with his dead wife via mediums. When the mediums seemed to consistently supply verifiable facts that shouldn't have been known to them, Rhine suspected telepathy.[11] Thomas had documented all of his seances, in the process accumulating 750 pages of information on both American and British mediums which he gave to Rhine and McDougall for their nascent Parapsychology Laboratory.

In April 1934 the Lab tested its first medium, Eileen Garrett. Garrett was one of the models for the novelist Patrick Dennis's celebrated character 'Auntie Mame'; in 1934 Garrett was 41 and had been a medium for eight years. Although Rhine started Garrett's testing with extrasensory perception (ESP) cards, he also held seances with her, where her spirit guide Uvani would present and offer information about the sitters. Her results were higher than chance, but neither ESP nor spirit communication could be confirmed.

In 1934 Rhine published his book *Extra-sensory Perception*, and his fame grew exponentially. He corresponded with Carl Jung, who was holding seances of his own. He also exchanged letters with anthropologist Margaret Mead, eager to know if she'd encountered any parapsychological data in her own research (she hadn't).

Over the next decade, Rhine endured criticism, refined his techniques and expanded to study psychokinesis and clairvoyance as well. In 1950 the Parapsychology Laboratory was removed from the Psychology Department and made its own creature. At that point Rhine expanded into other psychical research, including possession and poltergeists. The lab offered both studies and the public guidance that McDougall had talked about: in responding to a letter regarding use of a Ouija board, one staff member wrote that 'material gained in such a fashion is not authentic, but is the product of the unconscious just as is that of a nightmare. Therefore may I suggest for your own health that you get rid of the Ouija Board and dismiss the whole thing from your mind.'[12]

Rhine retired in 1965, at the age of seventy. At that time he redirected the laboratory's endowment into a non-university-affiliated Foundation for Research on the Nature of Man. Rhine passed away in 1980, but his foundation – renamed the Rhine Research Center in 1995 – continues to operate in Durham. Rhine himself is now credited with being the most serious investigator of psychic phenomena to date; sceptic and author Martin Gardner praised him as the scientist 'who has done more than any one man in history to give scientific respectability to the investigation of psychic forces'.[13]

In 1967 a former actress and screenwriter-turned-psychologist, Dr Thelma Moss, started a parapsychology laboratory out of the University of California, Los Angeles (UCLA). The lab received no funding from the university, but was given space to operate on the fifth floor of the Neuropsychiatric Institute (now the Semel Institute). Without serious financial backing, the lab depended largely on the work of volunteers, chiefly assistants Kerry Gaynor and Barry Taff. The lab investigated hundreds of cases, with possibly the best known being that of Doris Bither, a Culver City housewife who provided the inspiration for Frank DeFelitta's novel *The Entity* and the 1982 movie based on it. In DeFelitta's story, a woman is first haunted and then sexually assaulted by a spirit; when Moss, Taff and Gaynor investigated the story in 1974, they found no evidence of spectral rape, but did encounter 'a rather disturbingly real poltergeist outbreak'.[14] Moss eventually decided to focus primarily on Kirlian photography, a form of photography in which an object is placed directly on film or a photographic plate (no camera is required) and which some believe to show evidence of an aura. Moss wrote two books on the subject, even though Kirlian photography wasn't taken seriously within scientific circles. When grants failed to materialize and a new chairman of the Neuropsychiatric Institute took over, the lab was shut down and Moss was terminated from UCLA soon thereafter.

Although many of Moss's students felt that she was a positive influence on their life (Taff described her as 'a brilliant, accomplished, and dedicated medical psychologist and parapsychologist'[15]), others were disdainful of her methods. 'She was very casual and pleasant and easy to get along with,' said renowned sceptic, magician and debunker James Randi. 'The problem is [parapsychologists] aren't doing scientific research at all. They're allowing the so-called psychics to run the game.'[16]

Electronic Voice Phenomena (EVP)

The only reason that there weren't audio equivalents to William Mumler's spirit photographs in the nineteenth century was that sound-recording technology lagged slightly behind photography, not really arriving until the 1900s, but then – as phonographs, radios and telephones became standard household items – the spirits made themselves heard as well as seen.

One of the first to consider the possibility of directly communicating with spirits via machines rather than mediums was Thomas Edison. In 1920 Edison shocked his followers when he gave an interview in *American Magazine* in which he discussed his intention of building a device to talk to the dead. He claimed to be in the process of constructing his 'spirit phone' (he didn't use that name, but the media popularized that phrase after the publication of the interview), saying it would be completed in a few months. Edison's apparatus was dependent on his theory of life and its survival after death, which was, to put it mildly, unique:

I believe [our bodies] are composed of myriads and myriads of infinitesimally small individuals, each in itself a unit of life, and that these units work in squads – or swarms, as I prefer to call them – and that these infinitesimally small units live forever. When we 'die' these swarms of units, like a swarm of bees, so to speak, betake themselves elsewhere, and go on functioning in some other form or environment.[17]

Did Edison actually build and test his machine? Speculation has circled those questions for decades now.

There were some early attempts to capture spirit voices on phonograph records, but recording ghost voices didn't really catch on until the 1950s, when reel-to-reel tape recorders became affordable. Raymond Bayless, who would later write the book *Phone Calls from the Dead*, believed he successfully recorded spirit voices on reel-to-reel tape when he began working with Attila von Szalay, who had been investigating spirit recordings since 1941. Together, they presented their work in an article for the *Journal of the American Society for Psychical Research*.

In 1968 a Latvian psychologist named Konstantin Raudive published a book called *Breakthrough: An Amazing Experiment in Electronic Communication with the Dead* (the English translation followed in 1971), in which he detailed his experiences capturing spirit voices in tape recordings. Raudive had over 100,000 recordings, in some of which he had isolated small bits of speech. Most of these seemed to form nonsense phrases, but a few ('I follow you tonight') seemed more coherent (Raudive also claimed that some of the unintelligible bits of speech were because the spirit had either spoken in multiple languages or even backwards). During the 1980s spirits began to communicate via both computers and televisions. By the 1990s recording electronic voice phenomena (EVPs) had become a common technique. An article from a 1992 issue of *The National Spiritualist Summit* entitled 'Is This the Mediumship of the Future?' laid out the methods for creating EVPs: the first step was to purchase a tape recorder with speed control (because 'some spirits talk so fast'), a good microphone and headphones. When taping, it's recommended to have a steady background noise, like a radio tuned to the white noise between stations (although running water had been successfully used by some). Once the equipment was set up and the background noise in place, the recorder was turned on, a simple question asked and the recorder left running for about five minutes. The author of the article notes that it took him about a week of steady attempts to receive his first message.[18]

The recording of spirit voices is built on the theory that ghosts use the energy of electromagnetic frequencies to form spoken words. Building on this theory, in 2002 Frank Sumption created one of the most popular EVP devices, known as either a 'Spirit Box' or simply 'Frank's Box'. This is a small handheld player that rapidly scans the AM or FM radio band, creating a wash of white noise that is occasionally broken by a word or two. Believers say spirits use energies to form words; sceptics suggest that the device periodically brings up a split second of a radio broadcast, and that pareidolia – the tendency for the human mind to attempt to find meaning in meaningless or random stimuli – supplies the rest.

Mobile phones have transformed the notion of calls from the dead, with texts from the deceased being reported often. Texts from the dead usually have a simple explanation: with texting now a preferred form of communication for many, someone grieving for a lost loved one may send a text simply as a way of self-consolation, but may be unaware that the deceased's phone number has been reassigned, meaning they may receive a text back.

In 2015 an expert in artificial intelligence, Eugenia Kuyda, was devastated when her best friend died in an accident. She took an extensive history of him, integrated it into an artificial intelligence and was able to text with a convincing replica of her friend. These text-based 'griefbots' may provide the surest method of communicating with deceased loved ones in the very near future.[19]

The Philip Experiment

One of the most unusual paranormal investigations of all time was conducted in 1972 by eight members of the Toronto Society for Psychical Research. Composed of three men and five women, the group behind the Philip Experiment set out to prove that: 1) psychokinesis could be generated by a group; and 2) that a group already primed to see a ghost could experience shared hallucinations. To conduct their experiment, they first created a biography of 'Philip', a sixteenth-century British aristocrat who had fallen in love with a Romani girl named Margo. When Philip's wife Dorothea discovered the affair, she manoeuvred to have Margo executed as a witch, and Philip was so distraught that he threw himself from the battlements of his manor.

All members of the group studied Philip's history and offered their own details, including the idea that Philip's ghost had manifested at various points throughout history. They agreed to meet once a week for a year, conducting their meetings in a well-lit room around a table, without the use of a medium. They began their sessions by meditating, since they believed there was some proof to suggest that this would 'still the conscious mind so that the energies or powers within the subconscious mind are released'.[20] They recorded sessions with both audio equipment and cameras, but nothing more than casual conversation materialized.

After a year, their efforts had proven unsuccessful; however, when they read accounts of similar experiments being conducted within the framework of a traditional seance, they decided to move to a more conventional model. In a few weeks they achieved results, starting with table-rappings and movement of the table across the floor. On one occasion they believed that the table levitated completely off the floor about one or two centimetres; they never, however, succeeded in generating an apparition of Philip. They maintained that their results could be replicated by other groups that followed their model, and that their experiment suggested that group psychokinesis was actually behind the phenomena attributed to both mediums in seances and hauntings involving poltergeists. In 2004 the Humphrey Experiment attempted to recreate the effects achieved by the Philip group, but the results recorded nothing more than a few minor temperature anomalies.

The Afterlife Experiments

In the 1990s a university professor named Dr Gary Schwartz attempted to set up what he thought of as the first scientific study of mediums. Working out of the University of Arizona in Tucson, Schwartz and his associates conducted what came to be known as the Afterlife Experiments. Schwartz set out the project's goals as this: 'We started with the hypothesis, the working assumption, that science can establish that love exists, that consciousness exists, and that survival of consciousness exists, in the same way that science has established that gravity exists, that electrons exist, and that photons from "deceased" stars continue to exist.'[21] Their project was partly inspired by a meeting with Susy Smith, an elderly and well-known psychic who had written two books about her conversations with the spirit of pioneering psychologist William James (it's not uncommon for psychics to converse with the spirits of nineteenth-century scientists). Initial results with just two psychics (Smith and a southern California woman named Laurie Campbell) convinced Schwartz to continue his research with a larger number of sessions, sitters and psychics, and he'd soon convinced such stars of the field as John Edward, George Anderson and Suzane Northrop to participate. In the main experiments, Schwartz made sure that the mediums had no advance knowledge of the sitters; they were separated during the actual sessions by a screen in order to ensure that the psychics couldn't work from any visual cues. He asked the sitters to rate the psychics on the accuracy of their information.

He claimed very high success rates from the psychics, as much as 95 per cent. The psychics supplied some specific details, like the suicide of one woman's son; when Schwartz tested a control group of non-mediums, their highest scores were 54 per cent. Schwartz did return to the age-old speculation that the mediums were actually reading the minds of the sitters, but also speculated that they might be 'reading the mind of the deceased'. He tried to take into account a factor he called 'rater bias', that is, the fact that it was up to the sitters to score the accuracy results of the readings. Oddly, Schwartz required sitters to already have a favourable opinion of the existence of spirits and the abilities of mediums. He addressed the issue of why mediums seldom perform well with sceptics by suggesting that sceptical sitters invoked stress, which prevented the mediums from performing fully.

In conclusion, Schwartz said, 'After precise scoring, the findings showed remarkable replication across mediums and sitters, and across experiments as well. Probability values extend from the millions to the trillions. Guessing and chance cannot account for the accuracy of the information being provided.'[22] The experiments were filmed for an HBO documentary called *Life Afterlife*; however, both critics and sceptics were less than convinced by Schwartz's arguments. *Publishers Weekly*, in reviewing Schwartz's book about the experiments, said 'the narrative had the suspect tone of a sideshow barker',[23] and scientist and cold-reading expert Ray Hyman called the experiments 'methodologically defective' and saw no difference between what Schwartz's 'dream team' of celebrity mediums provided and any mentalist or fraudulent psychic.[24] Michael Shermer also noted that Schwartz's methodology was seriously flawed:

In one bizarre twist, one of Schwartz's mediums inquired if the sitter's husband had died. Although it was her son who had passed away, it was mistakenly relayed to the psychic that it was the husband who died, and he proceeded to channel from the other side the still living spouse. When the woman's husband was later killed in an accident, Schwartz proclaimed the psychic reading to be *prophetic*.[25]

The Fall of Parapsychology

At the beginning of the megahit 1984 film *Ghostbusters*, parapsychologist Peter Venkman (Bill Murray) and his team are fired from Columbia University. Dan Aykroyd, co-writer and co-star of the film and a lifelong fan of the paranormal, based that opening on the fall of Duke Parapsychology Laboratory. With the ending of both the Duke and the UCLA labs – to say nothing of the response to Gary Schwartz's experiments out of the University of Arizona – the study of parapsychology seemed to have failed at the academic level. Parapsychologists argued that sceptics seriously hurt their science, but sceptics offered another reason. 'It's fallen into disuse due to the fact that there's just nothing there,' said Michael Shermer, editor of the quarterly journal *Skeptic* and columnist for *Scientific American*. 'Parapsychology has been around for more than a century … [Yet] there's no research protocol that generates useful working hypotheses for other labs to test and develop into a model, and eventually a paradigm that becomes a field. It just isn't there.'[26] John Kruth, Executive Director of the Rhine Research Center, responded, 'The sceptics who say we have an evidence problem – they're not reading the evidence.'[27]

Shermer would address the issue again in his 2018 book *Heavens on Earth*, noting that science isn't about compiling anecdotes.[28] He also suggested that emotion had no place in the university setting: 'The emotional interpretations of such anomalous events grant them significance regardless of their causal account.'[29]

In the end, *Ghostbusters* had the last laugh: the film's depiction of the courageous parapsychologists facing off against frightening apparitions, and the equipment they carried (especially the 'PKE

Who you gonna call? Bill Murray, Harold Ramis and Dan Aykroyd in *Ghostbusters* (dir. Ivan Reitman, 1984).

meter', which bears a resemblance to a real k-ii meter, used to measure electromagnetic radiation), inspired a generation of young fans to grow up into the investigators who resurrected interest in the paranormal in the 2000s, largely via reality television shows.

The New Psychical Researchers

On 25 May 2002 a new reality series began airing on Britain's Living tv. *Most Haunted* was presented by Yvette Fielding (whose husband Karl Beattie directed). Each week, Fielding led a team comprised of a paranormal investigator, a medium and a historian to investigate a haunted location; they might hold a seance, use a Ouija board and record evps in an effort to contact spirits (and create ratings).

Despite being off the air between 2010 and 2013, the show continues to air and has produced more than 275 episodes.

On 6 October 2004 a series called *Ghost Hunters* premiered on the cable channel SyFy. The programmer called it a 'docu-soap', since it followed both the adventures of a group of amateur paranormal investigators and their daily lives. The real stars of the show, Jason Hawes and Grant Wilson, were plumbers who had formed a group called the Atlantic Paranormal Society (TAPS) to pursue their hobby of ghost hunting. *Ghost Hunters* substituted high-tech equipment for old-fashioned seances and mediums, eschewing the theatrical lighting of *Most Haunted* by instead presenting its investigations in a bare-bones documentary style.

After ten years of the original series, spin-offs, merchandising and more, it's safe to say that Hawes and Wilson will never have to return to the vocation of plumbing.

Ghost Hunters inaugurated not just a tsunami of television shows (which the *New York Times* dismissed as all 'call and no response'[30]), but created a new way for everyone to interact with spirits. No longer was it necessary to find a circle of like-minded friends and someone willing to enter a trance state to act as medium; although the Ouija board could be used by anyone anywhere, no one had ever pretended there was anything scientific about it. Now, for a small investment in equipment, anyone can venture to a supposedly haunted location and stage a scientific (or at least it *seems* like science) investigation as they attempt to contact the dead.

Most Haunted and *Ghost Hunters*, which inspired a spate of imitators including *Ghost Adventures*, *Paranormal State* and even *Psychic Kids: Children of the Paranormal*, created the template: a group of everyman investigators journey to a haunted location, interview residents and/or employees for stories of what they've experienced and then set up their equipment. During the ensuing investigation, ominous horror movie music will punctuate any exclamation of, 'Something touched me!' or 'I feel cold here.' At the conclusion of the episode, data gathered from the equipment – EVPs, infrared video, greenish night-vision footage – is examined for any anomalies. And the investigation is, of course, declared a success.

Critics may bemoan the repetitive nature of these shows (and even compare them to soft-core pornography[31]), but they also led to an explosion on the major networks (*Medium, Ghost Whisperer, Evil*) and have now been a mainstay of television programming for over a decade. They also created a cottage industry in equipment.

The most common piece of equipment is the handheld K-II meter. The K-II existed prior to the explosion of ghosthunting, when its sole purpose was to detect potentially harmful radiation from wiring or appliances, but after Grant Wilson used it on *Ghost Hunters*, it became a paranormal investigator's chief tool for detecting the presence of spirits. The K-II has a tiny screen with a simple meter that moves from green to yellow to red when it reads a bump in the electromagnetic field (EMF); since ghosts theoretically consist of energy, a fluctuation in the meter within a haunted location seems like a dead giveaway. Sceptics, however, point out that K-II meters are usually unshielded, meaning they can be set off by something as small and overlooked as a computer or a battery pack.

In the recent past the amateur ghosthunter might also have invested in a small digital audio recorder, a thermometer and (for those with extra money to spend) an infrared video camera; they could even purchase an entire kit from a web retailer dedicated to selling only ghosthunting equipment. Ghosthunting, though, has moved on to become even more egalitarian. 'Anybody can be a ghost-hunter,' noted Jill Pingleton, co-creator of the Spirit Story Box app, 'anybody can put an app on their phone.'[32] Inexpensive and even free apps can now mimic nearly all of the functions of expensive hardware, and do even more: phones can now detect EMF, locate ghosts on a small radar-like scanner, record EVPs or act as a Ouija board (complete with graphics imitating the look of a traditional board). At least one app, iOvilus, employs 'Instrumental

A ghost detector app spots a spirit (the green dot).

Trans Communications' (ITC), and works on the principle that the app uses changes to the phone's sensors to produce speech. Several apps both find ghosts and automatically take a photo if a ghost is within range; however, users have compared photos and discovered that these apps often insert the same ghostly figures, strange mist or glowing orbs.

'This is where ghosts live,' noted author Colin Dickey, 'in static, in glitches and in blurs.'[33]

The New Trance Mediums

By the 1980s the term 'medium' had become passé, and 'psychic' was the favoured word to describe those who commune with spirits. Psychics no longer channelled the dead in a dark living room; they performed on telephones and televisions. They wrote best-selling books, assisted in police investigations and became tabloid celebrities. If they were less photogenic or skilled, they could be found throughout most cities (depending on local laws regarding fortune tellers), laying out tarot cards, scrying into crystal balls or palm reading.

Doris Stokes was a perfect bridge between the Spiritualist mediums of the past and the modern psychics. Born in 1920 in Grantham, Lincolnshire, in England, Stokes was first recognized as a medium by the Spiritualists' National Union in 1949. However, she didn't achieve popular success until the late 1970s, when she started appearing on television talk shows. An early controversy on *The Don Lane Show* probably helped Doris's fame: she was a guest on an episode with Uri Geller and sceptic James Randi in 1980, but Lane took exception to Randi's suggestions that Stokes was a fraud and told Randi to 'piss off' (he later apologized).[34] She was the first medium to sell out the London Palladium, and she went on to produce a string of autobiographical books, selling more than two million copies. Much of Stokes's reputation rested on her warm personality; she was described by the press as 'like a favourite grannie', and one woman who went to Stokes for help in locating her missing mother ended up acknowledging that although the medium had been unable to assist with the crime, she'd assisted the family in coming to terms with the loss.[35]

Doris was one of the first psychics to tour and appear live before thousands, opening the way for the modern superstar psychics like George Anderson. Although he may not be as well-known to the greater public as John Edward and James Van Praagh, he is (according to his website) 'widely considered, by those in the medical, scientific and religious fields to be the world's greatest living medium'.[36]

Anderson says he gained his ability at the age of six, after a bout of chicken pox led to encephalomyelitis (other psychics, like Peter

Hurkos, similarly claimed to develop psychic abilities after surviving a traumatic illness or accident). His 1988 book *We Don't Die* became a best-seller (Anderson claims it was the first book written by a medium to achieve that status[37]). He has held more than 35,000 sessions, and says he has never conducted a sitting in which the spirits didn't come through (although he also freely admits that mediumship is not a perfect science, and that he's not 100 per cent accurate: 'Every time a ballplayer steps up to the plate, he doesn't hit a home run. But that doesn't mean he can't play ball'[38]).

Anderson compares contacting the spirits to taking a Polaroid photograph in which the picture slowly begins to appear. On his website, Anderson advises his sitters about what to expect:

> Within seconds, the souls are able to communicate, and the souls start coming forward. The souls already know why you have come to a session, and know who you are hoping to hear from. There may be more souls who come forward than you had expected – but they know who you have the most need to hear from, and that soul will most likely do the most communicating.[39]

Sitters aren't allowed to video their sessions, but audio recordings are encouraged. Anderson says he loses contact with the other side during heavy lightning storms.

Anderson's sessions are held in a hotel conference room (the hotel offers a room discount to those who fly in for sessions and stay overnight). Private sessions range from $1,200 (also the price for a private telephone session) to $2,000, depending on the number of family members who are present. Sessions last for one hour.[40] Anderson also holds large seminars which typically last ninety minutes and may draw six or seven hundred attendees.

While Gary Schwartz touted Anderson's accuracy rate in the *Afterlife Experiments* as 90 per cent,[41] sceptical response to Anderson (as well as to other psychics) has emphasized his skills at using both 'cold' and 'hot' reading techniques.

In 'cold reading' – contrary to the popular misconception that it consists entirely in reading body language – the reader uses a series of broad questions that increasingly narrow to reveal seemingly unknowable knowledge about someone. Writing in *The Skeptical Inquirer*, James Underdown described how '[The psychics] rattle off gobs of guesses until they find a vein of hits with one of their audience members. They are very adept at steering out of dead ends and helping the crowd forgive and forget their mistakes.'[42] Sceptical writer Gary P. Posner listened to a recording of one of Anderson's sessions and described the series of questions posed by the psychic:

> At thirteen minutes: 'He is now telling me his first name is short.' Eve offers a 'yes' but no more, and Anderson abandons this attempt. At about sixteen minutes he tries again: 'He doesn't have the most common first name . . . but you can shorten it? [Actually, no.] He showed me six letters, but it's less than that?' [Eve offers another 'yes.'] A bit later: '[The] letter "J" – anything to do with him?' Then, 'Now why did your son say "A, B, C, D" and he stopped, understood?' He offers the names 'Kyle' and 'Keith', both incorrect.

Posner concludes, 'One needs to listen to the entire recording to appreciate the endless stream of wild guesses and proffered questions that don't offer any specific information from or about the "next level" of existence.'[43] Another technique of cold reading is to offer a comment that, on the surface, seems sympathetic and insightful, but is really related more to common sense than a sixth sense. James Randi cited an example in which parents would tell a psychic that they'd lost a child. The psychic might respond with, 'You're wondering what to do with his toys, aren't you?' and the bereaved person will nod yes. 'But,' notes Randi, 'that applies to every parent of a deceased child.'[44]

Cold-reading expert Ray Hyman notes that there are three assumptions at the heart of the technique:

(1) that we all are basically more alike than different;
(2) that our problems are generated by the same major transitions of birth, puberty, work, marriage, children, old age, and death; (3) that, with the exception of curiosity seekers and troublemakers, people come to a character reader because they need someone to listen to their conflicts involving love, money, and health.[45]

Hyman also notes that cold readers have a repertoire of 'stock spiels' that they pull from; these routines further allow them to tailor the reading to the individual (that is, the reader won't use a 'stock spiel' for a teenager on an elderly woman').

Part of the success of a cold reader, too, must be in convincing their sitter that they are genuinely compassionate and interested. An actress, Kari Coleman, who studied cold-reading techniques to play a psychic medium, performed 'readings' in a Las Vegas casino, and was astonished at how easy it was to convince others that she was communing with spirits. After allowing one man to believe that he'd just conversed with his dead mother, Coleman confessed to him, but he wasn't angry. 'People', says Coleman, 'were happy just to have the chance to talk. They really just wanted someone to listen to their problems, their hopes and dreams.'[46]

In the 'hot-reading' technique, the psychic knows specific information about the sitter before the session even begins. A century ago, a Spiritualist medium might check family history in a graveyard or the offices of the town newspaper. In the twenty-first century, the celebrity psychic may obtain information about someone by investigating the data a sitter supplied when they purchased their session online. The website 'Bad Psychics' shared this anecdote of a woman who paid $1,000 for a phone session with Anderson after losing her son and husband in an accident: 'I can't explain what a horrible sinking feeling it was while listening to George and slowly realizing he was only telling me things that anyone could find through public records, like my husband's name, cause of death, how long we'd been married and that it was the first marriage for both of us, where we got married, etc.' Anderson went on to tell the woman that she and her husband had never had children; afterwards, the woman realized that her son's birth and death had both happened in another country, so records about him were hard to find.[47]

In a larger, group setting, the psychic may have confederates sprinkled in the crowd, listening in on conversations and relaying information to the psychic.

However, Anderson's fans also praise his abilities and the comfort he's provided. 'As a bereaved parent', said Nancy Schroeder, who attended a group session with Anderson after losing her twenty-year-old son Scott, 'losing a child can totally change your life, change your future. By attending the session, it gave me great comfort and peace of mind to have that one-on-one communication with my son.'[48]

Among the most charismatic of the new mediums is John Edward. Edward has seen spirits since at least his teen years, when he asked a schoolmate if he saw dead relatives (the 'no' he received was a turning point for Edward[49]). After publishing his first book *One Last Time* in 1998 and becoming a hit on the talk show circuit, Edward starred in his own series, *Crossing Over with John Edward*, on the SyFy Channel from 2001 to 2004. A second series, *John Edward Cross Country*, ran on WeTV from 2006 to 2008. In both series, Edward gave readings of particular members in a large group setting, and those individuals were interviewed for their response to the accuracy of the readings.

In 2002 James Underdown attended a taping of John Edward's *Crossing Over* television show, and in the process unearthed a third technique that the television psychics use more than even cold reading: editing. Underdown secretly audio-taped the show and then compared it to the final version that aired. He ended up concluding, 'John Edward's editor fine-tuned many of the dead-ends out of a reading riddled with misses.'[50]

British medium Derek Acorah, who passed away on 3 January 2020, remains possibly the only television psychic who was terminated after being caught lying on camera. While working on *Most Haunted* in 2005, Acorah was fed fictitious characters created by parapsychologist Dr Ciaran O'Keeffe; when Acorah later claimed to be in contact with 'Rik Eedles' (an anagram of 'Derek lies'), he was let go.[51] However, he went on to star in his own series *Derek Acorah's Ghost Towns*.

James Van Praagh's website introduces him as a 'Psychic Medium, Author & Master Teacher'.[52] Van Praagh's official bio touts his work as a spiritual teacher, his celebrity clients and the 'many famous deceased personalities' he has brought through, including 'Slim Pickins' [*sic*] and 'Ghandi' [*sic*],[53] whose spirits at the time of writing seem to have neglected to convey the proper spelling of their names.

Van Praagh, who stopped giving private readings in 1996, has authored or co-authored a dozen books, and hosted his own paranormal talk show, *Beyond*, on the WB network from 2002 to 2003. A 2002 CBS mini-series, *Living with the Dead*, was based on Van Praagh's life, and Van Praagh also served as an Executive Producer on the popular CBS series *Ghost Whisperer*, starring Jennifer Love Hewitt.

On his website, James Van Praagh promotes his 'James Van Praagh School of Mystical Arts', which provides an eight-week course that asserts 'This Is Mediumship Made Simple! Connecting with Spirit doesn't have to be difficult.' The course offers videos, 'field work', access to Van Praagh and an actual certificate, and costs (via Van Praagh's website) $987.[54]

Theresa Caputo has appeared on the TLC series *Long Island Medium* since 2011. Known for her down-to-earth sass, teased tower of blonde hair and open emotionalism, Caputo has also authored books and toured with *Theresa Caputo Live! The Experience* (which she says offers 'witnessing first-hand spirit communications'[55]). Her website emphasizes her fan club and her branded merchandise. Caputo also clearly embraces the title 'medium' over 'psychic': 'I only speak on how I communicate with spirits. I don't predict the future, I don't give out lottery numbers, I'm not telling people what to do with their lives.'[56]

Mediums and Crime

In January 1981 'psychic detective' Noreen Renier gave a lecture to about fifty police officers and Federal Bureau of Investigation (FBI) agents; present during that lecture was Special Agent Robert Ressler, the man who would coin the term 'serial killer' and become one of the most highly esteemed agents in the Bureau's history. During her lecture, Renier made two predictions: first, that President Ronald Reagan would be shot in the chest, but would survive; and second, that Reagan would be killed later that year during a parade. When Reagan did indeed survive an assassination attempt two months later, Renier's first prediction seemed accurate; although Reagan did not die later on during a parade, Egyptian president Anwar Sadat did. Ressler was so impressed that he asserted his belief in Renier's powers during a deposition[57] and introduced her to other law enforcement officials.

Yet, two years earlier, a study in the *Journal of Police Science and Administration* had concluded that 'the research data do not support the contention that psychics can provide significant additional information leading to the solution of major crimes.'[58]

Renier's method of crime-solving was 'psychometry', in which she held something related to the victim – a lock of hair, a scrap of clothing – and received images of the victim's future or whereabouts. Rather than spirits, Renier suggested that psychometry (or remote viewing) was a mental ability.

Others, however, were happy to claim the assistance of spirits. Sylvia Browne, the late psychic who wrote best-selling books, frequently prophesied in legal cases, most famously in the 2004 case of missing girl Amanda Berry, when Browne went on *The Montel Williams Show* with Berry's mother and told her, 'She's not alive, honey.'[59] Berry was found alive in 2013, but her mother died in 2006 believing her daughter was dead. Browne's speciality was 'deep trance channelling'.

Despite the continuing lack of documented success from psychics' involvement in criminal investigations, the Central Intelligence Agency (CIA) issued a paper in 2000 entitled 'Use of Psychics in Law Enforcement' that laid out the following bullet points:

A talented psychic can assist you by helping to:
- Locate a geographic area of a missing person,
- Narrow the number of leads to be concentrated on,
- Highlight information that has been overlooked, or
- Provide information previously unknown to the investigator.[60]

A 2015 bulletin from the UK's College of Policing suggested that 'Any information received from psychics should be evaluated in the context of the case.'[61] However, the Missing People charity, in responding to this, noted that there had been 'no significant findings through psychics or mediums'.[62] Confirming the Missing People charity assessment, a 2019 report from the Center for Inquiry noted, 'Despite claims to the contrary, there is not a single documented case of a missing person being found or recovered due to psychic information.'[63]

There's certainly a long history of mediums engaging in large-scale fraud, going all the way back to the generous patrons of Katie Fox, D. D. Home and Florence Cook. Felony theft on behalf of the spirits is still a modern-day problem as well: witness the case of a man in New York City who, beginning in 2013, paid more than $700,000 to a psychic who he believed would reunite him with a lost love named Michelle. When, in 2014, he discovered that Michelle had passed away, the psychic told him that she 'could reincarnate her'.[64] The victim contacted Bob Nygaard, a private investigator who specializes in cases regarding psychic crime; the fortune teller and a cohort were apprehended and charged with grand larceny.

Seances and mediums sometimes find themselves tangling with the law in other ways as well. In the case North Carolina v. Kimbrell,[65] the defendant was on trial for being an accessory to second-degree murder. During the trial, the prosecution questioned the defendant about statements he'd made previously admitting to involvement in 'devil worshipping' and attending a seance. This line of questioning was eventually ruled prejudicial towards the defendant, and demonstrates how seances are often thought to involve black magic.

In Idaho v. Charboneau, a capital murder case from 1989, the defence tried to admit as evidence a claim made by the defendant's niece that the identity of the actual killer had been revealed to her in a seance. The defendant was found guilty.[66]

In July 2018 an Ethiopian man was arrested after failing to resurrect a dead man in front of a crowd. A would-be prophet named Getayawkal Ayele had the body of a recently deceased man, Belay Biftu, exhumed. A video (which went on to receive considerable sharing on social media) shows Ayele prostrating himself on the corpse while shouting into the decomposing face; Ayele may be attempting a resurrection à la St Martin, who was described as stretching himself out full length on the corpse of a man he resurrected (although it took two hours). Ayele was arrested for abusing a dead body.[67]

Seances in the Twenty-first Century

Spiritualism is alive and well in Lily Dale, the Spiritualist enclave in southwestern New York. With a population of less than three hundred, Lily Dale remains an immensely popular tourist destination. In addition to housing a Spiritualist museum and a memorial to the Fox Sisters, Lily Dale is home to numerous mediums, some of whom offer traditional Spiritualist seances complete with spirit cabinets, levitations and materializations. In his book *Heavens on Earth*, Michael Shermer describes the modern-day rules he had to observe while attending a Lily Dale sitting:

> He gave us all very specific instructions [no mobile phones or cameras, no leaving after the start of the seances], and warned that to veer from them in any way was extremely dangerous ... A breach of these rules, even the smallest, could result in terrible consequences and could prove fatal to the medium.[68]

Meanwhile, some Christians still take exception. Adam Blai, a therapist and exorcist who runs a website called religiousdemonology.com, recently penned an article called 'The Devil Is Real: Combating Spiritualism':

> A new spiritualist movement has exploded in the United States, as well as many other countries, with the help of every form of media ... Human spirits in Purgatory generally only communicate a need for prayer, or a need for help with unfinished restitution of a sin. There are rare exceptions to

A 2019 seance with Bridget Marquardt, Patti Negri and Holly Madison
is livestreamed on Facebook.

this but generally if there is ongoing dialogue it is not with a
human spirit.[69]

Despite the persistence of some customs and beliefs from the
nineteenth century, the seance itself has, in most instances, evolved.
The modern seance is likely to still include an invocation and possibly even singing, although now pop songs are preferred; it may
also include ritualistic practices lifted from Wicca and paganism,
including the lighting of candles, the use of oils or herbs, or even
a protective circle of salt.

Seances may now be recorded and shared online, or even livestreamed as they happen. In 2019, for example, psychic-medium and
'Good Witch of Hollywood' Patti Negri acted as medium in a seance
(held on 30 October) at the (haunted) home of Holly Madison,
former girlfriend of Hugh Hefner and star of the reality series *The
Girls Next Door*. The seance also included Bridget Marquardt, co-star

of *The Girls Next Door* and host of the popular podcast *Ghost Magnet*, and Marquardt's fiancé. The seance was livestreamed on Facebook, allowing followers to view in real time and comment. The seance table combined all the modern seance paraphernalia: candles, phones with ghost-detecting apps, dowsing rods, K-11 meters and cameras. During the seance, Negri produced messages from Marquardt's grandfather and Hugh Hefner, among others.[70]

Welcome to the future of speaking with spirits from the past.

8

(WHY) DO WE NEED THE SEANCE?

In the 170 years since two teenage girls started a religion with a practical joke, thousands of mediums have held seances attended by millions; spirits (and attendant phenomena) have been consulted, studied, questioned, photographed, recorded and measured. True believers have gathered and celebrated, founded churches, organizations and towns, and cherished a few words of comfort from deceased loved ones.

And yet, with all of that, not a single verifiable shred of scientific evidence has been obtained to confirm the existence of spirits or the ability to communicate with them. Sceptics have revealed the fraud behind the miracles, the gross imposture of the mediums and the credulity of the faithful. For everyone who has exclaimed 'I have seen,' there have been debunkers pulling back the curtain to display the trickery.

So why against all evidence do we persist in believing that we can talk to the dead? Throughout all of human history and around the world, we have been consistent in thinking that we exist after death and are willing to continue relations with the living. 'The idea of immortality', said Jung, 'is a psychic phenomenon that is disseminated over the whole earth.'[1] Religions change, the methods of calling the spirits evolve, but our relationships with ghosts are fundamentally the same. Our gods may come and go, but our dead remain constant.

Cesare Lombroso and Charles Richet 'control' while Eusapia Palladino levitates a table in Milan, 1892.

Both the doubters and the doubtless agree on one point: that humans possess an innate desire to believe that they somehow continue after death. 'Plainly, there's something within me that's ready to believe in life after death. And it's not the least bit interested in whether there's any sober evidence for it,' said one of the great science writers of the last century, Carl Sagan.[2]

On the other end of the spectrum, superstar psychic George Anderson noticed a recurring theme in the letters he receives: 'People need to know not only that their loved ones continue to exist in some form and dimension, but that they still play a role in their lives here on earth.'[3]

Where debate arises is in continuing to believe in the face of overwhelming evidence to the contrary. In the prologue to his book *Heavens on Earth*, Michael Shermer notes that more than 100 billion human beings have preceded us here on earth, and then makes this observation: 'Of those 100.5 billion people who have come and gone, not one of them has returned to confirm the existence of an afterlife, at least not to the high evidentiary standards of science.'[4] Shermer was certainly wise to add that second clause, although many would debate even that. Certainly devoted Spiritualists would aver that many mediums have withstood scientific scrutiny.

That leads to the question: why did so many Spiritualists, especially those from the nineteenth century, feel that it was necessary to scientifically prove the reality of seances? William James, who established the psychology department at Harvard University and served as the president of the Society for Psychical Research (SPR), unquestionably felt the need for scientific confirmation of his own Spiritualist leanings. He believed that he had discovered at least one genuine medium, Leonora Piper, and he suggested that only one genuine medium was necessary to legitimize the scientific possibility of the survival of the human soul after death. 'If you wish to upset the law that all crows are black,' he said in an address to the SPR, 'you mustn't seek to show that no crows are; it is enough if you prove one single crow to be white.'[5] He believed that Leonora Piper was his white crow.

How could men like James and William Crookes have been duped (if, indeed, we accept that they were)? In their landmark study *The Psychology of the Psychic*, David Marks and Richard Kammann discuss the human bias to focus on successes and ignore failures, a bias that is possessed even by men of science. They point to a 1973 experiment in extrasensory perception (ESP) conducted by the SPR, and note that, while the SPR touted the *number* of successful matches between transmitters and receivers in the experiment, they ignored the *percentage* of successful matches, which was actually only 1.4 per cent. In fact, the experiment 'produced a definitive demonstration of non-ESP'.[6] Another seminal study in dedicated commitment to a non-rational idea, *When Prophecy Fails*, first set out the idea of 'cognitive dissonance'. Although the book was an examination of millennial cults, its findings could well be applied to both the scientists and the faithful at the heart of Spiritualism: 'When people are committed to a belief and a course of action, clear disconfirming evidence may simply result in deepened conviction and increased proselytizing ... the introduction of contrary evidence can serve to increase the conviction and enthusiasm of a believer.'[7]

What about the mediums themselves – were they all frauds? If we accept that, how then to explain someone like Georgiana Houghton, the nineteenth-century medium who, while in a trance state, produced such extraordinary works of art that she's now seriously discussed as one of the first great abstract painters?

In an essay on the channellers that sprang up in the 1970s and '80s, psychologist Graham Reed offers multiple reasons for why people engage in channelling (and his reasons are also applicable to mediums and their craft): while some may seek ego-enhancement, compensation or material rewards and so may be deliberately engaging in fraud, others may suffer from psychosis or dissociation. Certainly Jung's teenaged medium-patient S. W., whose spirit control, Ivenes, had called up a number of spirits during seances that Jung participated in, fits the profile of a medium suffering from a psychological condition:

> [The spirits she produces] disclose the independent
> growth of repressed thoughts ... They teach Ivenes
> the secrets of the Beyond, they tell her all those fantastic
> stories about the extraordinariness of her personality,
> they create situations in which she can appear dramatically
> with the attributes of their power, wisdom, and virtue.
> They are nothing but dramatized split-offs from her
> dream-ego.[8]

Professor George M. Robertson, Physician-Superintendent of the Royal Edinburgh Mental Hospital, thought (in 1917) that Spiritualism held particular dangers for 'neurotics':

I would remind inquirers into the subject that if they would meet those who are hearing messages from spirits every hour of the day, who are seeing forms, angelic and human, surrounding them that are invisible to ordinary persons, and who are receiving other manifestations of an equally occult nature, they only require to go to a mental hospital to find them . . . I desire to warn those who may possibly inherit a latent tendency to nervous disorders to have nothing to do with practical inquiries of a spiritualistic nature, lest they should awaken this dormant proclivity to hallucinations within their brains.[9]

Epileptic aura (which typically precedes seizure, but may also be experienced without seizure) is another possibility behind the creation of mediums. One study of those suffering from temporal lobe epilepsy found that they not only suffered from hallucinations (that could easily explain ghostly visits) but were also

easily distinguishable by their humorlessness, excessive moral zeal, and tendency to find profound meaning in mundane events. They were obsessed with details and often kept voluminous diaries, intending to work them into great metaphysical tomes. Their preoccupation with idiosyncratic religious, mystical, and cosmological speculation was invested with a strong sense of divine guidance and personal destiny. Repeated conversions were common, as was suspicion of those who failed to grasp the truth of their revelations.[10]

There is, however, also an argument to be made that there is one other significant reason people may have taken up mediumship, especially in the nineteenth century: it was a vocation that liberated them from the stultifying strictures of their gender and class. Most of the Spiritualist mediums came from working-class

The Fox Sisters in 1884: Leah, Kate and Maggie.

or impoverished backgrounds; becoming a medium allowed them to escape dull parents or spouses, and to move among the privileged (including royalty) they would otherwise have no access to.

Is it also possible that some mediums suffered from nothing worse than a desire to provide comfort to others? Mary Roach, after attending a modern school for mediums, said, 'I was wrong about mediums. I no longer think they are intentionally duping their clients. I believe that they believe, honestly and with conviction, that they are getting information from paranormal sources.'[11] Derren Brown, a British mentalist and magician whose 2004 television special *Séance* demonstrated ways in which sitters might be deceived, believes there are two groups of mediums: 'the out-and-out frauds and the people who are well-meaning and believe they do have powers'.[12] Jung's patient S. W. seems to have found solace from believing in the reality of her spirits:

> I do not know if what the spirits say and teach me is true, nor do I know if they really are the people they call themselves; but that my spirits exist is beyond question. I see them before me. I can touch them. I speak to them about everything I wish as naturally as I'm talking to you. They must be real.[13]

What about those who attend seances, and receive genuine peace from believing that they have communicated with a dead loved one? Should this be considered a criminal offence or an act of compassion? When Helen Duncan was put on trial in 1944, dozens of witnesses testified on her behalf, citing both her abilities and the comfort they derived as a result. Witness Mary Jane Blackwell offered a particularly poignant account of the seance when Duncan had produced an aunt:

> My aunt said that she had learned that the things of this world are ephemeral. She had been a connoisseur of silver and that sort of thing. Her whole life had been wrapped up in old silver, and when she materialized, she said, 'It was not worthwhile, it was absolutely silly.' I have learned that there is no person really dead. They are there waiting, and their love abides. This is a great consolation.[14]

Even sceptic Michael Shermer doesn't entirely condemn Spiritualism, which he said 'presented a relationship to the divine that was broad-minded, without dogma, hopeful, and liberating'.[15]

Patti Negri offers a philosophy that combines Spiritualism, positivity and Wicca:

> I believe that magick is all around us in many forms and many names. I believe that we can connect into that magickal energy and use and harness it to have a better, fuller life. I believe that spirit is all around us – and is truly there to help us if only we are aware of and acknowledge it.[16]

Harry Houdini, however, was less kind to the promotion of paranormal beliefs. Although he had been a believer in seances as a young person, after performing as a stage medium for many years he finally condemned the practice:

As I advanced to riper years of experience I was brought to
a realization of the seriousness of trifling with the hallowed
reverence which the average human being bestows on the
departed, and when I personally became afflicted with
similar grief I . . . realized that it bordered on crime.[17]

Marina Warner has also suggested that our interest in seances
can be a detrimental distraction. In discussing the ascendancy of
post-First World War Spiritualism, she said, 'Taking strength from
this form of spiritual consolation diverts energy from attacking the
cause of the young men's deaths.'[18]

Perhaps the final word should come from the woman who,
with her sister, created the seance in a farmhouse in 1848. Maggie
Fox, co-inventor of Spiritualism and certainly one of the greatest
mediums in history, wrote this in 1888 as part of her admission to
years of acting out fraud in the name of spirit communication:

I have been in graveyards at dead of night, having
permission to enter from those in charge. I have sat
alone on a gravestone, that the spirits of those who
slept underneath might come to me. I have tried to
obtain some sign. Not a thing! No, no, the dead shall
not return, nor shall any that go down into hell. So says
the Catholic Bible, and so say I. The spirits will not come
back. God has not ordered it.[19]

Here's hoping Maggie truly rests in peace, wherever she may be.

REFERENCES

INTRODUCTION

1 Lucy Ann Lamont, 'A Séance in Liverpool', *The Spiritualist*, LX, III/21 (15 September 1873), p. 334.
2 Vagrancy Act 1824, www.legislation.gov.uk.
3 'Society in Paris – Somnambulism', *Weekly Waterford Chronicle* (17 June 1843), p. 1.
4 'Portadown: Mr. Robinson's Lecture on Animal Magnetism. – Gross Deception', *Banner of Ulster* (21 February 1843), p. 3.
5 Erika Bourguignon, 'Necromancy' (2005), www.paulbourguignon. com/writing, published in *Encyclopedia of Religion*, X, ed. Lindsay Jones (2nd edn, Detroit, MI, 2005).
6 C. A. Dubray, 'Necromancy', *The Catholic Encyclopedia*, www.catholicity.com, accessed 10 September 2019.
7 Joseph E. Worcester, *A Dictionary of the English Language* (Boston, MA, 1860), p. 893.
8 'Spirit Revelations', *Galway Mercury, and Connaught Weekly Advertiser* (2 October 1852).
9 *New York Daily Times* (27 December 1852), p. 4.

1 SUMMONING THE OLD SPIRITS

1 Flavius Philostratus, *On Heroes*, trans. Ellen Bradshaw Aitken and Jennifer K. Berenson Maclean, §7.3, https://chs.harvard.edu.
2 Statius, *Thebaid*, Book IV, trans. Jane Wilson Joyce (Ithaca, NY, and London, 2008), p. 96.
3 E. R. Dodds, *The Ancient Concept of Progress* (Oxford, 1973), p. 206, quoted in Georg Luck, *Arcana Mundi: Magic and the Occult in the Greek and Roman Worlds* (Baltimore, MD, and London, 1985), p. 165.

4 Plato, *Laws*, Book 10, Section 909b, trans. R. G. Bury (Cambridge, MA, and London, 1967 and 1968), www.perseus.tufts.edu.

5 Irving L. Finkel, 'Necromancy in Ancient Mesopotamia', *Archiv für Orientforschung*, XXIX/30 (1983), pp. 1–17, p. 1.

6 Ibid., p. 1.

7 Ibid., p. 5.

8 Ibid., p. 14.

9 *Gilgamesh, Enkidu and the Nether World*, Electronic Text Corpus of Sumerian Literature (Oxford, 2002), http://etcsl.orinst.ox.ac.uk.

10 Ibid.

11 Clement of Alexandria, *Exhortation to the Heathen*, Chapter 2, trans. William Wilson, from Alexander Roberts, James Donaldson and A. Cleveland Coxe, *Ante-Nicene Fathers* (Buffalo, NY, 1885), vol. II, revised and edited for New Advent by Kevin Knight, www.newadvent.org.

12 Hans Dieter Betz, *The Greek Magical Papyri in Translation: Including the Demotic Spells* (Chicago, IL, and London, 1986), p. 42.

13 K. Preisendanz, *Papyri Graecae Magicae* (Leipzig, 1928–31), p. 118.

14 S. J. Tambiah, 'The Magical Power of Words', *Man*, III/2 (1968), pp. 175–208.

15 Preisendanz, *Papyri*, I, pp. 82f.

16 Pliny, *The Natural History of Pliny*, trans. John Bostock and H. T. Riley, Book XXX, Chapter 6 (London, 1866), p. 429.

17 Ian S. Moyer, *Egypt and the Limits of Hellenism* (Cambridge, 2011), pp. 209–10.

18 Heliodorus, *Aethiopica* or *Ethiopian Tales*, 6.14–15, from Luck, *Arcana Mundi*, pp. 223–5.

19 Apuleius, *The Golden Ass or Metamorphoses*, trans. E. J. Kenney, Book 2, Chapter 28 (London, 1998), pp. 36–7.

20 Herodotus, *The Histories*, trans. A. D. Godley, Book 4, Chapter 172, Section 3 (Cambridge, 1920), www.perseus.tufts.edu.

21 John Wilkes, *Encyclopædia Londinensis; or, Universal Dictionary of Arts, Sciences, and Literature*, vol. XVI (London, 1819), p. 667.

22 Homer, *The Odyssey*, trans. Samuel Butler, Book X, http://classics.mit.edu.

23 Ibid., Book XI, http://classics.mit.edu.

24 Aeschylus, *Psuchagogoi*, F273a, as quoted in Daniel Ogden, *Greek and Roman Necromancy* (Princeton, NJ, and Oxford, 2001), p. 48.

25 Aristophanes, *The Birds*, Internet Classics Archive, http://classics.mit.edu.

26 Strabo, *The Geography of Strabo*, vol. I, trans. H. C. Hamilton and W. Falconer (London, 1903), p. 434.

27 Yulia Ustinova, *Caves and the Ancient Greek Mind: Descending Underground in the Search for Ultimate Truth* (Oxford, 2009), p. 74.

28 Herodotus, *The Histories*, trans. A. D. Godley (Cambridge, 1920), 5.92G.2, www.perseus.tufts.edu.

29 Ogden, *Greek and Roman Necromancy*, p. 17.

30 Plutarch, *The Parallel Lives* (Boston, MA, 1914), http://penelope.uchicago.edu.

31 Pausanias, *Description of Greece*, trans. W.H.S. Jones, www.theoi.com, 3.25.5.

32 Aelian, Fragment 80, trans. William Hutton (2002), www.cs.uky.edu.

33 Virgil, *Publii Virgilii Maronis Georgicorum libri quatuor. The Georgicks [sic] of Virgil, with an English Translation and Notes*, trans. John Martyn, 2nd edn (London, 1746), Book IV, pp. 475–85.

34 Philostratus, *On Heroes*, §11.9.

35 Statius, *Thebaid*, Book IV.

36 Leonidas of Tarentum, *Epigrams*, 7.657, www.attalus.org.

37 Aeschylus, *The Persians*, trans. Robert Potter, http://classics.mit.edu.

38 Flavius Philostratus, *Life of Apollonius*, trans. F. C. Conybeare (Boston, MA, 1912), Book 4, Chapter 16, www.livius.org.

39 Lucian, *Menippus: A Necromantic Experiment*, from *The Works of Lucian of Samosata*, trans. H. W. Fowler and F. G. Fowler (South Australia, 2014).

40 Lucian, *Lucian*, vol. III, trans. A. M. Harmon (London, 1921), p. 341.

41 Horace, *The Book of the Epodes of Horace*, www.authorama.com.

42 Seneca, *Medea*, vv. 670–843, quoted in Luck, *Arcana Mundi*, pp. 86–7.

43 Lucan, *Pharsalia*, quoted in Luck, *Arcana Mundi*, p. 197.

44 Lucan, *Pharsalia*, trans. S. H. Braund, www.u.arizona.edu.

45 Cicero, *The Speech of M. T. Cicero against Publius Vatinius; Called Also, the Examination of Publius Vatinius*, trans. C. D. Yonge, Section VI, http://pages.pomona.edu.

46 Ogden, *Greek and Roman Necromancy*, p. 154.

47 C. Suetonius Tranquillus, *The Lives of the Twelve Caesars* (Boston, MA, 1914), 34.4, http://penelope.uchicago.edu.

48 Dio Cassius, *Roman History*, 52.36.2–4 [1917], http://penelope.uchicago.edu.

49 Plutarch, *Consolatio ad Apollonium* (Boston, MA, 1928), XIV, http://penelope.uchicago.edu.

50 Virgil, *The Eclogues*, VIII, www.gutenberg.org.

51 *Ammianus Marcellinus*, vol. III, trans. John Rolfe (London, 1958), pp. 203–7.

52 Attributed to Bartholinus, as quoted in Thomas Gray, *The Works of Thomas Gray* (London, 1816), vol. I, p. 87.

53 Ibid.

54 *Ynglinga* saga, as quoted in Stephen A. Mitchell, 'Óðinn, Charms and Necromancy: Hávamál 157 in Its Nordic and European Contexts', in *Old Norse Mythology: Comparative Perspectives* (Boston, MA, 2017), p. 292.

55 Saxo Grammaticus, *The Danish History*, trans. Oliver Elton, Book One (2006), www.gutenberg.org.

56 Þorleifs þáttr jarlsskálds, Chapters 5–8, pp. 222–9, as quoted in Mitchell, 'Óðinn, Charms and Necromancy', p. 300.

57 *Grógaldr; or, The Spell of Gróa*, trans. W. H. Auden and P. B. Taylor, *Germanic Mythology*, www.germanicmythology.com.

58 Kirsi Kanerva, 'From Powerful Agents to Subordinate Objects? The Restless Dead in Thirteenth- and Fourteenth-century Iceland', in *Death in Medieval Europe: Death Scripted and Death Choreographed* (New York and Oxford, 2017).

59 'The Adventures of Nera', trans. Kuno Meyer, Celtic Literature Collective, www.ancienttexts.org.

60 John Carey, 'Varia II. The Address to Fergus's Stone', *Ériu*, vol. LI (2000), p. 185.

61 M. Martin, *A Description of the Western Islands of Scotland*, 2nd edn (London, 1716), p. 391.

62 Ibid., p. 110.

63 Ibid., pp. 111–12.

64 Ibid.

65 Ibid., p. 112.

66 Andrew E. M. Wiseman, 'Caterwauling and Demon Raising: The Ancient Rite of the Taghairm?', *Scottish Studies*, 35, doi 10.2218/ss.v35.2694, p. 182.

2 EARLY NECROMANCY

1 St Augustine, *On the Care to Be Taken for the Dead* (*De cura pro mortuis gerenda*), trans. Glen L. Thompson, H. Browne and Catherine T. Rapp, Chapter 16, AD 422, www.fourthcentury.com.

2 Tertullian, *A Treatise on the Soul*, trans. Peter Holmes, LVII, www.tertullian.org.

3 Thomas Aquinas, *Summa Theologiae*, Question 64 ('The Punishment of the Demons'), Objection 2, www.newadvent.org.

4 Justin Martyr, 'The First Apology', Chapter 18, from *Ante-Nicene Fathers*, vol. I, trans. Marcus Dods and George Reith, ed. Alexander

Roberts, James Donaldson and A. Cleveland Coxe (Buffalo, NY, 1885), revised and edited for New Advent by Kevin Knight, www.newadvent.org.

5 Herbert J. Thurston, SJ, and Donald Attwater, *Butler's Lives of the Saints: Complete Edition* (Westminster, MD, 1990), p. 94.

6 *The Sayings of the Desert Fathers, The Alphabetical Collection*: Macarius the Great, 38, https://classicalchristianity.com.

7 Sulpitius Severus, 'On the Life of St Martin', in *A Select Library of Nicene and Post-Nicene Fathers of the Christian Church*, Second Series, vol. XI (New York, 1894), www.holybooks.com.

8 J. O'Beirne Crowe, 'Siabur-Charpat Con Culaind. From "Lebor na h-Uidre" (Fol. 37, Et Seqq.), a Manuscript of the Royal Irish Academy', *Journal of the Royal Historical and Archaeological Association of Ireland*, I, Fourth Series, 1870–71 (Dublin, 1878), pp. 371–2.

9 T. W. Rolleston, *Myths and Legends of the Celtic Race* (London, 1911), p. 239.

10 Babylonian Talmud: Tractate Gittin, Folios 56b and 57a, www.come-and-hear.com.

11 Richard Kieckhefer, *Magic in the Middle Ages* (Cambridge, 2000), p. 156.

12 'The Acts of Peter', in *The Apocryphal New Testament*, trans. M. R. James (Oxford, 1924), Chapters IV–XXXII, www.earlychristianwritings. com.

13 *Clementine Recognitions*, Book II, Chapter XIII, www.ccel.org.

14 Tertullian, 'On the Resurrection of the Flesh', Chapter 22, in *Ante-Nicene Fathers*, vol. II, trans. Peter Holmes, ed. Alexander Roberts, James Donaldson and A. Cleveland Coxe (Buffalo, NY, 1885), revised and edited for New Advent by Kevin Knight, www.newadvent.org.

15 Reginald Scot, *The Discoverie of Witchcraft* (London, 1886), p. 101.

16 Sofia Torallas Tovar and Anastasia Maravel-Solbakk, 'Between Necromancers and Ventriloquists: The ἐγγαστρίμυθοι in the Septuaginta', *Sefarad*, LXI/2 (January 2001), p. 420.

17 E. M. Butler, *Ritual Magic* (Cambridge, 1949), pp. 102–3.

18 Benvenuto Cellini, *The Life of Benvenuto Cellini*, trans. John Addington Symonds (New York, 1930), pp. 176–7.

19 *Acta Sanctorum*, II (Paris and Rome, 1866), pp. 49–50.

20 'The Testament of Solomon', trans. F. C. Conybeare, *Jewish Quarterly Review* (October, 1898), verse 113, p. 40.

21 Butler, *Ritual Magic*, p. 48.

22 S. Liddell Macgregor Mathers, *The Key of Solomon the King* (London, 1889), p. 84.

23 Butler, *Ritual Magic*, p. 43.
24 M. Gaster, *The Sword of Moses: An Ancient Book of Magic* (London, 1896), www.esotericarchives.com.
25 'Necromancy', *The Jewish Encyclopedia* (1901), www.studylight.org.
26 Henry Cornelius Agrippa, *Agrippa's Four Books of Occult Philosophy* (2014), p. 636.
27 Ibid., p. 739.
28 Ibid., p. 537.
29 Ibid., p. 810.
30 Johann Georg Faust, *The Black Raven or also called The Threefold Coercion of Hell*, trans. Karl Hans Welz (Decatur, GA, 1993), www.grimoires.com.
31 Johannes Faust, *Magia Naturalis et Innaturalis*, trans. Nicolás Álvarez Ortiz (2016–17), pp. 216–21.
32 Kieckhofer, *Magic in the Middle Ages*, p. 179.
33 Jean Bodin, *On the Demon-mania of Witches*, trans. Randy A. Scott (Toronto, 1995). p. 104.
34 Ibid., p. 105.
35 Scot, *The Discoverie of Witchcraft*, pp. 344–6.
36 Ibid., p. 26.
37 Robin Briggs, *Witches and Neighbours: The Social and Cultural Context of European Witchcraft* (New York, 1998), p. 8.
38 Matthew Hopkins, *The Discovery of Witches: In Answer to Severall Queries, Lately Delivered to the Judges of Assize for the County of Norfolk* (London, 1647), www.gutenberg.org.
39 'The Trial of Martha Carrier, at the Court of Oyer and Terminer, Held by Adjournment at Salem, August 2, 1692', in Cotton Mather, *The Wonders of the Invisible World* (Boston, MA, 1693), www.hawthorneinsalem.org.
40 Edward Kelly, *The Alchemical Writings of Edward Kelly* (London, 1893), pp. ix–x.
41 John Weever, *Ancient funerall monuments within the vnited monarchie of Great Britaine, Ireland, and the Islands adjacent, with the dissolved Monasteries therein contained* (London, 1631), pp. 45–6.

3 DARKNESS ACROSS THE ENLIGHTENMENT AND THE ROMANTIC GOTHIC

1 Alonso de Salazar Frías, 'Salazar's Second Report to the Suprema, 1611', in *Witchcraft in Europe, 400–1700: A Documentary History*, 2nd edn, ed. Alan Charles Kors and Edward Peters (Philadelphia, PA, 2001), p. 409.

2 Henry Ridgely Evans, 'Cagliostro – A Study in Charlatanism', *The Monist*, XIII/4 (1903), pp. 531–2.

3 Ibid., p. 534.

4 Thomas Carlyle, *Critical and Miscellaneous Essays*, vol. II (London, 1887), p. 481.

5 Arthur Edward Waite, *The Brotherhood of the Rosy Cross: A History of the Rosicrucians* (New York, 1993), pp. 499–500.

6 James Randi, 'Cagliostro, Conte Alessandro', *An Encyclopedia of Claims, Frauds, and Hoaxes of the Occult and Supernatural*, https://web.randi.org, accessed 10 July 2019.

7 'Christaan Huygens: The True Inventor of the Magic Lantern', *de Luikerwaal* (2015), www.luikerwaal.com.

8 Nicolai Karamsin, *Travels from Moscow, through Prussia, Germany, Switzerland, France, and England*, vol. I *(Letters of a Russian Traveler)* (London, 1803), pp. 167–9.

9 N. William Wraxall, *Memoirs of the Courts of Berlin, Dresden, Warsaw, and Vienna, in the Years 1777, 1778, and 1779* (London, 1800), pp. 279–94.

10 X. Theodore Barber, 'Phantasmagorical Wonders: The Magic Lantern Ghost Show in Nineteenth-century America', *Film History*, III/2 (1989), pp. 73–86.

11 Marina Warner, *Phantasmagoria: Spirit Visions, Metaphors, and Media into the Twenty-first Century* (Oxford, 2006), p. 147.

12 Paul de Philipsthal, playbill for show at Lyceum, London, 1802, quoted in Hermann Hecht, 'Some English Magic Lantern Patents', *New Magic Lantern Journal*, II/2 (January 1982), p. 2.

13 Jim Steinmeyer, *Hiding the Elephant: How Magicians Invented the Impossible and Learned to Disappear* (Philadelphia, PA, 2004), p. 32.

14 'Anecdotes of Mr. B—W. Dublin, 1785', *Supernatural Magazine*, I/1 (June 1809), p. 25.

15 Emanuel Swedenborg, *True Christian Religion*, trans. John Whitehead (Loschberg, 2018), p. 283.

16 Letter of Dr John Grieve as quoted in *The Life and Letters of Joseph Black MD*, ed. Sir William Ramsay (London, 1918), pp. 84–5.

17 Letter by A.-J.-M. Servan to M.-A. Julien, 17 August 1781, quoted in Robert Darnton, *Mesmerism and the End of the Enlightenment in France* (New York, 1970), p. 60.

18 Arthur Schopenhauer, 'Animal Magnetism and Magic', in *On the Fourfold Root of the Principle of Sufficient Reason and On the Will in Nature: Two Essays by Arthur Schopenhauer*, trans. Madame Karl Hillebrand, revised edition (London, 1903), p. 342.

19 Henry Cornelius Agrippa, *Agrippa's Four Books of Occult Philosophy* (2014), p. 136.

20 Darnton, *Mesmerism and the End of the Enlightenment in France*, p. 58.

21 Quoted ibid., pp. 65–6.

22 George Bush, *Mesmer and Swedenborg; or, The relation of the developments of mesmerism to the doctrines and disclosures of Swedenborg*, Appendix C, 'Letter to the "Societie des Amis Reunis," at Strasburg' (New York, 1847), p. 266.

23 'Animal Magnetism: Its History – Theory – and Phenomena No. 11', *Cheltenham Looker-on*, Third Series, No. CLXXV (7 May 1842), p. 14.

24 'Animal Magnetism', *Supernatural Magazine*, 1/1 (June 1809), pp. 7–9.

25 'Animal Magnetism', *Bath Chronicle and Weekly Gazette*, LX/2909 (27 November 1817), p. 2.

26 Wirth, 'Animal Magnetism', quoted in *John O'Groat Journal* (8 June 1838), p. 4.

27 'Oneiromancie Artistique', *Morning Post* (24 April 1847), p. 6.

28 Percy Bysshe Shelley, 'The Magnetic Lady to Her Patient' (1832), www.infoplease.com.

29 P. Stanbury, 'Reflections of Mesmerism in Literature,' *Anaesthesia and Intensive Care*, 40/1 (suppl) (July 2012), p. 14.

30 Edgar Allan Poe, 'The Facts in the Case of M. Valdemar' (1845), https://poestories.com.

31 Justinus Kerner, *The Seeress of Prevorst Being Revelations Concerning the Inner-life of Man, and the Inter-diffusion of a World of Spirits in the One We Inhabit*, trans. Mrs Crowe (London, 1845), p. 73.

32 Ibid., p. 77.

33 Ibid., p. 201.

34 C. G. Jung, 'On the Psychology and Pathology of So-called Occult Phenomena', in *Psychology and the Occult*, trans. R.F.C. Hull (Princeton, NJ, 1977), pp. 30–40.

35 Andrew Jackson Davis, *The Principles of Nature, Her Divine Revelations, and a Voice to Mankind* (New York, 1847), p. 33.

36 Ibid., p. 42.

37 Andrew Jackson Davis, *The Fountain with Jets of New Meaning* (Boston, MA, 1870), p. 209.

38 Lord Warburton, 'Episodes of Eastern Travel', Chapter VI: 'Magic – Masonry – Magnetism', *Dublin University Magazine*, XXIII/130 (October 1843), p. 433.

39 Ibid.

40 Ibid., p. 434.

41 Kerner, *Seeress of Prevorst*, p. 24.

42 Catherine Crowe, *The Night-side of Nature; or, Ghosts and Ghost-seers* (London, 1848), vol. II, p. 378.

43 John Nevil Maskelyne, *Modern Spiritualism: A Short Account of Its Rise and Progress, with Some Exposures of So-called Spirit Media* (London, 1876), p. 3.

44 'Cruel Rumours about an Authoress', *London Daily News* (29 April 1854), p. 2.

45 Crowe, *The Night-side of Nature*, vol. I, p. 4.

4 THE VICTORIANS AND SPIRITUALISM; OR, THE SEANCE IS BORN

1 David S. Landes, *The Unbound Prometheus: Technological Change and Industrial Development in Western Europe from 1750 to the Present* (Cambridge, 1988), p. 4.

2 Janet Oppenheim, *The Other World: Spiritualism and Psychical Research in England, 1850–1914* (Cambridge, 1985), p. 267.

3 C. G. Jung, 'On Spiritualistic Phenomena', in *Psychology and the Occult*, trans. R.F.C. Hull (Princeton, NJ, 1977), p. 93.

4 Emma Hardinge, *Modern American Spiritualism: A Twenty Years' Record of the Communion between Earth and the World of Spirits* (New York, 1870), p. 547.

5 E. E. Lewis, *A Report of the Mysterious Noises, Heard in the House of Mr. John D. Fox, in Hydesville, Arcadia, Wayne County, Authenticated by the Certificates, and Confirmed by the Statements of the Citizens of That Place and Vicinity* (Rochester, NY, 1848), p. 9.

6 Ibid., p. 19.

7 Ibid., p. 33.

8 A. Leah Underhill, *The Missing Link in Modern Spiritualism* (New York, 1885), www.gutenberg.org.

9 Reuben Briggs Davenport, *The Death-blow to Spiritualism: Being the True Story of the Fox Sisters, as Revealed by Authority of Margaret Fox Kane and Catherine Fox Jencken* (New York, 1888), p. 118.

10 Barbara Weisberg, *Talking to the Dead: Kate and Maggie Fox and the Rise of Spiritualism* (New York, 2008), e-book.

11 See letter from George Willets in Underhill, *The Missing Link in Modern Spiritualism*, p. 105.

12 Eliab W. Capron and Henry D. Barron, *Singular Revelations: Explanation and History of the Mysterious Communion with Spirits, Comprehending the Rise and Progress of the Mysterious Noises in Western New-York, Generally Received as Spirit Communications*, 2nd edn (Auburn, NY, 1850), p. 70.

13 Ibid., p. 7.

14 Quoted in Weisberg, *Talking to the Dead: Kate and Maggie Fox and the Rise of Spiritualism*, p. 94.

15 Quoted in James Parton, *The Life of Horace Greeley* (Boston, MA, 1889), pp. 287–8.

16 F. W. Evans, *Compendium of the Origin, History, Principles, Rules and Regulations, Government, and Doctrines of the United Society of Believers in Christ's Second Appearing* (New York, 1859), www.passtheword.org.

17 'Shakers, Spiritualism, and Seances: Part II', Shaker Heritage Society of Albany New York, http://home.shakerheritage.org, accessed 27 August 2019.

18 'The Spiritual Telegraph, No. 1 Is Issued This Morning', *New-York Daily Tribune* (8 May 1852), p. 9.

19 Ibid.

20 S. B. Brittan, 'Address to the Reader', *Spiritual Telegraph* (8 May 1852), p. 2.

21 Augustus H. Strong, *Reminiscences of Early Rochester* (Rochester, NY, 1916), p. 5.

22 William Lloyd Garrison, 'Modern Phenomena', *The Liberator* (3 March 1854), later reprinted by the American Liberal Tract Society (Boston, MA), pp. 2–4.

23 'The Ghost of the Cock Lane Ghost', *Household Words* (20 November 1852), p. 220.

24 Letter of W. R. Hayden, 4 February 1853, as printed in 'Mrs. Hayden's Visit to England 1852–3 and the Conversion of Robert Owen', *Psypioneer*, II/10 (October 2006), p. 214.

25 Ibid., p. 221.

26 Joseph Mathews, 'Hymn for a Circle', *Spiritual Telegraph*, II/7 (18 June 1853), p. 27.

27 Emma Hardinge Britten, *Nineteenth Century Miracles; or, Spirits and Their Work in Every Country of the Earth* (New York, 1884), p. 137.

28 Letter of T. Clapp dated 19 July 1852, from *Columbus Enquirer* (24 August 1852), p. 3.

29 E. W. Capron, *Modern Spiritualism: Its Facts and Fanaticisms, Its Consistencies and Contradictions* (Boston, MA, 1855), pp. 117–19.

30 Michael Faraday, 'On Table-turning', in *Experimental Researches in Chemistry and Physics* (London, 1859), p. 382.

31 Michael Faraday, 'Experimental Investigation of Table-moving', in *Experimental Researches in Chemistry and Physics*, p. 391.

32 Cromwell Fleetwood Varley, 'Phenomena I Have Seen', in *Psychic Facts: A Selection from the Writings of Various Authors on Psychical Phenomena* (London, 1880), pp. 37–9.

33 'Petitioning Congress: 1854 Memorial of the Spirit Rappers',
   http://iapsop.com, accessed 2 September 2019.
34 *Fourth Annual Spiritual Register* (1860), http://iapsop.com.
35 Hardinge, *Modern American Spiritualism*, pp. 491–2.
36 Ibid., p. 494.
37 Ibid., p. 498.
38 Ibid., p. 507.
39 Ibid., p. 560.
40 Orrin Abbott, *The Davenport Brothers: Their History, Travels, and
   Manifestations. Also, the Philosophy of Dark Circles, Ancient and Modern*
   (New York, 1864), p. 27.
41 Ibid., p. 40.
42 John Mulholland, *Beware Familiar Spirits* (New York, 1938), p. 77.
43 Harry Houdini, *A Magician among the Spirits* (New York and London,
   1924), p. 25.
44 'The Feud over Fraud: The Davenport Brothers Vs. Maskelyne' (2017),
   www.geniionline.com.
45 Joe Nickell, *Real Life X-Files: Investigating the Paranormal* (Lexington,
   KY, 2001), p. 23.
46 Houdini, *A Magician among the Spirits*, p. 38.
47 D. D. Home, *Incidents in My Life*, 6th edn (New York, 1874), p. 17.
48 S. B. Brittan, as quoted in Mme. Dunglas Home, *D. D. Home: His Life
   and Mission* (London, 1888), pp. 9–10.
49 Mulholland, *Beware Familiar Spirits*, pp. 84–5.
50 'A Spirit-Rapper at the Tuileries', *Burnley Advertiser* (21 March 1857),
   p. 4.
51 Ruth Brandon, *The Spiritualists: The Passion for the Occult in the
   Nineteenth and Twentieth Centuries* (New York, 1983), p. 67.
52 Stuart Cumberland, *That Other World: Personal Experiences of Mystics
   and Their Mysticism* (London, 1918), pp. 23–4.
53 'Mr. Home's Levitations', *Stroud News and Gloucestershire Advertiser*
   (28 July 1871), p. 2.
54 Mme. Dunglas Home, *The Gift of D. D. Home* (London, 1890),
   p. 231.
55 Home, *D. D. Home: His Life and Mission*, pp. 252–64.
56 D. D. Home, *Lights and Shadows of Spiritualism*, 2nd edn
   (London, 1878), p. 284.
57 Sir David Brewster, letter reprinted in *Dublin Evening Mail*
   (5 October 1855), p. 4.
58 'Sir David Brewster and the Spirit-rappers', *The Witness*, XVI/1700
   (20 October 1855), p. 2.

59 John Nevil Maskelyne, *Modern Spiritualism: A Short Account of Its Rise and Progress, with Some Exposures of So-called Spirit Media* (London, 1876), p. 44.

60 Houdini, *A Magician among the Spirits*, p. 57.

61 As quoted in Count Perovsky-Petrovo-Solovovo, 'Some Thoughts on D. D. Home', *Proceedings of the Society for Psychical Research*, XXXIX/114 (March 1930), p. 248.

62 Ibid., p. 251.

63 Nathaniel Hawthorne, *Passages from the French and Italian Note-books of Nathaniel Hawthorne* (Boston, MA, and New York, 1913), p. 296.

64 Robert Browning, *Dramatis Personæ*, 2nd edn (London, 1864), p. 171.

65 Ibid., p. 191.

66 Frank Podmore, *Modern Spiritualism: A History and a Criticism* (London, 1902), vol. II, p. 240.

67 William Crookes, 'Experimental Investigation of a New Force', *Quarterly Journal of Science* (1 January 1871), www.survivalafterdeath.info.

68 Ibid.

69 From 'Tom Waits Meets Jim Jarmusch', *Straight No Chaser* (1992), excerpted in *Tom Waits on Tom Waits: Interviews and Encounters*, ed. Paul Maher Jr (Chicago, IL, 2011), p. 235.

70 William Crookes, *Quarterly Journal of Science* (October 1871), as quoted at www.survivalafterdeath.info.

71 Quoted in Trevor H. Hall, *The Spiritualists: The Story of Florence Cook and William Crookes* (New York, 1963), p. xvi.

72 'Miss Florence Cook's Mediumship', *The Spiritualist*, No. 33/II-5 (15 May 1872), p. 36.

73 Ibid.

74 'An Exposure of Imposture', *The Spiritualist*, No. 317/XIII-12 (20 September 1878), p. 133.

75 Roger Luckhurst, *The Invention of Telepathy, 1870–1901* (Oxford, 2002), p. 155.

76 'Miss Florence Cook's Mediumship', p. 36.

77 Ibid.

78 'The Systematic Appearance of Spirits', *The Spiritualist*, No. 37/II-9 (15 September 1872), p. 69.

79 'Spirit Forms and Faces', *The Spiritualist*, No. 48/III-9 (15 March 1873), p. 133.

80 British Association of Progressive Spiritualists, collection of papers (1874), p. 22.

81 Christopher Sandford, *Houdini and Conan Doyle* (London and New York, 2011), p. 128.

82 William Crookes, *Researches in the Phenomena of Spiritualism* (London, 1874), p. 111.

83 William Crookes, 'The Last of "Katie King": The Photographing of "Katie King" by the Aid of the Electric Light', *The Spiritualist*, No. 93/iv-23 (5 June 1874), p. 274.

84 Trevor H. Hall, *The Spiritualists*, pp. 99–102.

85 D. D. Home, *Lights and Shadows of Spiritualism*, p. 326.

86 Ibid.

87 'Mr. Serjeant Cox on Materialisations and the Mediumship of Miss Showers', *The Spiritualist*, No. 90/iv-20 (15 May 1874), p. 230.

88 William Crookes, 'President's Address', *Proceedings of the Society for Psychical Research*, vol. xii (1896–7), p. 352.

89 Tom Dardis, *Some Time in the Sun* (New York, 1976), p. 214.

90 Oppenheim, *The Other World: Spiritualism and Psychical Research in England, 1850–1914*, p. 109.

91 John Tyndall, *Fragments of Science for Unscientific People: A Series of Detached Essays, Lectures, and Reviews* (London, 1871), p. 435.

92 John Tyndall, *Fragments of Science for Unscientific People: A Series of Detached Essays, Lectures, and Reviews*, 6th edn (London, 1879), vol. 1, p. 504.

93 *Report on Spiritualism, of the Committee of the London Dialectical Society, Together with the Evidence, Oral and Written, and a Selection from the Correspondence* (London, 1871), pp. 2–5.

94 Benjamin Coleman, 'Miss Catherine Fox', *Spiritual Magazine* (November 1871), p. 525.

95 'Miss Kate Fox's Mediumship', *The Spiritualist*, 1/28 (15 December 1871), p. 1.

96 Richard F. Burton, *A Glance at the Passion-play* (London, 1881), pp. 164–8.

97 Robert Dale Owen, 'The Life to Come', originally printed in *Atlantic Monthly*, reprinted in *The Spiritualist at Work*, 1/8 (21 November 1874), p. 88.

98 Robert Dale Owen, *Footfalls on the Boundary of Another World* (London, 1860), p. 20.

99 'A Painful Surprise', *Light*, xxvii/1373 (4 May 1907), p. 210.

100 'How to Form a Spirit Circle', *Spiritual Scientist*, ii/24 (19 August 1875), p. 288.

101 'Materialization', *Spiritual Scientist*, iv/2 (16 March 1876), p. 18.

102 Houdini, *A Magician among the Spirits*, p. 218.

103 William H. Harrison, 'The Systematic Appearance of Spirits in London', *The Spiritualist*, No. 33/ii-5 (15 May 1872), p. 33.

104 'Marvellous Spirit Manifestations', *The Spiritualist*, I/22 (15 June 1871), p. 169.

105 Moncure Daniel Conway, *Autobiography: Memories and Experiences of Moncure Daniel Conway* (Boston, MA, and New York, 1904), vol. II, pp. 343–4.

106 Houdini, *A Magician among the Spirits*, pp. 217–23.

107 Mulholland, *Beware Familiar Spirits*, pp. 231–40.

108 Hiraf, 'Rosicrucianism', *Spiritual Scientist*, II/17 (1 July 1875), p. 199.

109 Charles R. Flint, *Memories of an Active Life: Men, and Ships, and Sealing Wax* (New York and London, 1923), pp. 118–32.

110 'Spiritualism in Massachusetts', *Cambridge Chronicle and Journal* (18 April 1857), p. 3.

111 George Cruikshank, *A Discovery concerning Ghosts: With a Rap at the 'Spirit Rappers'*, 2nd edn (London, 1864).

112 'Old Ghosts and New', *Punch*, LXII (6 January 1872), p. 2.

113 Lionel A. Weatherly and J. N. Maskelyne, *The Supernatural?* (Bristol and London, 1891), p. 183.

114 'Messrs. Maskelyne and Cooke's Performance', letter 26 June 1873 by Algernon Joy to *The Spiritualist*, No. 55/III-16 (1 July 1873), p. 253.

115 'Trial of Dr. Slade, Evidence of Mr. Maskelyne, the Conjuror', *Ossett Observer* (14 October 1876), p. 3.

116 'The Case of Dr. Monck, Spiritualist', *South Wales Daily News* (27 January 1877), p. 7.

117 'Archdeacon Colley and Mr. Maskelyne', *Light*, XXVII/1373 (4 May 1907), p. 208.

118 'Manifestations in the Far East', *Spiritualist Newspaper*, No. 463/XIX-2 (8 July 1881), p. 2.

119 'Marvellous Spirit Manifestations', p. 170.

120 'Séance', The London Dungeons, www.thedungeons.com, accessed 2 October 2019.

121 Advertisement in *The Spiritualist*, No. 166/VII-18 (29 October 1875), p. ii.

122 'Imperator', 'Spirit Teachings. No. XXVIII', *The Spiritualist*, No. 132/VI-10 (5 March 1875), p. 1.

123 'The Late "M. A. (Oxon.)": Spiritualist', *Pall Mall Gazette* (12 September 1892), p. 7.

124 J. Simmons, 'Further Experiments with Dr. Slade in Russia', *The Spiritualist*, No. 295/XII-16 (19 April 1878), p. 186.

125 'Prosecution of Dr. Slade', *The Scotsman* (3 October 1876), p. 6.

126 'Anent Mrs. Carpenter, of Boston', *The Spiritualist*, No. 166/VII-18 (29 October 1875), pp. 206–7.

127 'Angels Daguerreotyped', *Spiritual Telegraph and Fireside Preacher*, No. 380/VIII-16 (13 August 1859), p. 190.

128 'Angels Daguerreotyped', *Spiritual Telegraph and Fireside Preacher*, No. 393/VIII-29 (12 November 1859), p. 343.

129 William Mumler, quoted in Peter Manseau, *The Apparitionists: A Tale of Phantoms, Fraud, Photography, and the Man Who Captured Lincoln's Ghost* (Boston, MA, and New York, 2017), p. 203.

130 'The Mumler Swindle', *Illustrated Photographer* (11 June 1869), p. 276.

131 British Association of Progressive Spiritualists, collection of papers (1874), p. 23.

132 Ibid., p. 24.

133 'Spirit Photography on Trial', Graphic Arts Collection, Special Collections, Firestone Library, Princeton University (2017), https://graphicarts.princeton.edu, accessed 12 August 2019.

134 Mulholland, *Beware Familiar Spirits*, p. 150.

135 'The Case of M. Leymarie', *Spiritual Scientist*, II/24 (19 August 1875), p. 286.

136 Florence Marryat, 'A Midsummer's Nightmare; or, The Amateur Detective', *The Ghost of Charlotte Cray and Other Stories* (Leipzig, 1883), p. 265.

137 Marina Warner, *Phantasmagoria: Spirit Visions, Metaphors, and Media into the Twenty-first Century* (Oxford, 2006), p. 281.

138 Edward A. Pace, 'Spiritism', *The Catholic Encyclopedia* (New York, 1912), vol. XIV, p. 224.

139 Ibid., p. 221.

140 Ibid.

141 Owen Davies, *A Supernatural War: Magic, Divination, and Faith during the First World War* (Oxford, 2018), p. 77.

142 As quoted in Manseau, *The Apparitionists: A Tale of Phantoms, Fraud, Photography, and the Man Who Captured Lincoln's Ghost*, p. 40.

143 J. Godfrey Raupert, *The Dangers of Spiritualism: Being Records of Personal Experiences with Notes and Comments and Five Illustrations*, 2nd edn (London, 1907), pp. 7–10.

144 Archbishop of Canterbury, from a letter quoted in *Borderland*, I/1 (July 1893), p. 10.

145 Bishop of Durham, letter quoted in *Light*, XIII/654 (22 July 1893), p. 337.

146 Ibid.

147 Ibid.

148 William Stainton Moses, *Spirit Teachings*, 6th edn (London, 1907), p. 9.

149 Oppenheim, *The Other World*, p. 240.

150 *The Spiritualist*, vi/i (1 January 1875), p. ii.

151 William L. Courtney, 'The New Psychology', *Fortnightly Review*, vol. xxvi, New Series (London, 1879), p. 372.

152 Gordon Pennycook, James Allan Cheyne et al., 'On the Reception and Detection of Pseudo-profound Bullshit', *Judgment and Decision Making*, x/6 (2015), pp. 549–63.

153 John Nevil Maskelyne, *The Fraud of Modern 'Theosophy' Exposed* (London, 1912), p. 5.

154 Ibid., p. 32.

155 Letter to W. H. Burr dated 19 November 1877, in W. H. Burr, *Madame Blavatsky* (London, 1893), pp. 5–6.

156 H. P. Blavatsky, *The Key to Theosophy, Being a Clear Exposition, in the Form of Question and Answer, of the Ethics, Science, and Philosophy for the Study of Which the Theosophical Society Has Been Founded* (Pasadena, CA, 1972), reprinted from 1889 edn, p. 194.

157 'The Alleged Himalayan Brothers', *Spiritualist Newspaper*, No. 462/xix-i (1 July 1881), p. 1.

158 J. Malcolm Bird, *My Psychic Adventures* (New York, 1924), p. 26.

159 H. Carvill Lewis et al., 'Accounts of Some So-Called "Spiritualistic" Seances', *Proceedings of the General Meeting of the Society for Psychical Research* (23 April 1887), p. 350.

160 William James, 'Review of Report on the Census of Hallucinations', *Psychological Review*, ii/i (1895), pp. 69–75, http://dx.doi.org.

161 Hereward Carrington, *Eusapia Palladino and Her Phenomena* (New York, 1909), p. 183.

162 William F. Barrett, 'A Note on Direct Voice Phenomena', *Light*, xxxiv/1765 (7 November 1914), p. 530.

163 *Spiritualism Shown as It Is!: Boston Courier Report of the Proceedings of Professed Spiritual Agents and Mediums, in the Presence of Professors Peirce, Agassiz, Horsford, Dr. B. A. Gould, Committee, and Others, at the Albion Building, Boston, on the 25th, 26th, and 27th of June, 1857*, 2nd edn (Boston, MA: *Boston Courier*, 1859), p. 2.

164 Ibid., p. 10.

165 Ibid., p. 24.

166 'One of the Fox Sisters Arrested', *New York Times* (5 May 1888), p. 5.

167 As quoted in Davenport, *The Death-blow to Spiritualism: Being the True Story of the Fox Sisters, as Revealed by Authority of Margaret Fox Kane and Catherine Fox Jencken*, p. 56.

168 Margaret Fox Kane, 'The Curse of Spiritualism', *New York Herald* (14 May 1888), as quoted in Davenport, *The Death-blow to Spiritualism*, pp. 30–31.

169 As quoted ibid., p. 42.

170 Ibid., p. 33.

171 Ibid., p. 57.

172 Ibid., p. 58.

173 Ibid., p. 51.

174 H. H. Furness, Jr, *Preliminary Report of the Commission Appointed by the University of Pennsylvania to Investigate Modern Spiritualism in Accordance with the Request of the Late Henry Seybert* (Philadelphia, PA, and London, 1920), p. 5.

175 Ibid., p. 8.

176 Ibid., p. 12.

177 Ibid., p. 26.

178 Edmund Richardson, 'Nothing's Lost Forever', *Arion: A Journal of Humanities and the Classics*, www.bu.edu, accessed 14 September 2019.

179 'A Discovery or a Delusion', *Brooklyn Daily Eagle* (29 March 1888), p. 2.

180 'All Perjurers Except the Saintly Princess of Spookdom', *Brooklyn Daily Eagle* (13 June 1888), p. 6.

5 WARS AND OUIJA: SPIRITUALISM IN THE TWENTIETH CENTURY

1 Max Weber, 'The Disenchantment of Modern Life', in *Max Weber: Essays in Sociology*, trans. and ed. H. H. Gerth and C. Wright Mills (New York, 1946), pp. 129–56.

2 Edvard Radzinsky, *The Last Tsar: The Life and Death of Nicolas II* (New York, 1993), p. 64.

3 William James, 'Review of Human Personality and Its Survival of Bodily Death by F.W.H. Myers', *Proceedings of the Society for Psychical Research*, 18 (1903), p. 23.

4 G. Stanley Hall, 'A Medium in the Bud', *American Journal of Psychology*, XXIX (April 1918), p. 156.

5 Harry Price, *Leaves from a Psychist's Case Book* (London, 1933), p. 200.

6 'Links Alchemists with Spiritualism: S. F. Damon, Named by Doyle, Says Ectoplasm May Have Been "First Matter"', *New York Times* (14 April 1922), p. 14.

7 'Doyle Reaffirms Ectoplasm Belief', *New York Times* (1 October 1922), p. 46.

8 Harry Houdini, *A Magician among the Spirits* (New York and London, 1924), p. 169.

9 Baron von Schrenck-Notzing, *Phenomena of Materialisation: A Contribution to the Investigation of Mediumistic Teleplastics* (London, 1923), p. 30.

10 Mark W. Richardson, E. E. Dudley and L.R.G. Crandon, 'The Margery Mediumship', *Quarterly Transactions of the British College of Psychic Science*, VII/2 (July 1928), p. 101.

11 Letter from Eric J. Dingwall to Baron Schrenck-Notzing, quoted in Richardson, Dudley and Crandon, 'The Margery Mediumship', p. 97.

12 Letter from Grant Code quoted in Mary Roach, *Spook: Science Tackles the Afterlife* (New York, 2005), p. 137.

13 Dan Burton and David Grandy, *Magic, Mystery, and Science: The Occult in Western Civilization* (Bloomington and Indianapolis, IN, 2004), p. 206.

14 Marina Warner, *Phantasmagoria: Spirit Visions, Metaphors, and Media into the Twenty-first Century* (Oxford, 2006), p. 300.

15 'Our Soldiers in the World Beyond: Notes on the Address Delivered by Dr. Ellis T. Powell at York on October 27th, 1918', *Light*, XXXVIII/1977 (30 November 1918), p. 379.

16 J. Carleton Bell, 'War and Credulity (Editorial)', *Journal of Educational Psychology*, IX/5 (May 1918), pp. 299–300.

17 'The Uncanny Under Fire', *The Globe* (13 October 1914), p. 2.

18 Hereward Carrington, *Psychical Phenomena and the War* (New York, 1919), p. 250.

19 Ibid., pp. 251–2.

20 Ibid., p. 237.

21 Ibid., p. 239.

22 Ibid., p. 248.

23 Ibid., p. 296.

24 Ibid., pp. 302–6.

25 'Ministering Spirits on the Battlefield: Address by Mrs. M. H. Wallis', *Light*, XXXIV/1, 765 (7 November 1914), p. 536.

26 'Sir A. Conan Doyle', *Sheffield Daily Telegraph* (9 April 1926), p. 2.

27 Advertisement from *Light*, XXXVI/1869 (4 November 1916), p. ii.

28 Sir Oliver Lodge, *Raymond or Life and Death* (New York, 1916), p. 98.

29 Sir Arthur Conan Doyle and Joseph McCabe, *A Debate on Spiritualism between Sir Arthur Conan Doyle and Joseph McCabe* (Girard, KS, 1919), pp. 22–3.

30 Sir Arthur Conan Doyle, 'A New Revelation: Spiritualism and Religion', *Light*, XXXVI/1869 (4 November 1916), p. 357.

31 As quoted in Christopher Sandford, *Houdini and Conan Doyle* (London and New York, 2011), p. 104.

32 As quoted ibid., p. 100.

33 Houdini, *A Magician among the Spirits*, p. 152.

34 Ibid., p. 137.

35 Houdini, 'Spirit Compacts Unfulfilled', *New York Sun* (30 October 1922), p. 18.

36 'Independent Voice Development with Mrs. Osborne Leonard', *Light*, LXVII/3321 (January 1947), p. 17.

37 C. D. Broad, *Lectures on Psychical Research: Incorporating the Perrott Lectures Given in Cambridge University in 1959 and 1960* (London, 1962), p. 253.

38 Ibid., p. 254.

39 J. Malcolm Bird, *My Psychic Adventures* (New York, 1924), pp. 136–7.

40 Ibid., pp. 162–92.

41 Claude F. Jacobs and Andrew J. Kaslow, *The Spiritual Churches of New Orleans: Origins, Beliefs, and Rituals of an African-American Religion* (Knoxville, TN, 1991), p. 34.

42 Zora Hurston, 'Hoodoo in America', *Journal of American Folklore*, XLIV/174 (October–December 1931), p. 319.

43 Jacobs and Kaslow, *The Spiritual Churches of New Orleans: Origins, Beliefs, and Rituals of an African-American Religion*, p. 73.

44 'The Cult of Black Hawk', *Chicago Tribune* (6 December 1998), www.chicagotribune.com.

45 Laine Kaplan-Levenson, 'Mother Catherine Seals and The Temple of the Innocent Blood', *New Orleans Public Radio* (1 December 2016), www.wwno.org.

46 U.S. Patent Office, No. 446054 (10 February 1891), https://pdfpiw. uspto.gov.

47 Museum of Talking Boards blog (21 December 2016), www.museumoftalkingboards.com.

48 Kate Field, ed., *Planchette's Diary* (New York, 1868), p. 7.

49 C. G. Jung, 'On the Psychology and Pathology of So-called Occult Phenomena', in *Psychology and the Occult* (Princeton, NJ, 1977), p. 28.

50 E. W. and M. H. Wallis, *A Guide to Mediumship, and Psychical Unfoldment* (London, 1898), p. 183.

51 Gioia Diliberto, 'Patience Worth: Author from the Great Beyond', *Smithsonian Magazine* (September 2010), www.smithsonianmag.com.

52 'Darby and Joan', *Our Unseen Guest* (Los Angeles, CA, 1947), p. 14.

53 Ibid., p. 68.

54 Merikay Waldvogel, Rosalind Webster Perry and Marian Ann J. Montgomery, PhD, *The Quilters Hall of Fame: 42 Masters Who Have Shaped Our Art* (Minneapolis, MN, 2011), pp. 79–81.

55 Takahiro Shitara, Vibol Yem and Hiroyuki Kajimoto, 'Reconsideration of Ouija Board Motion in Terms of Haptic Illusions (IV): Effect of Haptic Cue and Another Player', *Proceedings*

of siggraph *'19* – Posters (2019).

56 J. Godfrey Raupert, *The New Black Magic and the Truth about the Ouija Board* (New York, 1919), pp. 60–61.

57 Ibid., pp. 5, 82.

58 Ibid., pp. 224–5.

59 Bernard Vaughan, foreword to Elliot O'Donnell, *The Menace of Spiritualism* (New York, 1920), p. xi.

60 Ibid., p. 90.

61 Ibid., p. 121.

62 Ibid., p. 89.

63 Ibid., p. 90.

64 J. Edward Cornelius, *Aleister Crowley and the Ouija Board* (Los Angeles, ca, 2005), p. 97.

65 Ibid., p. ii.

66 'The "Spiritualist" Case', *Gloucester Citizen* (24 July 1928), p. 6.

67 'Blows at a Séance', *Nottingham Evening Post* (19 June 1928), p. 7.

68 'Spiritualistic Influence', *Sunderland Daily Echo and Shipping Gazette* (16 June 1931), p. 1.

69 'Police Attend Séance', *Aberdeen Press and Journal* (2 July 1940), p. 4.

70 'Attended Séance: Solicitor Is Now "Convinced"', *Nottingham Evening Post* (3 November 1942), p. 4.

71 Raymond Buckland, *The Spirit Book: The Encyclopedia of Clairvoyance, Channeling, and Spirit Communication* (Detroit, mi, 2005), p. 360.

72 Peter Underwood, *Into the Occult* (London, 1972), p. 126.

73 Harry Price, 'Brilliant Phenomena in the Home of the Schneiders', *British Journal of Psychical Research*, i/2 (July–August 1926), p. 54.

74 'Says He Heard Row between Ghost and Medium', *Daily Mirror* (24 March 1944), quoted in Nina Shandler, *The Strange Case of Hellish Nell: The Story of Helen Duncan and the Witch Trial of World War ii* (Cambridge, 2006), p. 46.

75 Price, *Leaves from a Psychist's Case Book*, p. 203.

76 Ibid., pp. 209–10.

77 Ibid., p. 35.

78 Court transcript as quoted in Shandler, *Strange Case of Hellish Nell*, p. 107.

79 '"Spirit" Freed Medium from Police Handcuffs', *Newcastle Journal* (30 March 1944), p. 4.

80 Letter of 3 April 1944, Winston Churchill to Home Secretary, as quoted in Shandler, *Strange Case of Hellish Nell*, p. 3.

81 'Fraudulent Mediums Act 1951', www.legislation.gov.uk, accessed 20 July 2019.

82 'Against Fraudulent Mediums', *The Scotsman* (2 December 1950), p. 7.

83 'Medium Faces "Fraudulent Device" Charge', *Belfast Telegraph* (7 February 1952), p. 6.

84 Derek Lambert, '"I Am Not Satisfied," Says Husband of Woman Whose Death Was Foretold by a Wineglass', *Daily Mirror* (23 July 1956), pp. 1 and 20.

85 Ibid.

86 Suzanne Riordan, 'Channeling: A New Revelation?', in *Perspectives on the New Age*, ed. James R. Lewis and J. Gordon Melton (Albany, NY, 1992), p. 125.

87 Seth Learning Center, Testimonials (2005), www.sethlearningcenter. org, accessed 4 October 2019.

88 'Who is Seth?', www.sethlearningcenter.org, accessed 4 October 2019.

89 Ramtha's School of Enlightenment, www.ramtha.com, accessed 4 October 2019.

90 Peter Hoffer and Hugh Davies, 'Copyright in Ghost Case Passes to the Other Side', *Daily Telegraph* (2 March 1995), p. 1; Andrew Kollar, 'Coverdale Avoids Debt with Bankruptcy in JZ Lawsuit', *Nisqually Valley News* (21 December 2017), www.yelmonline.com.

91 Graham Reed, 'The Psychology of Channeling', *Skeptical Inquirer*, XIII/4 (Summer 1989), p. 390.

92 Tom Driberg, *Swaff: The Life and Times of Hannen Swaffer* (London, 1974), p. 210.

93 Sinister Pointe, www.haunting.net, accessed 10 October 2019.

94 Lyn Gardner, '*Blithe Spirit* and Theatre as Séance: the Lasting Appeal of Spiritualism on Stage', *The Guardian* (4 March 2014), www.theguardian.com.

95 Henry W. Simon, *100 Great Operas and Their Stories* (New York, 1989), p. 322.

96 Gina Covina, *The Ouija Book* (New York, 1979), p. 18.

6 HOW UNIVERSAL IS THE SEANCE?

1 'Akawaio' (3 October 2019), www.encyclopedia.com.

2 Christopher Heaney, 'The Fascinating Afterlife of Peru's Mummies', *Smithsonian Journeys Quarterly* (28 August 2015), www.smithsonianmag.com.

3 Kevin Lo, 'Black Magic Baby: The Macabre History of *Kuman Thong*', *Atlas Obscura* (27 February 2014), www.atlasobscura.com.

4 Chao Wei-pang, 'The Origin and Growth of the Fu Chi', https://nirc.nanzan-u.ac.jp/nfile/1048, accessed 20 October 2019.

5 Philip Clart, 'Moral Mediums: Spirit-writing and the Cultural

Construction of Chinese Spirit-mediumship', *Negotiating Transcendence*, xxv/1 (2003), p. 171.

6 Claudine Michel, 'Vodou in Haiti: Way of Life and Mode of Survival', *Journal of Haitian Studies*, viii/1 (2002), p. 101.

7 Kim Wall and Caterina Clerici, 'Vodou Is Elusive and Endangered, but It Remains the Soul of Haitian People', *The Guardian* (7 November 2015), www.theguardian.com.

8 Kathy Weiser, 'Kachinas of the Puebloans', *Legends of America* (November 2019), www.legendsofamerica.com.

9 Patrick Polk, 'Black Folks at Home in the Spirit World', in *Activating the Past: Historical Memory in the Black Atlantic World*, ed. Andrew Apter and Lauren R. Derby (Cambridge, 2010), p. 372.

7 THE MODERN SEANCE

1 Jamie Ballard, '45% of Americans Believe That Ghosts and Demons Exist', YouGov (21 October 2019), https://today.yougov.com.

2 'James Van Praagh', Celebs Trending Now (11 September 2019), https://celebstrendingnow.com.

3 'John Edward', Celebs Trending Now (29 August 2019), https://celebstrendingnow.com.

4 'Zak Bagans', Celebs Trending Now (19 September 2019), https://celebstrendingnow.com.

5 'Yvette Fielding Networth', NetworthBuzz (9 June 2019), https://networthbuzz.com.

6 Hereward Carrington, *The Physical Phenomena of Spiritualism*, 3rd edn (New York, 1920), p. v.

7 H. H. Furness, Jr, *Preliminary Report of the Commission Appointed by the University of Pennsylvania to Investigate Modern Spiritualism in Accordance with the Request of the Late Henry Seybert* (Philadelphia, PA, and London, 1920), p. 19.

8 David Marks and Richard Kammann, *The Psychology of the Psychic* (Buffalo, NY, 1980), p. 194.

9 William McDougall, 'Psychical Research as University Study', in *The Case For and Against Psychical Belief*, ed. Carl Murchison (London, 1927), p. 157.

10 Stacy Horn, *Unbelievable: Investigations into Ghosts, Poltergeists, Telepathy, and Other Unseen Phenomena, from the Duke Parapsychology Laboratory* (New York, 2009), p. 22.

11 Ibid., p. 16.

12 Ibid., p. 90.

13 Martin Gardner, *Fads and Fallacies in the Name of Science* (New York, 1957), p. 299.

14 Dr Barry Taff, 'The Real Entity Case' (7 August 2011), http://barrytaff.net.

15 Dr Barry Taff, 'Legacy's End: The Rise and Fall of the UCLA Parapsychology Lab' (15 November 2012), www.teemingbrain.com.

16 James Randi, quoted in Sean Greene, 'UCLA Lab Researched Parapsychology in the '70s', *Daily Bruin* (26 October 2010), http://dailybruin.com.

17 B. C. Forbes, 'Edison Working on How to Communicate with the Next World', *American Magazine* (October 1920), p. 11.

18 Rev. Rupert Sigurdsson, 'Is This the Mediumship of the Future?', *National Spiritualist Summit* (August 1992), pp. 6, 31.

19 Patricia Hartley, 'Texting the Dead is Definitely a Thing . . . From Sick Pranks to Griefbots' (15 April 2019), https://connectingdirectors.com.

20 Iris M. Owen with Margaret Sparrow, *Conjuring Up Philip: An Adventure in Psychokinesis* (New York, 1976), p. 7.

21 Gary Schwartz with William L. Simon, *The Afterlife Experiments: Breakthrough Scientific Evidence of Life After Death* (New York, 2003), e-book.

22 Ibid.

23 Review, '*The Afterlife Experiments*: Breakthrough Scientific Evidence of Life After Death', *Publishers Weekly*, www.publishersweekly.com, accessed 22 September 2019.

24 Ray Hyman, 'How *Not* to Test Mediums: Critiquing the Afterlife Experiments', *Skeptical Inquirer*, XXVII/1 (January–February 2003), pp. 20–30.

25 Michael Shermer, *Heavens on Earth: The Scientific Search for the Afterlife, Immortality, and Utopia* (New York, 2018), p. 111.

26 Glenn McDonald, 'Whatever Happened to Parapsychology?' (24 June 2013), www.seeker.com.

27 Ibid.

28 Ibid., p. 115.

29 Shermer, *Heavens on Earth*, p. 114.

30 Mike Hale, 'Consigning Reality to Ghosts', *New York Times* (10 December 2009), www.nytimes.com.

31 Ibid.

32 Jill Pingleton in interview, 'Spirit Story Box: The App That Claims to Reach the Dead', CNET, 21 November 2016, www.youtube.com.

33 Colin Dickey, 'The Broken Technology of Ghost Hunting', *The Atlantic* (14 November 2016), www.theatlantic.com.

34 Troy Lennon, 'Magician the Amazing Randi Has Dedicated His Life to Promoting Critical Thinking', *Daily Telegraph* (7 August 2018), www.dailytelegraph.com.au.

35 Roy Robert Smith, 'Brighton Dome – Doris Stokes', *The Stage* (14 July 1983), p. 5; John O'Connor, 'A Heartache That Refuses to Go Away', *Evening Herald* (2 August 1986), p. 8.

36 'About' (2019), https://georgeanderson.com.

37 Ibid.

38 George Anderson quoted in J. D. Reed, 'Across the Great Divide', *People* (25 October 1999), https://people.com.

39 'FAQ' (2019), https://georgeanderson.com.

40 'Sessions', https://georgeanderson.com, accessed 6 October 2019.

41 Schwartz and Simon, *The Afterlife Experiments*, e-book.

42 James Underdown, 'They See Dead People – or Do They?: An Investigation of Television Mediums', *Skeptical Inquirer*, XXVII/5 (September/October, 2003), p. 43.

43 Gary P. Posner, 'Close Encounter of the Secondhand Kind with "Psychic Medium" George Anderson', *Skeptical Briefs*, XX/2 (31 January 2011), https://skepticalinquirer.org.

44 Reed, 'Across the Great Divide'.

45 Ray Hyman, 'Cold Reading: How to Convince Strangers That You Know All About Them', in *Paranormal Borderlands of Science*, ed. Kendrick Frazier (Buffalo, NY, 1981), p. 82.

46 Ibid.

47 'George Anderson – Psychic Medium and One Unhappy Customer', www.badpsychics.com, accessed 5 October 2019.

48 Reed, 'Across the Great Divide'.

49 Johanna McDiarmid, 'John Edward: The Making of a Psychic Superstar', ABC (3 November 2015), www.abc.net.au.

50 Underdown, 'They See Dead People – or Do They?: An Investigation of Television Mediums', p. 44.

51 Matt Roper, 'Spooky Truth: TV's Most Haunted Con Exposed', *Mirror* (13 May 2013), www.mirror.co.uk.

52 James Van Praagh, www.vanpraagh.com, accessed 5 October 2019.

53 'About', www.vanpraagh.com, accessed 5 October 2019.

54 'JVP School of Mystic Arts', www.jvpschoolofmysticalarts.com, accessed 5 October 2019.

55 'Live the Experience' (30 June 2017), www.youtube.com.

56 Theresa Caputo on *The Wendy Williams Show* (23 February 2017), www.youtube.com.

57 'Deposition of FBI Agent Robert Ressler', https://skeptiko.com.

58 M. Reiser, L. Ludwig, S. Saxe and C. Wagner, 'Evaluation of the Use of Psychics in the Investigation of Major Crimes', *Journal of Police Science and Administration*, VII/1 (March 1979), pp. 18–25, www.ncjrs.gov.

59 Stephen Hudak, 'Amanda Berry Is Dead, Psychic Tells Her Mother on Montel Williams' Show', *Plain Dealer* (18 November 2004) https://web.archive.org.

60 'Use of Psychics in Law Enforcement', Central Intelligence Agency (CIA), www.cia.gov.

61 See https://twitter.com/CollegeofPolice, accessed 8 October 2019.

62 Duncan Campbell, 'Why Involve Psychics in Police Investigations When Their Track Record Is So Poor?', *The Guardian* (1 September 2015), www.theguardian.com.

63 Benjamin Radford, 'Another Abducted Girl, Another Psychic Fail', Center for Inquiry (16 January 2019), https://centerforinquiry.org.

64 Ben Tufft, 'Fortune Teller "Scams Lovesick Man Out of $700,000"', *The Independent* (7 June 2015), www.independent.co.uk.

65 State of North Carolina v. Charles Ray Kimbrell, No. 83A87 (1987), https://law.justia.com, accessed 10 October 2019.

66 Idaho v. Charboneau, 116 Idaho 129, 774 P.2d 299 (1989), www.courtlistener.com.

67 Phoebe Southworth, 'Ethiopian "Prophet" Who Tried (and Failed) to Raise a Man from the Dead Is Arrested by Police', *Daily Mail* (23 July 2018), www.dailymail.co.uk.

68 Shermer, *Heavens on Earth*, p. 73.

69 Adam Blai, 'The Devil Is Real: Combating Spiritualism', St Paul Center, https://stpaulcenter.com, accessed 15 October 2019.

70 *Ghost Magnet with Bridget Marquardt*, Séance (30 October 2019), www.facebook.com.

8 (WHY) DO WE NEED THE SEANCE?

1 C. G. Jung, foreword to 'Phénomènes Occultes', in *Psychology and the Occult* (Princeton, NJ, 1977), p. 3.

2 Carl Sagan, *The Demon-haunted World: Science as a Candle in the Dark* (New York, 1996), p. 203.

3 Joel Martin and Patricia Romanowski, *We Are Not Forgotten: George Anderson's Messages of Love and Hope from the Other Side* (New York, 1992), p. 3.

4 Michael Shermer, *Heavens on Earth: The Scientific Search for the Afterlife, Immortality, and Utopia* (New York, 2018), p. 1.

5 William James, 'Address by the President', *Proceedings of the Society for Psychical Research*, XII (1896–7), p. 5.

6 David Marks and Richard Kammann, *The Psychology of the Psychic* (Buffalo, NY, 1980), pp. 161–3.

7 Leon Festinger, Henry W. Riecken and Stanley Schachter, *When Prophecy Fails: A Social and Psychological Study of a Modern Group That Predicted the Destruction of the World* (2012, Kindle edition), Chapter 1.

8 C. G. Jung, 'On the Psychology and Pathology of So-called Occult Phenomena', *Psychology and the Occult*, p. 81.

9 Quoted in Charles A. Mercier, *Spiritualism and Sir Oliver Lodge* (London, 1917), p. vii.

10 D. M. Bear, 'The Temporal Lobes: An Approach to the Study of Organic Behavior Changes' (1979), quoted in Barry L. Beyerstein, 'Neuropathology and the Legacy of Spiritual Possession', *Skeptical Inquirer*, XII/3 (Spring 1988), pp. 253–4.

11 Mary Roach, *Spook: Science Tackles the Afterlife* (New York, 2005), p. 177.

12 Derren Brown, 'Mystics – Frauds or Believers?', *The Sun* (14 May 2018), www.thesun.co.uk.

13 Jung, 'On the Psychology and Pathology of So-called Occult Phenomena', p. 26.

14 Court transcript, as quoted in Nina Shandler, *The Strange Case of Hellish Nell: The Story of Helen Duncan and the Witch Trial of World War II* (Cambridge, 2006), p. 150.

15 Shermer, *Heavens on Earth*, p. 45.

16 Patti Negri, *Old World Magick for the Modern World* (Atlanta and Houston, 2019), p. 14.

17 Harry Houdini, *A Magician among the Spirits* (New York, 1972), p. xi.

18 Marina Warner, *Phantasmagoria: Spirit Visions, Metaphors, and Media into the Twenty-first Century* (Oxford, 2006), p. 244.

19 Reuben Briggs Davenport, *The Death-blow to Spiritualism: Being the True Story of the Fox Sisters, as Revealed by Authority of Margaret Fox Kane and Catherine Fox Jencken* (New York, 1888), p. 37.

SELECT BIBLIOGRAPHY

Bebergal, Peter, *Strange Frequencies: The Extraordinary Story of the Technological Quest for the Supernatural* (New York, 2018)

Boston Courier, *Spiritualism Shown as It Is!: Boston Courier Report of the Proceedings of Professed Spiritual Agents and Mediums, in the Presence of Professors Peirce, Agassiz, Horsford, Dr. B. A. Gould, Committee, and Others, at the Albion Building, Boston, on the 25th, 26th, and 27th of June, 1857*, 2nd edn (Boston, MA, 1859)

Brandon, Ruth, *The Spiritualists: The Passion for the Occult in the Nineteenth and Twentieth Centuries* (New York, 1983)

Butler, E. M., *Ritual Magic* (Cambridge, 1949)

Capron, Eliab W., and Henry D. Barron, *Singular Revelations: Explanation and History of the Mysterious Communion with Spirits, Comprehending the Rise and Progress of the Mysterious Noises in Western New-York, Generally Received as Spirit Communications*, 2nd edn (Auburn, NY, 1850)

Carrington, Hereward, *Eusapia Palladino and Her Phenomena* (New York, 1909)

—, *Psychical Phenomena and the War* (New York, 1919)

Crowe, Catherine, *The Night-side of Nature; or, Ghosts and Ghost-seers*, 2 vols (London, 1848)

'Darby and Joan', *Our Unseen Guest* (New York and London, 1920)

Darnton, Robert, *Mesmerism and the End of the Enlightenment in France* (New York, 1970)

Davenport, Reuben Briggs, *The Death-blow to Spiritualism: Being the True Story of the Fox Sisters, as Revealed by Authority of Margaret Fox Kane and Catherine Fox Jencken* (New York, 1888)

Davies, Owen, *A Supernatural War: Magic, Divination, and Faith during the First World War* (Oxford, 2018)

Furness, Jr, H. H., *Preliminary Report of the Commission Appointed by the University of Pennsylvania to Investigate Modern Spiritualism in Accordance with the Request of the Late Henry Seybert* (Philadelphia, PA, and London, 1920)

Hall, Trevor H., *The Spiritualists: The Story of Florence Cook and William Crookes* (New York, 1963)

Hardinge, Emma, *Modern American Spiritualism: A Twenty Years' Record of the Communion between Earth and the World of Spirits* (New York, 1870)

Home, D. D., *Incidents in My Life*, 6th edn (New York, 1874)

Horn, Stacy, *Unbelievable: Investigations into Ghosts, Poltergeists, Telepathy, and Other Unseen Phenomena, from the Duke Parapsychology Laboratory* (New York, 2009)

Houdini, Harry, *A Magician among the Spirits* (New York and London, 1924)

Kieckhefer, Richard, *Magic in the Middle Ages* (Cambridge, 2000)

Lewis, E. E., *A Report of the Mysterious Noises, Heard in the House of Mr. John D. Fox, in Hydesville, Arcadia, Wayne County, Authenticated by the Certificates, and Confirmed by the Statements of the Citizens of That Place and Vicinity* (Rochester, NY, 1848)

London Dialectical Society, *Report on Spiritualism, of the Committee of the London Dialectical Society, Together with the Evidence, Oral and Written, and a Selection from the Correspondence* (London, 1871)

Luck, Georg, *Arcana Mundi: Magic and the Occult in the Greek and Roman Worlds* (Baltimore, MD, and London, 1985)

Manseau, Peter, *The Apparitionists: A Tale of Phantoms, Fraud, Photography, and the Man Who Captured Lincoln's Ghost* (Boston, MA, and New York, 2017)

Maskelyne, John Nevil, *Modern Spiritualism: A Short Account of Its Rise and Progress, With Some Exposures of So-called Spirit Media* (London, 1876)

Mulholland, John, *Beware Familiar Spirits* (New York, 1938)

O'Donnell, Elliot, *The Menace of Spiritualism* (New York, 1920)

Ogden, Daniel, *Greek and Roman Necromancy* (Princeton, NJ, and Oxford, 2001)

Oppenheim, Janet, *The Other World: Spiritualism and Psychical Research in England, 1850–1914* (Cambridge, 1985)

Owen, Iris M., with Margaret Sparrow, *Conjuring Up Philip: An Adventure in Psychokinesis* (New York, 1976)

Raupert, J. Godfrey, *The Dangers of Spiritualism: Being Records of Personal Experiences with Notes and Comments and Five Illustrations*, 2nd edn (London, 1907)

Roach, Mary, *Spook: Science Tackles the Afterlife* (New York, 2005)

Sandford, Christopher, *Houdini and Conan Doyle* (London and New York, 2011)

Shandler, Nina, *The Strange Case of Hellish Nell: The Story of Helen Duncan and the Witch Trial of World War II* (Cambridge, 2006)

Shermer, Michael, *Heavens on Earth: The Scientific Search for the Afterlife, Immortality, and Utopia* (New York, 2018)

Underhill, Leah A., *The Missing Link in Modern Spiritualism* (New York, 1885)

Warner, Marina, *Phantasmagoria: Spirit Visions, Metaphors, and Media into the Twenty-first Century* (Oxford, 2006)

Weisberg, Barbara, *Talking to the Dead: Kate and Maggie Fox and the Rise of Spiritualism* (New York, 2008)

ACKNOWLEDGEMENTS

When your friends find out you're writing a book about seances, the resulting suggestions and offered materials are gratifying and sometimes overwhelming. I apologize in advance to anyone I've omitted, but thanks are certainly due to Richard Brewer, Kevin Cazares, Rob Cohen, James Derrick, Del Howison, Sean Patrick Traver and Lisa Tuttle.

Brandon Hodge and Marc Demarest founded and maintain an extraordinary archive, the International Association for the Preservation of Spiritualist and Occult Periodicals. I am deeply indebted to them for this invaluable collection of source materials on Spiritualism, and I highly recommend that anyone who desires to read more first-hand accounts from the people who invented the seance visit www.iapsop.com.

Special thanks to my editor, David Watkins, for suggesting this whole thing in the first place, and Ricky Grove, for keeping me calm and fed throughout the writing of it.

PHOTO ACKNOWLEDGEMENTS

The author and publishers wish to express their thanks to the below sources of illustrative material and/or permission to reproduce it. Some locations of artworks are also given below, in the interest of brevity:

Albertina, Vienna: p. 161; Biblioteca Nazionale Marciana, Venice (MS Lat. VI, 245): p. 66; Bibliothèque interuniversitaire de Santé, Paris: p. 79; from Olive Bray, ed., *The Elder or Poetic Edda, Commonly Known as Sæmund's Edda*, vol. I (London, 1908): p. 45; from Emma Hardinge Britten, *Nineteenth Century Miracles, or, Spirits and their Work in Every Country of the Earth* (New York, 1884): p. 303; The Cleveland Museum of Art, OH: pp. 55, 110; photo Rob Cohen: p. 296; from William Crookes, *Researches in the Phenomena of Spiritualism* (London, 1874): p. 143; from George Cruikshank, *Second Edition of a Discovery Concerning Ghosts* (London, 1864): pp. 172, 173; from *The Davenport Brothers, the World-renowned Spiritual Mediums: Their Biography, and Adventures in Europe and America* (Boston and New York, 1869): pp. 126, 127; from Justus Doolittle, *Social Life of the Chinese*, vol. II (New York, 1865): p. 263; from Henry Ridgley Evans, *Hours with the Ghosts, or Nineteenth Century Witchcraft* (Chicago, 1897): p. 299; from Johann Georg Faust, *Magia naturalis et innaturalis, oder dreifacher Höllenzwang, letztes Testament und Siegelkunst* (Stuttgart, 1849): p. 67; from Louis Figuier, *Les mystères de la science* (Paris, 1887): p. 136; Library of Congress, Prints and Photographs Division, Washington, DC: pp. 13, 223; from Oliver J. Lodge, *Raymond; or, Life and Death* (New York, 1916): p. 220; from Fulgence Marion, *L'Optique* (Paris, 1867): p. 86; photo Adrian Mira: p. 262; photos Lisa Morton: pp. 259, 285; Museo del Prado, Madrid: p. 163 (*top*); Národní galerie Praha (Prague): p. 164 (*bottom*); Nationalmuseum, Stockholm: p. 164 (*top*); photo Michael Nicht: p. 31; from *Revelations of the Great Modern Mystery Planchette, and Theories Respecting It* (Boston, 1868), photo courtesy

PHOTO ACKNOWLEDGEMENTS

the Harry Elkins Widener Memorial Library, Harvard University: p. 234;
Wellcome Collection: pp. 70, 92.

INDEX

Page numbers in *italics* refer to illustrations